WRITING UNEMPLOYMENT

Worklessness, Mobility, and Citizenship in
Twentieth-Century Canadian Literatures

Writing Unemployment

Worklessness, Mobility, and Citizenship in Twentieth-Century Canadian Literatures

JODY MASON

UNIVERSITY OF TORONTO PRESS
Toronto Buffalo London

ISBN 978-1-4426-4433-5

Printed on acid-free, 100% post-consumer recycled paper with vegetable-based inks.

Library and Archives Canada Cataloguing in Publication

Mason, Jody, 1976–
Writing unemployment : worklessness, mobility, and citizenship in twentieth-century
Canadian literatures / Jody Mason.

Includes bibliographical references and index.
ISBN 978-1-4426-4433-5

1. Canadian literature – 20th century – History and criticism.   2. Unemployment –
Canada – History – 20th century.   3. Liberalism – Canada – History – 20th century.
4. Unemployment – Political aspects – Canada.   5. Working class – Canada – Social
conditions.   6. Unemployment in literature.   7. Liberalism in literature.
8. Working class in literature.   I. Title.

PS8101.U46M37 2013   c810.9'3553   C2013-900503-X

University of Toronto Press acknowledges the financial assistance to its publishing
program of the Canada Council for the Arts and the Ontario Arts Council.

Canada Council   Conseil des Arts
for the Arts   du Canada

ONTARIO ARTS COUNCIL
CONSEIL DES ARTS DE L'ONTARIO
50 YEARS OF ONTARIO GOVERNMENT SUPPORT OF THE ARTS
50 ANS DE SOUTIEN DU GOUVERNEMENT DE L'ONTARIO AUX ARTS

This book has been published with the help of a grant from the Canadian Federation
for the Humanities and Social Sciences, through the Awards to Scholarly Publications
Program, using funds provided by the Social Sciences and Humanities Research
Council of Canada.

University of Toronto Press acknowledges the financial support of the Government of
Canada through the Canada Book Fund for its publishing activities.

Contents

Acknowledgments

A book requires resources intellectual, emotional, and financial. This last is not to be sniffed at. I am grateful for the financial assistance provided by the Social Sciences and Humanities Research Council of Canada, the estate of Frank Waddell, and the research and travel support provided by the Faculty of Arts and Social Sciences at Carleton University.

I wish to thank the editors of *Canadian Literature* and the *Papers of the Bibliographical Society in Canada*, who published portions of my work on Irene Baird. Librarians and archivists across the country have provided me with indispensable assistance and expertise. In particular, I thank Bev Buckie at the McLaughlin Archives at the University of Guelph; Gaby Divay at University of Manitoba Archives and Special Collections; Cathy Garay and Carl Spadoni at the William Ready Division of Archives and Research Collections McMaster University; Heather Home at the Queen's University Archives; and Jenna Smith at Library and Archives Canada. To those scholars who first turned my attention to the study of literature in Canada and who modelled a critical nationalism to me – Diana Brydon, Frank Davey, the late Tom Tausky, and Gillian Whitlock – I want to say a respectful thank you for this early mentorship. Marlene Goldman, Linda Hutcheon, and Russell Brown were later, but similarly influential, interlocutors and guides. Others who certainly deserve acknowledgment for their advice, research assistance, and expertise include Stephanie Doerksen, Colin Hill, Dean Irvine, Smaro Kamboureli, Eli MacLaren, Siobhan McMenemy, Nick Mount, Heather Murray, Lora Senechal Carney, Kelly Wadson, my fine and generous colleagues at Carleton University (especially Brenda Carr Vellino, Franny Nudelman, and Jennifer Henderson for their suggestions and for comments on draft material), the members of the Canadian literature discussion group at the University of Toronto, the students and colleagues in the Cultural Mediations seminar group at Carleton University that hosted me in the fall of 2009, and students in my graduate courses in 2010, particularly Laura Dunbar, whose research on transience and travel informed me of the existence of Harold Baldwin's *A Farm for Two Pounds* (1935). The assessors of this manuscript were critical and careful readers, and I acknowledge their time and effort. I am also indebted to James Leahy, who patiently edited the manuscript.

A large and loving family surrounds me. My scholarly work emerges at least in part from the stories my parents told me of grandparents who were tenement farmers, mechanics, and road builders, and from the tales of the Depression conjured by my late grandmother, Mabel Uens Cook. For their support and affection, I thank Will Mason and Amy Nilsson, Davin and Michelle Mason, Oliver MacLaren and Jean Chia, and Julia MacLaren. Ian and Margaret MacLaren made doctoral studies imaginable and inhabitable. My parents, Bill and Linda Mason, have always encouraged me to consider how my own work is dependent on the work of others, and I thank them for this. The respective births of my three sons, Xavier, Simon, and Charles, occurred at various stages of the life of this project. This book is for them, and for Eli.

WRITING UNEMPLOYMENT

Worklessness, Mobility, and Citizenship in
Twentieth-Century Canadian Literatures

Introduction

Canada, by her neglect of her unemployed, her depressed areas and her youth during the 1930s, provides a striking example of a state that was not a national community. (Lewis and Scott 192)

In our current historical moment, unemployment has come to seem 'obvious, mundane,' 'self-evident' – the 'eternal opposite of "work"' (Walters 1). How did this come to be? At earlier moments in the twentieth century, and particularly during the unemployment crisis of the Depression, worklessness was not assumed to be a fixed feature of everyday life, and protests of its increasing ubiquity were loud, insistent, and pervasive. In the concluding lines of Dorothy Livesay's 1936 poem 'Dominion Day at Regina,' for example, the unemployed voice an urgent request: 'Give us the work / and it shall be done!' (*Right Hand* 186). Despite the imperative that opens these lines and the exclamatory mood marked at their end, 'Dominion Day at Regina' offers a telling example of the kind of conciliatory appeal to the would-be benevolent state that flourished in the 1930s. This book argues that such appeals to the state subsequently shaped much of the discourse of unemployment in the latter half of the twentieth century. The interwar conception of worklessness as a problem that required the intervention of the state influenced understandings of unemployment in the context of the postwar compact between state and labour and the decades that concluded the twentieth century. The 'mundane' character of contemporary unemployment must be understood via this history.

Writing Unemployment asks how writers – activists of the radical left, social democrats, and reformists – participated in and protested against the discursive framing of unemployment and its normalization in every-day life. Prior to the Depression, there were certainly writers and activists whose work strove to represent the mobility and seasonal fluctuation that were entrenched features of the early twentieth-century labour market, but the realist fiction of the period and subsequent literary histories tend to privilege the figure of the settler-pioneer because this figure enables settler-invader claims regarding territory. In the tumultuous 1930s, unemployment and the related phenomena of transience were more frequently represented in cultural texts, even if the period's poetry, short stories, manifestos, agitprop, and novels were not subsequently canonized in the postwar period, which was largely hostile to the nation's leftist traditions of protest. In this era of crisis, writers affiliated with a diversity of political perspectives called for federal state intervention in the labour market and urged a federal solution to what was clearly articulated as the 'problem' of unemployment. The discourse of unemployment that emerged during the Depression – even from the communist left – thus anticipated and inflected welfare-state policy and conceptions of the unemployed in the postwar period. By the 1960s, literary representations of unemployment, particularly Depression-era experiences of unemployment, were absorbed into national allegories and other nation-making narratives that figure the experience of the transient, unemployed male as a crucial element of the nation's coming of age. Via such narratives, the state thus becomes, as social democrats David Lewis and F.R. Scott have it in their 1943 book *Make This Your Canada*, a national community. As historian Ian McKay observes, Lewis and Scott's book, which sold 25,000 copies in less than a year (Whitehorn 159), urges a collective awareness of 'nation,' effectively supplanting an interwar discourse of class in order to promulgate a national purpose that would be rooted in an effectively managed state ('For a New Kind' 99–109; *Rebels* 177–82). In the argument of *Make This Your Canada*, and, I would contend, in the literary and cultural texts of many writers who interpret unemployment from the perspective of the latter half of the twentieth century, 'it is nationalism, not socialism, which serves as the Other of capitalism' (McKay, 'For a New Kind' 106). Yet New Leftists and socialist-feminists in the 1960s and '70s were not uncritical of this postwar compact between state and labour, sealed as it was in the welfare state that promised to make a nation, and the fault lines of this postwar project became particularly apparent as unemployment rates escalated in the 1970s.

William Walters observes that unemployment has arguably received more attention from social scientists than any other social question (1).

Indeed, in Canada, economists, social policy analysts, labour and social historians, sociologists, and psychologists have analysed unemployment with admirable rigour. James Struthers's 1983 study, *No Fault of Their Own: Unemployment and the Canadian Welfare State, 1914–1941,* remains the most important historiographical contribution to the literature, not least because he elucidates the ways in which liberal thought influenced twentieth-century constructions of both unemployment and the unemployed individual. *Writing Unemployment* is unique insofar as it examines unemployment from the perspective of literary studies, arguing that the cultural left, broadly construed, both participated in *and* sought to amend liberal constructions of unemployment and the unemployed.

Literary and cultural studies of leftist formations in Canada have been proliferating in recent years. In a 2007 article on Irene Baird's Depression-era strike novel *Waste Heritage,* critic Herb Wyile contends that

> Despite a rich and interesting history of labour in Canada, representations of work, labour agitation, and unemployment are fairly uncommon in Canadian literature, and, although there is some criticism that focuses on considerations of class and labour in the work of particular writers, the broader profile of such considerations in Canadian literature falls far short of that of, say, postcolonialism, multiculturalism, or feminism, about which numerous monographs, essay collections, and individual articles have been published over the last thirty years. (62)

I am less convinced than Wyile that work, labour unrest, and unemployment appear rarely in literary texts in Canada; he is much more suggestive when he notes that 'those who write about these issues tend to remain outside the canon' (63); however, in terms of the scholarly attention that such texts have attracted, Wyile is correct to note that the tendencies he observes have diminished to some extent in recent years. He points to the work of James Doyle and Roxanne Rimstead, and I would add Larry McDonald, Caren Irr, Alan Filewod, Candida Rifkind, and Dean Irvine to the list (and still it would not be exhaustive).[1] Yet much work remains to be done in this field of study. In what follows, I will outline the ways in which this book builds on the impressive contemporary scholarship of the cultural left in twentieth-century Canada and, along the way, will describe the methodological and theoretical underpinnings of this study.

Attentive to the methodologies of book- and print-culture studies, each chapter of *Writing Unemployment* analyses the linkages between conditions of creative labour and discursive constructions of unemployment, and it is my hope that this approach, which I use whenever archival materials allowed me to do so, will yield new dialogues in the study of the cultural left. As labour and social historians have documented, twentieth-century Canada witnessed the emergence of a labour force that was construed as national – rather than local or regional – and that possessed specific social rights of citizenship. In the context of an emerging welfare state in the interwar and postwar periods, for example, social rights of citizenship such as unemployment insurance, a universal family allowance, and old-age security appeared. As the Massey Commission and the attendant development of the Canada Council and the National Library (among many other institutions) attest, the postwar period was also a time of intense national self-examination, particularly in terms of the nation's cultural identity and the function of the state vis-à-vis that identity. Of course, these new roles for the federal state, which created an unprecedented level of intervention in everything from unemployment insurance to the funding of literary magazines, must not be read as indications that phenomena like joblessness and creative writing did not exist in late nineteenth- or early twentieth-century Canada. Yet along with the growth of the state came new discursive representations of such phenomena: for example, joblessness became the predictable and to some extent manageable problem of 'unemployment,' and literature, as a bearer of what Paul Litt calls 'liberal humanist nationalism,' became one means of compensating the nation for its economic dependency on the United States (Litt 104–20; Dowler 342).

   Throughout the chapters, I have attempted to maintain a parallel focus on representations of unemployment and the material conditions in which such creative and political work was undertaken. To this end, chapter 1 considers the linkages between pioneer-settler ideologies and romantic conceptions of authorship and analyses the influence of both on literary nationalism in Canada. I have also consulted archival collections across the country in order to reconstruct the publishing histories of many narratives of protest and have thus been able to argue that conditions of constraint in the interwar and postwar fields of cultural production militated against novels that directly engaged the state's unwillingness to deal with unemployment. This book also offers a contribution to the study of little-magazine culture in Canada, building on the work of Doyle and Irvine, among others, whose studies have helped to expand this history to include the interwar period and the leftist periodicals that proliferated in it. Adding periodicals such as *The Worker* and the *Daily Clarion* to the more commonly cited triad of the *Canadian Forum,*

Masses, and *New Frontier,* this book places the leftist periodical culture of the 1930s in a wider context and uses the issue of unemployment to show the shared cultural and political work of these ostensibly antagonistic publications. In the final chapter, the methodology is slightly different but is similarly indebted to the insights of print-culture studies insofar as it seeks to analyse the relations between labour-market policy and artistic production in 1970s Canada.

This book also contributes to recent thinking about the internationalism of Canada's cultural lefts.[2] While *Writing Unemployment* attends to such cross-border connections in its analysis of interwar periodical cultures or Canada's only Depression-era strike novel, *Waste Heritage,* for example, I am more interested in the specifically national address that appears in the texts under consideration because this focus allows me to query the specific strategies that leftist cultural producers and activists employed in their attempts to render the unemployed a visible category within the nation and in relation to the state. As I point out in chapter 2, such strategies were not required to the same extent in the United States during the 1930s because state intervention in the crisis of joblessness was more vigorous there. The confluence of the New Left and the emerging cultural nationalisms of late-1960s Canada, which I discuss in chapters 4 and 5, also create a particular recuperation of the Depression-era transient that is unique to Canada, although New Left cultures in Canada were, like their predecessors, striated by international concerns.

Moreover, insofar as this book theorizes the confluences and ruptures between Old and New Left cultures, it realizes Rifkind's call, articulated in the conclusion to her 2009 book *Comrades and Critics,* to think beyond the 1930s in histories of the cultural left. She contends, for example, that 'the diagonal lines drawn by writers, artists, and critics between the 1970s and the 1930s are ripe for much more detailed analysis of the camaraderie, but also the conflicts, between the so-called old and new lefts' (210).[3] In chapters 4 and 5 I turn to this camaraderie and conflict, attempting to situate these engagements in the political economy of the welfare state.

It is in this analysis of the welfare state and its meanings for cultural producers, as well, that I hope this book will contribute to work on the history of leftist formations. Historians, economists, and public policy analysts have produced a tremendous body of scholarship on the subject of Canada's welfare state, much of which critiques its very incomplete project.[4] In Canada, literary and cultural studies of the welfare state have focused on the rise of state-sponsored culture in the wake of the 1952 Massey Report, but little attention has been paid to the ways in which writers and other cultural producers anticipated, called forth, and engaged the welfare state as it rose and declined in the latter half of the twentieth century.[5] To be sure, such an analysis requires forgoing rigid conceptions of left and right, the state and civil society. In his book *New Deal Modernism: American Literature and the Invention of the Welfare State*, Michael Szalay posits that the welfare state has proven 'curiously immune to strong ideological formulation,' and few critics or historians of leftist formations in the United States (or, I would add, in Canada) 'have been roused to treat the welfare state as an ideological formation coherent enough to be engaged at all' (4). Historians of the cultural left are attracted to the interwar period because it is admittedly so rich with cultural materials, but also, arguably, because it offers a chimera of polarized political ideologies, signalled, for example, by the now-infamous colour-coding of the 1930s – pink for bourgeois, red for radical. Such a schema is clearly inappropriate to the analysis of the postwar and contemporary cultural lefts. Michael Denning's identification of a broad postwar 'cultural front' in the United States and a 'labouring of American culture' in the wake of the New Deal offers an attractive model for the sort of work I undertake in this book; however, as Szalay points out, Denning's desire for 'an emancipatory cultural studies' jettisons the state – the 'presumably hegemonic, mainstream liberalism of the New Deal' – at great cost:

> If there has in fact been an end of history, if, cradled in the arms of liberal governance, this nation has slept through the death of non-capitalist ideology, then we need to trace our slumbers back to the New Deal, when the welfare state, visible in its newness perhaps only for a moment, becomes all too quickly the signpost of a bankrupt political compromise. (19–20)

Of course, there was no New Deal in Canada (although R.B. Bennett modelled his failed 1935 'New Deal' on Roosevelt's); nevertheless, Szalay's call to revisit the making of state in the latter half of the twentieth century clearly has great relevance and, indeed, urgency for those living in Canada in the early twenty-first century.

Following McKay, and those historians who have adapted his influential 'liberal-order framework,' I also strive to reconfigure the history of Canada's leftist formations in non-sectarian ways in order to illuminate the ground that diverse leftist cultures shared and share. McKay's 'liberal-order framework' provides an important, if admittedly contentious, framework for the chapters that follow. For those who are currently revisiting the political, social, and cultural histories of the left in Canada and British North America, it is difficult to ignore the work of McKay, whose 2000 essay 'For a New Kind of History: A Reconnnaissance of 100 Years of Canadian Socialism' presaged a four-volume history of the nation's lefts. This latter project is ongoing, and it, like McKay's related work on Canada's 'liberal-order framework,' has not failed to provoke debate.[6] In 'For a New Kind of History,' McKay offers a Gramscian analysis of Canada's liberal 'passive revolution' in the 1940s, 'whereby a threatened liberal order transformed both itself (into a "new democracy" answerable to its "citizens") and many of its socialist adversaries (into "new democrats" comfortable with Fordism at home and American globalism abroad) in response to an apprehended social insurrection' (71). Such a 'passive revolution' (and not the infamous 'Tory tinge'), he contends, is responsible for the 'anomaly of a relatively influential Canadian socialist movement in a continent otherwise quite hostile to formal socialist politics' (70). Antonio Gramsci's concept of the 'passive revolution,' particularly as he applied the concept to the United States in the context of the New Deal in his analysis of 'Americanism and Fordism,' clearly offers much potential for what labour historians in Canada have called the postwar compact between the state and labour, or the 'price Liberalism is willing to pay to prevent socialism' (Palmer, *Working-Class* 276). However, as Bruce Curtis argues, McKay's reading of liberalism tends to pit a liberal state against civil society, such that 'the social' is 'reappropriate[d]' for 'working-class struggle' (180). Curtis thus contends that McKay's 'state conception remains firmly located in the state / civil society binary,' despite 'Gramsci's own tendencies to see state hegemony as increasingly anchored in civil society,' and suggests that 'Gramsci's interest in the creation of the "new man" of Fordism could certainly be extended by Michel Foucault's analysis of the constitution of subjectivity' (178–9, 180).[7]

In this book, I maintain McKay's broad conceptualization of Canada's 'left formations.' In particular, I rely on his identification of a second formation (1917–39), which coalesced around a call to proletarian revolution; a third formation (1935–70), which urged national economic and social management; and a fourth, 'New Left,' formation (1965–80), which critiqued older, bureaucratized lefts and pursued direct democracy (*Rebels* 146–7). Yet this study seeks to avoid simplistic state / civil society binaries, and consistently pursues the ruptures and contradictions that characterize McKay's formations. As McKay recognizes, 'older paradigms of socialism are frequently (and often effectively) re-activated in subsequent periods' ('For a New Kind' 80), but it must also be said that leftist formations and their liberal antagonist(s) were (and are) far from cohesive or unified. In this latter sense, the argument of this book seeks to acknowledge the nuanced thinking about liberalism and liberal modes of government that has modified McKay's argument.[8] As Curtis's essay suggests, Foucault's theorization of governmentality is useful to the kind of work I am undertaking here, insofar as it analyses how power comes to target 'population' and manages population 'in depth, in all its fine points and details' (Foucault 107). A post-Marxist reading of an 'anatomy of power' (Goldstein 46–7), Foucault's theory of governmentality unsettles 'reductionist' conceptions of the state that ascribe to it a 'unity,' 'individuality,' 'rigorous functionality,' and 'importance' that it does not possess, and proposes a governmentality that is 'at once internal and external to the state' insofar as the means that government uses to achieve its ends (e.g., the welfare of the population) are 'all in some sense immanent to the population' (Foucault 109, 105). As François Ewald proposes, state insurance, such as the unemployment insurance developed by Mackenzie King's government in 1940, is a means of managing the population with the population's consent: 'In guaranteeing security, the state is equally guaranteeing itself its own existence, maintenance, permanence. Social insurance is also an insurance against revolutions' (209).

Constantly forming a part of the broader questions posed in this study are more specific interrogations of the ways in which class, gender, race, and sexuality intersect. How, for example, has the construction of unemployment participated in the differential distribution of power in Canada, including the making of classed, gendered, and racialized subjectivities? Labour history and histories of the left often emphasize the role of men and masculinity in relation to the problems of unemployment and transience, state responses to unemployment, and the political activism of the unemployed, yet attention to unemployment from a cultural perspective brings women and constructions of femininity to the fore, particularly because the scope of this study extends into the contemporary period, when socialist-feminists and New Leftists were interrogating the unprecedented rise of unemployment among women.[9] The literary and cultural texts examined in this book were produced between 1910 and 1975 – the years that witnessed the formation and subsequent deformation of the welfare state and its attendant social rights of citizenship, including the right to unemployment insurance: but who possesses these rights, and why? As Lara Campbell observes in her social history of Depression-era Ontario,

Liberal understandings of citizenship and male economic independence framed many of the popular concepts of welfare state formation ... Similarly, hierarchical gender roles based on the roles of male breadwinner and female homemaker were rarely challenged in popular discourse, state policy, or in radical left politics. Maternalist duties and the breadwinner ethos were celebrated and upheld throughout the Great Depression, and women working in the paid labour force were criticized at best and fired and attacked at worst. These ideals were encoded in welfare state policy and helped to ensure that the most generous postwar welfare benefits, such as unemployment insurance, were structured around the patterns of male employment. (187)

The gender politics of insurance for the unemployed has in some senses altered very little since the 1940s, as the continued exclusion of forms of domestic work from Canada's Employment Insurance program attests.

The anachronistic use of the term citizenship in the chapters that deal with the 1930s is meant to emphasize the ways in which cultural producers such as Irene Baird were actively involved in negotiating the emerging fault lines between concepts of class and nascent, liberal ideas about citizenship. National citizenship did not become a legal concept in Canada until the Citizenship Act of 1947. Prior to 1947, Canadian nationals (those born in Canada or naturalized under immigration law) were legally defined as British subjects.[10] Yet the interwar period was also a time of emerging nationalism that was bolstered by Canada's experiences in the First World War and the 1931 Statute of Westminster, which defined Canada legally as a self-governing nation. These years form a threshold over which both class and citizenship – what Marx formulated in 'On the Jewish Question' as human versus political emancipation – arguably could not pass: indeed, it was the advent of the Second World War and its aftermath that consolidated the idea of the national citizen who laboured in return for social and political rights. Linda Cardinal's research on the social rights of citizenship in Canada corroborates the importance of the interwar period in defining the relation between a rights-based politics and citizenship; she shows how the emergence of a civil-liberties movement, the appearance of a nascent welfare state, and the growth of an increasingly centralist and interventionist federal government in the arenas of social and economic rights coalesced in the 1930s to produce the idea of social rights that has been so central to the practice of Canadian citizenship in the contemporary period (164–6).[11] The interwar crucible in which class and citizenship are sundered is one in which national identity, ethnicity, and race begin to play increasingly determining roles. As my readings of interwar texts in chapters 2 and 3 demonstrate, agitation for social rights like unemployment insurance often anticipated a narrow definition of eligibility, presaging the restricted conceptions of the citizen that, in the postwar period, gave lie to liberal notions of the universal human subject. While the popular narrative of Canadian history suggests an increasing 'tolerance' of cultural diversity (more accommodating postwar immigration policy is often cited), this narrative is complicated by the fact that national citizenship in Canada, while theoretically available to all, is subject to the principle of what sociologist Nandita Sharma calls 'differential inclusion,' a process by which potential citizens and temporary migrants – especially migrant labourers – are distinguished from one another (18).

Enmeshed in the question of national citizenship – who qualifies for it and why – is the issue of mobility. The theorization of the politics of mobility, which considers 'the materiality of mobility alongside its differential production and reproduction' (Simpson xix) and which I assess in more detail in chapter 1, forms a line of inquiry that is followed throughout the book. As I argue in chapter 1, mobility has been a particularly important concept in Canada, where settler-invader ideologies have encouraged what anthropologist Liisa Malkki would call the 'sedentarist' mythology of the settler-pioneer. Against this mythology of place-based rootedness moves the transient labourer – often the immigrant, transient labourer – a ubiquitous figure in late nineteenth- and early twentieth-century Canada's resource-based economy, and one of the reasons why Canada's Depression-era crisis of joblessness disproportionately affected single, immigrant men, many of whom had no choice but to take to the road (Struthers, *No Fault* 97). The radical politics that some of these men espoused encouraged state fear and anxiety. R.B. Bennett's work camps for this workless population, run by the Department of National Defence in the early 1930s and intended to curtail the mobility of the transient unemployed, can be understood in this context. Moreover, the disenfranchisement of those in the camps (Brown, 'Unemployment' 539) is a particularly revealing instance of how transient mobility and citizenship were disarticulated during the Depression. As I argue throughout chapter 4, however, this disarticulation did not persist in the postwar period, when narratives of the Depression, and of Depression-era unemployment, in particular, came to serve as allegories of the nation in the making or of the coming of age of the national citizen. The narrowed distance between the liberal citizen and the unemployed worker – now at least a nominal beneficiary of state protection – enabled a new imagining of the relation of mobility to nation.

The chapters that follow proceed more or less chronologically, beginning in the first decades of the twentieth century and moving, in the final chapter, to the 1970s. The study begins in the first decades of the twentieth century because, as many labour historians have documented, the seasonal nature of work in nineteenth- and early twentieth-century Canada meant that occupational pluralism and geographical mobility characterized the labour market long before the advent of the Depression. Moreover, severe economic slumps between 1913 and 1915 and again in the half-decade following the end of the First World War offered preludes to the dire unemployment brought on by the Depression. Chapter 1, 'Towards a Politics of Mobility: Vagabonds, Hobos, and Pioneers,' considers the emergence of the category of the unemployed worker in the late nineteenth-century United States against residual Romantic ideologies of wandering and vagabondage and, pushing across the border into Canada, examines the contradictory coexistence of narratives of settlement and counter-settlement in the first decades of the twentieth century and considers why tropes of vagabondage, tramping, and hobodom have remained marginal elements in canonical Canadian literatures. To this end, the chapter first reads Frederick Philip Grove's peripatetic pseudo-autobiography *A Search for America* (1927) against and through the turn-of-the-century 'vagabondia' poems of Bliss Carman and Richard Hovey, and then engages in a comparative reading of Grove's pioneer-settler ideal and the less well-known narratives of mobility that documented experiences of itinerant labour in early twentieth-century Canada.

Chapters 2 and 3 focus specifically on discourses of unemployment and transience from the 1930s, the years during which the Great Depression sent thousands of men (and some women) out on the road in search of work. The second chapter, 'The Politics of Unemployment in Leftist Periodical Cultures, 1930–1939,' looks at poems, short stories, essays, editorials, and manifestos from a variety of periodicals ranging from the social democratic, League for Social Reconstruction (LSR)-affiliated *Canadian Forum* to the Communist Party of Canada's (CPC) the *Daily Clarion* in order to describe how contributors to these publications imagined the unemployment crisis and its potential solutions. Aesthetically and ideologically distinct, these periodical cultures of the left shared a commitment to agitating for a federal program of unemployment insurance.

Chapter 3, 'Novel Protest in the 1930s,' employs the insights of print-culture studies to analyse how the novel both circulated within and rested uneasily against the protest cultures of 1930s Canada. To this end, this chapter considers the material and symbolic production of the only two Depression-era novels in Canada – Claudius Gregory's all-but-forgotten *Forgotten Men* (1933) and Irene Baird's *Waste Heritage* (1939) – that protest the crisis of joblessness that plagued the decade.

Chapter 4, 'The Postwar Compact and the National Bildungsroman,' turns to the only other novel in Canada that explicitly protests Depression-era unemployment: Hugh Garner's *Cabbagetown* (1950; 1968). This chapter limits itself to the reading of a single text because the publication history that archival documents reveal, in this particular case, uniquely illuminates the unfolding of the postwar compact between labour and the state in Canada. Tracing the complex but largely unexamined textual history of this novel, which has its inception in two reportage pieces that appeared in the *Canadian Forum* during the 1930s, this chapter argues that the postwar compact between the worker and the state and, later, the rise of the New Left and the consolidation of Canada's literary field have shaped the aesthetics and politics of Garner's shifting text. In the latter part of this argument, I analyse the 1968 edition of *Cabbagetown* as a Bildungsroman that allegorizes the nation's and the national citizen's coming of age, and argue for the presence of this allegory in other literature of the Centennial period, such as John Marlyn's novel *Under the Ribs of Death* (1959) and Al Purdy's *The Cariboo Horses* (1965).

Chapter 5, 'New Left Culture and the New Unemployment,' builds on the previous chapter's analysis of New Left political and artistic cultures, turning to an examination of the ways that unemployment was discursively constructed in the 1970s as a new kind of 'problem' created by the increased participation of women and youths in the labour market. In the early 1970s, job creation strategies that emphasized citizenship participation were designed to ease this 'new' unemployment while assuaging the demands of youth, particularly a politicized youth culture in Quebec, and women. As in other chapters, where the material conditions of work that produce narratives of unemployment shape my understanding of texts, this final chapter examines the relation between labour market policy – especially job creation – and the arts in 1970s Canada. The diversity of texts examined in chapter 5 – the documentary plays of the alternative theatre movement, popular and academic histories of Depression-era unemployment, memoirs of the Depression-era unemployed, Jean-Jules Richard's 1965 novel *Journal d'un hobo*, Helen

Potrebenko's 1975 novel *Taxi!* and the socialist-feminist periodical *The Pedestal* – is suggestive of the complexity of responses to unemployment in this period. While nostalgia offers one well-worn explanation for the citation of Depression-era unemployment in the 1970s, I argue that a liberal mythology of the welfare state, on the one hand, and a diagnosis of the failures of the welfare state, on the other, characterize the polarized debate of the period. As I indicate in this final chapter, the study ends here, in the mid-1970s, because it is in this period that the post-Fordist global economy and the shift to monetarist economic policy transformed the relation between the state and workers, shifting labour-market policy toward 'real work' on infrastructure and private-sector initiatives and turning artistic labour to more narrowly economic ends via an emerging cultural industries strategy.

Chapter One

Towards a Politics of Mobility:
Vagabonds, Hobos, and Pioneers

The federal government did not regularly measure unemployment rates until after the Second World War, but it is clear from estimates that rates of joblessness were low in the 1920s compared to the Depression.[1] Yet as Ronald Liversedge insists in his 1973 *Recollections of the On to Ottawa Trek*, 'the great economic depression of the thirties did not start on that memorable day in November, 1929' (3). Struthers concurs:

> Canadians had become well acquainted with cyclical unemployment – or trade depressions as they were then called – well before the 'dirty thirties.' The 1870s, the early 1890s, and the years 1907–08, 1913–15, and 1920–25, were all periods of heavy unemployment in this country. From this perspective it's best to think of the Great Depression as simply the most intense and long-lasting of a series of 'waves' of unemployment which battered all western industrial economies during the last half of the 19th and the first third of the 20th centuries. ('Canadian Unemployment' 376)

The precariousness of working-class life in Canada in the first decades of the twentieth century had as much to do with a lack of employment as with the seasonal, temporary character of much unskilled labour in this period. Yet in the canonized modern fiction that preserves rural settings – novels by Laura Goodman Salverson, Frederick Philip Grove, and Robert Stead, for example – the settler-pioneer, rather than the mobile, unskilled labourer, prevails. As subsequent chapters will indicate, by the 1960s the young, unemployed male of the Depression was allegorized in relation to the nation's coming of age, but in the decade or so prior to the Depression, unemployment, labour mobility, and an unstable labour market caused specific problems for a nation being narrated to maturity in prose fiction.

Admittedly, in modern fiction with rural settings the 'invisible city' unsettles the pastoral ideal that Raymond Williams describes as the 'knowable community' (Willmott 146; *The Country* 178); nevertheless, a profound nostalgia persists in the modern fiction of western Canada – a nostalgia that locates in the figure of the white, male pioneer a foundational narrative for the nation, a narrative that followed in the wake of the settlement of the prairies and that emerged just as the Canadian west was being transformed by the second industrial revolution. Using the theoretical insights of the politics of mobility, this chapter considers how the valorization of the settler-pioneer serves to bolster the nationalist narrative and the romantic discourses of authorship that attend it. To this end, I read a variety of texts that negotiate tropes of mobility, such as the vagabondia poetry produced by Bliss Carman and Richard Hovey in the late nineteenth and early twentieth centuries, Frederick Philip Grove's novel *A Search for America* (1927), and the considerable, and largely unexamined, body of modern poetry, travel narratives, and fiction that I will call narratives of mobility.

The Vagabondia Poetics of Bliss Carman and Richard Hovey

On a blistering August afternoon in 1892, Fredericton-born poet Bliss Carman, who had recently taken up a job as the editor of the New York literary magazine the *Independent,* stumbled across an antiquated English statute regarding the social problem of vagabonds and vagrants, who 'wake on the night and sleep on the day, and haunt customable taverns and alehouses and routs about, and no man wot from whence they came, nor wither they go' (qtd in Miller, *Bliss Carman* 87). Stifled by desk work and urban life, Carman was enchanted with the vagabond and immediately began writing the poem that appeared as 'The Vagabonds' in his 1893 collection *Low Tide on Grand Pré.* Between 1895 and 1912, he and Richard Hovey wrote four extremely popular collections of vagabondia poetry that purported to critique urban life under capitalism, none of which has earned a significant place in Canadian literary history. Writing in the context of the southward migration of thousands of Canadians in the last decades of the nineteenth century (Mount 6), Carman felt no compulsion to put his vagabond figure in the service of Canadian cultural nationalism; indeed, the vagabondia poems revel in a peripatetic placelessness that has proved singularly unappealing to Canadian discourses of cultural nationalism. For example, in his pioneering 1924 study of the Canadian literary field – itself a product of the ebullient nationalism that followed the First World War – Archibald MacMechan laments that 'after his removal from Canada,' Carman's verse never 're-gained "the first fine careless rapture"' of *Low Tide on Grand Pré* – a 'thoroughly Canadian book of lyrics':

> Across the border, he fell under other influences – of Boston plus Browning in the weird days of Browning societies – and of a certain calculated Bohemianism which led him into a strange region yclept Vagabondia. Frankly, his later work became vague and affected. His tendency to be formless becomes confirmed; and much of his later verse seems purely experimental. (127)

Almost forty years later, MacMechan's judgment was echoed in another nationalist stock taking – Roy Daniells's assessment of the Confederation poets in the *Literary History of Canada*. Daniells reads Carman's vagabond persona – his 'haphazard way of life' and 'congenital indecisiveness' – as that which 'robbed his poetry of substance and vitiated its form' (429). He defends Carman's vagabondia verse by reading it in the tradition of a poetry of place that he finds in Charles G.D. Roberts and Archibald Lampman, but sounds remarkably uncommitted to his comment that the 'background' of vagabondia – the 'geographical continuum' of the Canadian Maritimes and the states of New England – is 'less of an affectation than it appears' (430). Malcolm Ross's New Canadian Library anthology of the *Poets of the Confederation* (1960) makes no mention of the vagabondia poetry in its introduction, and, although a few selections from both *Songs from Vagabondia* (1894) and *More Songs from Vagabondia* (1896) appear in its pages, Carman's work with Hovey is certainly the least represented aspect of his poetic career. Despite its tremendous popularity with readers in the United States, in particular, and the fact that Carman and Hovey shared with many writers in early twentieth-century Canada an anti-modernist nostalgia, the placeless vagabond proved an unattractive figure for the Canadian literary historians and critics who shaped an emerging canon during the nationalist periods that followed both world wars, and who tended to privilege place-based, realist fiction.[2]

Carman and Hovey's tremendously popular *Songs from Vagabondia*, which was published by Boston's Copeland and Day in the fall of 1894 and reprinted fifteen times before Carman's death in 1929 (Mount 73), bristles with but refuses to represent directly the economic depression that plagued the United States (and other industrializing nations) in the 1890s. Carman and Hovey's poems reify the vagabond figure in anti-modern celebrations of drink, leisure, song, and homosocial camaraderie that ignore the dire economic conditions that gave rise to contemporary forms of vagabondage – the tramping of the unemployed – in the 1890s. The opening poem, 'Vagabondia,' revels in an unfettered wandering that resists the illusion of choice, freedom, and mobility that lies beneath the capitalist imperative of uniformity and stasis:

> Free as the whim
> Of a spook on a spree, –
> Free to be oddities,
> Not mere commodities,
> Stupid and saleable,
> Wholly available,
> Ranged upon shelves;
> Each with his puny form
> In the same uniform,
> Cramped and disabled;
> We are not labelled,
> We are ourselves. (2)

Playing the vagabond in Carman and Hovey's poems serves to invigorate and renew the alienated bourgeois male so that he may continue to consume in comfort (Mount 73).[3] Significantly, playing the vagabond also obscures the crisis of capital that beleaguered life in the United States in the 1890s. Carman and Hovey avoid employing 'tramp' as a noun in their four volumes of vagabondia poetry, although its usage was common in the United States after it was first nominalized in the context of the economic panic of the 1870s (Ringenbach 4). An 1894 review of *Songs from Vagabondia* in the New York *Mail and Express* mistook the poets for 'intellectual tramp[s],' which degraded their art, in Henrietta Hovey's view, to 'mere hoboism' (qtd in Miller, *Bliss Carman* 127–8).[4] Carman and Hovey's reification of the vagabond figure thus deliberately detaches it from all class relations or material determinations. If the vagabond was a popular literary trope around the turn of the century, other discourses of transient mobility emerged in this period that eventually came to dominate twentieth-century conceptions of worklessness.

The Tramp and the Hobo: Frederick Philip Grove's *A Search for America*

In that same summer of 1892 when Carman stumbled across the inspiring vagabond reference, Frederick Philip Grove – also known as Felix

Paul Greve – arrived in North America, or so he claimed in both his pseudo-autobiographical novel *A Search for America* and his autobiography, *In Search of Myself* (1946). In the former text, Grove's persona Phil Branden's search for a national identity culminates in a figure who is the vagabond's antithesis – the settler-pioneer. The key difference between Carman and Hovey's turn-of-the-century vagabondia series and Grove's *A Search for America* is that the latter, although ostensibly set in the 1890s, is an expression of the cultural nationalism of Canada in the 1920s.

Since its publication in 1927, Grove's popular *A Search for America* has been heralded repeatedly within discourses of cultural nationalism. For example, Russell Brown's essay 'The Road Home: Meditation on a Theme,' which was published in the mid-1990s, contends that the road motif, which is so central to U.S.-American tropes of mobility and progress, has its opposite in centrifugal Canadian road narratives like *A Search for America*, which emphasize not 'escape but the need to discover some larger truths about the Canadian homeland' (34). Drawing on Northrop Frye's well-known assessment of Grove's 'quest for the peaceable kingdom' (first published in his conclusion to the *Literary History of Canada*) (360), Brown finds in *A Search for America* 'the irony of the newly arrived narrator's decision to leave Canada in order to go in search of a mythic America that speaks to his dreams of New World promise – because we know that he will return, learning in the end the familiar moral of children's stories, that the object of the quest lay all along where the journey began' (38). This thematic reading of the centrifugal tendencies of *A Search for America* echoes but does not identify the nationalist moment in which the book was first published by Ottawa's quixotically nationalist and short-lived publisher The Graphic Publishers. Immediately after reading and accepting *A Search for America* for publication in November of 1926, H.C. Miller, the president of Graphic, wrote to Grove that the Canadian authors – including Grove – his house hoped to secure 'have a message for our country and its people, and I hope that I will prove to be the medium to spread that gospel of a bigger and better Canada.'[5] This discourse was similarly employed by the Association of Canadian Clubs when they solicited Grove for a national speaking tour in 1928–9. The association, which in 1920 had reinvented itself in keeping with the heady postwar nationalism of the day, found in *A Search for America* an 'ideal subject' – 'an immigrant who had tried life in the United States, spurned it, and chosen Canada,' and in Grove himself they found 'a New Canadian who could give voice to the silent strangers, who could reveal their needs, trials and dreams to their would-be helpers' (Stobie 120).[6]

Grove's persona Phil Branden may resist what he perceives as the crass materialism of late nineteenth-century life in the United States by literally moving away from it into the pristine space of the Canadian west, but what exactly are the politics of this movement? Moreover, as a road narrative that attempts to imagine home through the figure of the settler-pioneer in the Canadian west, how is the movement of *A Search for America* embedded in its publication history?

A textually complex narrative with a notoriously dissembling author, Grove's *A Search for America* has yet to be examined in light of what human geographer Doreen Massey calls the politics of mobility. This theoretical lens enables a reading of the often perplexing admixture of romance and realism in *A Search for America* – a reading that engages both the time-space it purports to represent (the northeastern United States in the early 1890s) and the milieu in which it was actually written and disseminated (Canada in the 1920s). Mark Simpson augments Massey's suggestive phrase and employs it to describe 'the contestatory processes that produce different forms of movement, and that invest these forms with social value, cultural purchase, and discriminatory power' (xii–xiv). Sidestepping the elusive spectre of what 'actually happened' – which in the case of *A Search for America* presents a constantly disappearing trace – the politics of mobility seeks to 'restore, at the forefront of critique, the materiality of mobility alongside its differential production and reproduction' (xix). Canada lacks the powerful mythology of mobility as progress that Simpson examines in the context of the nineteenth-century United States, but the work of Simpson, Massey, and scholars such as Caren Kaplan urges us to examine other cultural mythologies of movement and their material determinations.

Despite the uneven meanings of mobility in Canada, rootedness in the land is a powerful and enduring idea in the nation's cultural and literary histories. Indeed, what Malkki calls 'sedentarist' thought – ranging from the botanical tropes that have described Canada's literary 'growth' to the tropes of literary regionalism – is a central component of nationalist cultural discourse in post-colonial Canada. As Paul Hjartarson contends, the figure of the settler-pioneer has played a crucial role in asserting, by metonymical relation, the nation's ownership of an ostensibly unclaimed and unnamed land ('Staking a Claim' 26–8). Through the autobiographical tendencies of his fiction, Grove explored and often associated with himself the figure of the white, male settler-pioneer. In relation to the canonization of Grove's novels (particularly the novels that continue to be reprinted and read as examples of 'prairie realism'), critics such as

Hjartarson have examined the cultural power of the pioneer myth and its historical embedding in the racialized category of the preferred immigrant. I would like to push this work further by looking more closely at the mobilities of *A Search for America* and, in particular, how the text rejects the idealized mobilities of Carman and Hovey in favour of a more historically specific experience, only to resolve itself in a sedentarist ideal that is specifically located in the space of the Canadian west.

The work of reading *A Search for America* obliges one first and foremost to grapple with the difficult question of genre. Following Grove's ambiguous prompting in his author's notes for the various editions of *A Search for America* and in his autobiography *In Search of Myself*, critics of *A Search for America* have read it as both autobiography and, especially since D.O. Spettigue's unveiling of Grove's fabricated past in 1971, semi-autobiography or fictional autobiography.[7] Yet Gaby Divay argues that the book contains valuable biographical clues that Grove scholars should not fail to overlook ('Felix Paul Greve' 132). A materialist approach to *A Search for America* is complicated by the fact that Branden's experiences often correspond in some way to the three years that Grove actually spent in the United States (from 1909 to 1912), but, in accordance with the biography that Grove fabricated in order to obscure his early life in Germany and on the European continent, he sets the events of the narrative in the early 1890s. In other words, this is a text that reveals as much as it hides about the enigma we know as Frederick Philip Grove, and the often puzzling admixture of romance and realism in *A Search for America* testifies to its ambivalent relation to its spatio-temporal ground.

A Search for America opens by figuring Grove's persona, Phil Branden, in relation to the classic hero of the nineteenth-century Bildungsroman, a genre that was particularly popular in Grove's Germany and that influenced his 1902 collection of poems, *Wanderungen* (Divay, 'Frederick Philip Grove's *A Search for America*'). Set adrift from a spiritual or material inheritance by his father's descent into poverty and subsequent death, Branden arrives in North America and undergoes his apprenticeship first as a waiter in Toronto and then as a bookseller in New York. Drawing on the work of Franco Moretti, Glenn Willmott reads the modern Canadian novel as Bildungsroman, claiming that the 'image of youth as a figure of mobility and restlessness which focalizes for society its own, new modernity' was already present in the post-traditional world of the early nineteenth-century Bildungsroman (25), but adds that this earlier form 'still takes as its domain of action a circumscribed and self-sufficient national space in which all things are continuous and connected by some form of social logic' (39). Such knowable space is decidedly absent, Willmott concludes, from the modern Canadian Bildungsroman, which grapples with the globalized space of an emerging technological-industrial economy that exists in ambivalent relation to the British Empire, making it difficult for the protagonist to reconcile the actual – local life on the ground – with the ideal – those values and aesthetics that mark the imperial world (22, 39). In the case of Grove's canon, as Smaro Kamboureli has pointed out, such fissures also 'spill out of his diasporic condition' (37) – his complex connections to a (German, English, and French) European literary heritage and to the German ethnicity that he disavowed, as Rudy Wiebe states frankly, in a 'world that hated Germans' (357).

In *A Search for America*, the tension between the actual and the ideal is apparent in the contest between realism and romance. At the end of Book Two, Branden abandons his apprenticeships in favour of withdrawal from society and a period of wandering, during which he seeks the romantic ideal of life in its essentials on the U.S.-American frontier but finds, in its place, the reality of the tramp and the hobo. The narrative's development thus moves the protagonist from the ideal of the romance to the contingent and particular reality of late nineteenth-century life in the United States. Its conclusion attempts to reconcile the ideal and the actual in the space of the Canadian west: it is here that Grove locates the elusive agrarian life on the soil, but the move is an idealizing one. Despite the narrative's self-proclaimed embeddedness in history, its conclusion refuses to cast its glance on the labour market conditions of western Canada in the early decades of the twentieth century. Moreover, the move is predicated on the anti-modernist opposition of mass-produced art – the kind of art produced in an industrialized society in which periodic unemployment, and thus tramping, are common – and the organic art that might be created in what Grove represents as the pre-industrial Canadian frontier. Willmott remarks that Grove and his contemporaries understood realism 'not to oppose romance but to absorb it,' such that 'realism must always register an incomplete reality, and romance an historicized wish' (23). The extreme brevity and suddenness of the conclusion of *A Search for America* signals not just Grove's anxiety about narrating his own arrival in the nation he desired to write into existence, but also the historical and political uncertainty of the prospect of realizing the 'historicized wish' of the agrarian ideal in modern Canada – the individual's will to be rooted in unoccupied space.

In the United States, *A Search for America*'s Phil Branden confronts the national mythology that linked mobility with progress in the post-bellum period, and learns to disdain its threat to his ideal – the 'ground-mass of the nation,' or the local, autonomous forms of existence he cherishes (356). Simpson describes the 'entangled ideologies of national identity and progress' that deployed 'mobility as their prime sign or symptom' in the latter half of the nineteenth century, and observes how this 'synonymity' was 'in a sense, nothing less than the promise of American democracy' (xxv); however, as Simpson observes, the 'core' of a seductive modern mobility depends, paradoxically, on 'the strategic potential of *inertia*' (93). Put another way, the technologies of mobility are both unevenly available and deeply regulatory: one might think here, for instance, of the spatialization of class and race divisions within a nineteenth-century passenger train. This paradox at the heart of modern mobility forms a key component of the early stages of Phil Branden's apprenticeship in the Bildungsroman of *A Search for America*. Although the mass-produced art and knowledge inside the travelogues he peddles profess to be instant tools of democratization and class mobility, they actually function as a means of putting readers and salespeople alike in perpetual debt to the company; in other words, instead of mobility they offer constant regression and repetition. Branden's subsequent encounter with the railway augments his critical response to the conflation of speed and national progress. In Book Two, before he abandons urban life for the road in Book Three, Branden contrasts the velocity and arrogance of night-time train travel in a comfortable berth, which allows him to see nothing of the land around him, with his emerging ideal – a slower, more thoughtful encounter on foot with life on the land (217–18). In this sense, the technological mastery of the train actually impedes his search. This comparison recurs in Book Four when Branden takes a terrifyingly monotonous ride on the rods of a 'giant monster' of a train and regrets the 'delightful tramp it might have been – in the green river-valley with its flood-plain, its sandbanks, and its shady trees' (379–80).

At the end of Book Two, Branden actively chooses to resist the national mythology of mobility as progress and its collusion with the technologies of speed through the slow and deliberate practice of wandering, which he initially understands in purely romantic terms. His decision to go 'out west' at the end of Book Two marks a point in the narrative when romance triumphs over realism. Margaret Stobie observes the text's Kafkaesque combination of 'realistic exactness' and 'dream-like romanticism' (63), and notes that the latter aesthetic, in particular, colours the narrative's highly literary tramping episodes, which allude to, among other texts, Ovid's *Metamorphoses*, Homer's *Odyssey* (a cloth-bound copy of which Branden retains on his tramps), Defoe's *Robinson Crusoe*, Twain's *Adventures of Huckleberry Finn,* and Thoreau's *Walden; or, Life in the Woods* (63–6). Branden admits before he sets out that underlying the anti-industrial 'western exodus' of which he imagines himself a part is a 'literary movement' that 'crystallized' in the name of reputed naturalist, essayist, and transcendentalist John Burroughs (248).

In his early, somewhat aimless, rambles outside New York City, Branden describes himself as 'strangely weightless' and 'adrift on the world,' lacking in the corporeal presence that would mark him as that which he does not wish to be – a productive labourer in the service of a capitalist imperative that he is beginning to disdain (260). The wandering episodes also possess a highly symbolic quality: Branden's overnight rebirth in the 'humus' of America at the beginning of Book Three, for example, signals his Thoreauvian departure from the corruption of urban life. Moreover, he calls attention to the anti-realist quality of this section of the narrative, noting that his memory of his time on the road is unreliable, full of 'apparent contradictions,' 'detached scenes,' and 'disconnected visions, like mere pictures flashed upon the screen of memory' (257). Significantly, this aesthetic of the 'disconnected vision' is echoed in the narrative's lack of reference to crucial events that occurred in the period in which it is set – the years between 1892 and 1894. While Branden's tramping episodes begin in the autumn of 1893, six months after 'Industrial Black Friday' on 5 May 1893 and well into the five-year Depression that ensued, the narrative, like Carman and Hovey's *Songs from Vagabondia,* makes no mention of these events and Branden never relates his own experiences of unemployment to the economic panic, which was the most significant downturn of the century and led to the highest unemployment rates in the history of the United States to that point (Ringenbach 38).

Yet unlike *Songs from Vagabondia,* Grove's narrative ultimately turns to the suffering body of the disenfranchised individual in its attempt to narrate Phil Branden into his place and time. Initially, this physical suffering is merely an allegory for the spiritual transformation that must occur in order for Branden to leave 'the society of man' (262) and, following the advice of Thomas Carlyle and Thoreau, locate the 'essentials' of existence (249); however, as Book Three charts Branden's westward wanderings through the Ohio River Valley, the physical torture of constant mobility, fatigue, hunger, and exposure to the elements becomes increasingly literal. Parallel to this movement from the allegorical to the literal is the suggestion that the literary archetype of the wanderer is less appropriate to Branden's experience than the late nineteenth-century, U.S.-American social constructions of the tramp and hobo. Tim Cresswell demonstrates how the boom and bust cycles of the late nineteenth-century economy in the United States, the development of a transcontinental rail system after 1869, and the growing need for mobile labour in the Great Lakes region created a 'conflation of mobility options and economic pressures' that led to the creation of the tramp – who grew out of the more local social problem of vagrancy or vagabondage – as a new social type (24–38). The literary quality of Branden's wandering might be said to more or less cease somewhere in Ohio, where his Huck Finn–like raft – his home on the road – is dashed to pieces.[8] Later, in Indiana, Branden attempts to find employment and shelter for the winter months but is rejected as a tramp – the 'scum of the country, which comes down the river' (322). Thus, a key aspect of Branden's search in Book Three of *A Search for America* is his recognition that an entire culture of tramps and hobos underpins his movement. A distinction between tramp and hobo emerged around the turn of the century to differentiate those who wandered but did not seek work from migratory workers (Cresswell 48–9), and, as Book Three progresses, Branden learns the difference between the shiftless tramp whose 'rambles are always at random' and the hobo, who is 'lord of the world' and master of his own labour – a 'coarser and de-sublimated Henry David Thoreau' (368). While the hobo maintains agency and proximity to nature, he is nevertheless a 'desublimated' version of the transcendental ideals with which Branden commenced his wandering.

Attempting to narrow the gap between self and space that is the shaping convention of the classic Bildungsroman, Grove relied on late nineteenth-century accounts of the lives of single, unemployed men in the United States. He clearly drew on the documentary essays of Norwegian writer Knut Hamsun and, very likely, turn-of-the-century tramp writers like Josiah Flynt. These intertexts, which suggest that Grove needed to research this period of U.S.-American history that he had not actually experienced, are much less visible than the allusions to the Western canon that permeate the narrative and that shore up Grove's self-narration as labourer-cum-author.[9] Knut Hamsun, who is perhaps best known for his Nobel Prize–winning novel *Growth of the Soil* (1917), also published extensively on the subject of modern life in the United States, which he experienced during two sojourns in 1882–3 and 1887–8. Like Phil Branden, Hamsun was disillusioned with the materialism of life in the United States, its false promises of liberty and democracy, and its lack of cultural refinement – themes he explored in his book *On the Cultural Life of Modern America* (1889). From Hamsun Grove took the story of the Bonanza Farm, which appears as the sprawling Mackenzie Farm that Branden and his hobo companion Ivan work on in Book Four.[10] Bonanza Farms were huge, mechanized wheat farms that proliferated in the Red River Valley after the Sioux were dispersed and the development of railways opened the area for white settlement in the 1870s, and they were major employers of itinerant labour in this period (Cresswell 37). Hamsun worked on such a farm near Casselton, Dakota Territory in 1887, at the end of the boom in the area, and wrote about his experiences in essays such as 'On the Prairie,' which was first published in the collection *Brushwood: Stories and Sketches* in Copenhagen in 1903.[11]

Complementing Hamsun's accounts is a minor genre of 'life on the road' narratives produced around the turn of the century in the United States, the best-known of which is Josiah Flynt's *Tramping with Tramps* (1899). Flynt, who went on the tramp to escape a Puritanical upbringing, began to write about his experiences in 1891, producing a 'constant stream' of illustrated articles in popular magazines such as *Century Magazine* and *Atlantic Monthly* (Cresswell 60).[12] Cresswell describes Flynt's experimentation with what sociologists of the twentieth century would call participant observation – his predilection for studying the tramp in his habitat while posing as one of them. In his 'author's note' to *Tramping with Tramps*, Flynt describes his methodology by way of an analogy to the scientific study of 'parasitic forms of life,' and argues that 'in writing on what I have learned concerning human parasites by an experience that may be called scientific in so far as it deals with the subject on its own ground and in its peculiar conditions and environment, I seem myself to be doing similar work with a like purpose' (ix). In the book's first study, 'The Criminal in the Open,' Flynt suggests that the popular scientific practice of assessing physiognomy should be supplanted by the study of the criminal outcast's 'milieu' (26). Flynt thus literalized Carman's and Hovey's literary role playing as a means of advocating for social reform, although his recommendations were rarely sympathetic to the unemployed whom he studied. Like Flynt, Branden engages in a sort of participant observation: in Book Four, despite his continued inability to secure stable work, he claims that he could 'step out of this condition of hobodom whenever I chose to' (418) and increasingly assumes the posture of the observer gleaning knowledge about a 'particular brand of humanity' – the hobo (419). As an ostensibly detached observer, Flynt condemned tramps as morally degenerate and hopelessly lazy, suggesting that both free transportation on the railroads and comfortable jails only encouraged tramping (302–3, 99). Grove picks up this latter point in *A Search for America*: Branden's first encounter with another tramp, which occurs just after his raft is destroyed, introduces him to the idea that there are men in America who would not work if they were offered it, and who use jails as a means of sheltering and feeding themselves without labour.

By the end of Book Four, Branden is more sympathetic than Flynt with the hobo, who 'has or at any rate had a definite function in the nation's economy' (368), and contends that the hobo's lamentable existence is a structural feature of an industrial capitalism that relies on 'partial or seasonal employment' (416). In Branden's opinion, the hobo figure thus becomes one more symptom of what Grove later called a nation 'gone insane with transportation and speed' ('Nationhood' 161). The labour market prevents the hobo from remaining in place, and this in turn, as Branden laments, engenders a wanderlust 'mania' in the hobo for which 'they can no longer be held responsible' (416). In keeping with the paradox at the heart of modern mobility, the hobo's movement succeeds in perpetuating rather than alleviating his poverty. Through Branden, Grove thus deploys a discourse of reform that emerged in the United States in the mid-1890s. Historian Paul Ringenbach contends that social reformers in the northeastern United States did not link the category of the 'tramp' to structural problems in the labour market until after the 1893 economic panic (47–65). By participating in, and acting as visionary spokesman for, a contemporary social movement, Branden – and Grove – become significant men of their time, and also begin to shore up the final arguments in favour of Branden's rejection of the United States.

If Branden's apprehension of the political economy of the late nineteenth-century United States – that is to say, the move to realism from romance – functions as a means of closing the gap between self and space, he eventually decides that his knowledge of social and labour conditions in the United States has come at the cost of his romantic ideals, and that this exchange will not yield a meaningful life. Moreover, there are clues throughout the narrative that Grove's attempt to narrate Branden into the particular time-space of the United States in the late nineteenth century is not without slippage. One persistent problem is that the narrative is inevitably bound to Grove's actual distance from the time and place in which it is set. Grove claims in his author's note that the 'anachronisms,' such as the motor cars that appear throughout the book, are the 'inevitable consequence' of many decades of rewriting, and these, as well as the omission of crucial historical events such as the depression of the 1890s,

serve as constant reminders to the reader of the author's strained relation to the ground of his subject. Anachronisms and omissions have their
parallel in other textual clues: K.P. Stich points out that Branden's work
as a 'veneer man' and a tree pruner/grafter at the end of Book Three
and the beginning of Book Four functions as a metaphor for Grove's
own biographical 'pruning' and shaping (160). Although Branden's self-
recognition as a tramp and then hobo seems to acknowledge the social
and economic contingencies of the period in which the narrative is set,
the hobo role functions as another of the text's many masks. Grove did
not spend twenty (or any!) seasons as an itinerant farm labourer as he
claimed in *In Search of Myself* (195–6),[13] and the text's suggestive links to
both Knut Hamsun and Josiah Flynt perhaps serve, like the references
to veneering and pruning, as another of Grove's many cryptic textual
clues to his own dissembling. The short narratives of life in the United
States that Hamsun published in Norwegian and Danish newspapers in
the 1880s are 'presented as personal experiences' but, like *A Search for
America*, 'actually fuse fact and fiction' (Warken 30). Moreover, Josiah
Flynt was, like Grove, a wearer of masks: 'He successfully led a double
life as a tramp and as a figure on the margins of literary circles. He travelled widely in Europe as well as in the United States. He liked to dress
up, to play out different rôles, and he had a remarkable linguistic ability' (Cresswell 60). Educated in Germany and fluent in German, Flynt
reversed Grove's trajectory from Germany to North America, returning
to Germany many times as an undercover tramp in order to conduct his
field research.[14] In the concluding pages of *A Search for America*, Branden
insists that hobodom has similarly become for him a kind of 'disguise'
that he can don and discard at will: 'I have since gone out like that again,
a good many times; I have always enjoyed such holidays' (437). He thus
claims his ability to detach himself from the historical, political, and economic contingencies that he has taken such pains to apprehend, and it
is this unmooring that enables his seemingly untethered movement into
Canada at the conclusion of the narrative.

The Settler-Pioneer Ideal vs. Narratives of Mobility

For Phil Branden, taking up national subjecthood in Canada means re-
nouncing the U.S.-American myth of mobility and its underside – the
structural unemployment of masses of men – in favour of life in Canada
as a settler-pioneer. Branden finally, if very suddenly in the concluding
paragraphs of this vast narrative, realizes that his long-standing desire

to 'take root somewhere' (369) can only be realized in Canada. As Spettigue wrote in his classic 1969 study of Grove, Branden's choice to 'seek again the conditions of the agricultural way of life in the belief that it alone connotes freedom' is echoed in Abe Spalding's decision to abandon the 'settled East' in favour of the open west in Grove's 1933 novel *Fruits of the Earth* (131). This theme is also one that Grove used as the centrepiece of his 1928–9 lectures for the Association of Canadian Clubs. In 'Nationhood,' for example, the author pronounces that of all the peoples of North America, only the 'plain, rough people' of the Canadian prairies had preserved the 'tragic reaction of human souls to the fundamental conditions of man's life on earth' (155). In *A Search for America*, Canada becomes the open west of America's closed and morally corrupt east. This Canadian west is an idealized, rural space that will, as Branden tells us, 'inherit the world' because it has the capacity to feed the masses (436). In 'Nationhood,' Grove expands this notion of the ideal west, bringing it closer to the romantic individualism of Thoreau's philosophical tradition. In this lecture, he insists that the capacity to produce bread for the world is nothing for Canada to boast of; what the rural areas of the nation have preserved through their contact with the 'essentials and fundamentals of life' is the 'spiritual heritage' of Britain and Europe (158–9), and the 'soil' these pioneers till is the purely metaphorical ground from which 'new thought, new art, new religious feeling can spring' (162). In other words, armed with the right cultural inheritances, the new-world artist can write on blank space, just as the settler-pioneer is granted the power to settle and grant meaning to ostensibly uninhabited space. The actual work of farming the land, Grove implies, is incidental and perhaps even irrelevant to this idealistic vision. Appropriately, then, Branden moves to the Canadian west to become a teacher rather than a farmer, despite the fact that his ideal is, like Thoreau's, agrarian in nature. Upon his arrival in Canada, Branden immediately has 'a number of interviews' for teaching positions (448), and, in the seeming effortlessness of two short paragraphs, he becomes an intellectual and moral guide for the 'foreign settlements' of the Canadian west: 'I have been a teacher ever since; and not only a teacher, but the doctor, lawyer, and business-agent of all the immigrants in my various districts' (448). The brevity and marked suddenness of the conclusion of *A Search for America*, which is exacerbated by the fact that Grove's belief that Thoreau's ideal now exists only in the Canadian west appears as a mere footnote, signal the slippage between the actual experience of life on the land north of the border and Branden's romantic ideal.[15]

The forced mobility of the hobo figure becomes the opposite of the pioneer's rootedness in this conclusion; that is to say, it functions as a means of opposing an actually corrupt United States to a purer, agrarian ideal that exists in yet-to-be-settled Canada. Yet seeking the rapprochement of his ideal with the actual space of the Canadian west requires Grove to ignore some crucial aspects of that geopolitical space. For example, *A Search for America* suggests that labour mobility, which, as Branden continually tells us, has nefarious effects south of the border, is not a structural feature of the labour market in either late nineteenth- or early twentieth-century Canada. This portrait of Canada forms part of Grove's enduring appeal: as Hjartarson argues, the figure of the white, northern European, immigrant pioneer – and *not* the figure of the eastern or southern European or Asian mobile labourer – is 'central to the cultural production of a "national" literature in English-Canada' in the interwar and postwar periods ('Staking' 22). Central to the mythology of settlement is the process of forgetting – forgetting not just, as Hjartarson, Alan Lawson, and others point out, the indigenous presence on the land, but also, I would add, the emerging technological-industrial economy that depended on the mobile labour of officially non-preferred immigrants.

The seasonal and therefore mobile character of work in colonial British North America that historians such as Judith Fingard have documented continued well into the twentieth century. Historian Donald Avery contends that of the millions of mostly eastern and southern European workers who arrived in Canada during the young nation's first major wave of immigration between 1896 and 1932, most were unskilled workers who were more or less restricted to mobile forms of seasonal and temporary labour (15). Labour historians thus agree that 'geographical mobility' and 'occupational pluralism' typified the European immigrant experience of this period (Avery 8; Struthers, *No Fault* 4; Heron 32–3). These largely unskilled workers flocked to Canada as part of a transatlantic phenomenon of the second industrial revolution – the division of Atlantic economies and their colonies into industrializing and rural areas, a division that drew the absolute surplus population from less developed areas and attracted them to places, like the United States and Canada, where their unskilled labour was needed (Hoerder 6). This mass migration of a landless proletariat, then, had much to do with the uneven development patterns of industrial capitalism. Once in Canada, these immigrants tended to find work in waged employment (mining, lumbering, harvesting, and railroad construction) rather than setting up homesteads, which required considerable capital (Avery 16). British writer Harold Baldwin's retrospective account of his experience trying to secure a 'farm for two pounds' in the second decade of the twentieth century, *A Farm for Two Pounds: Being the Odyssey of an Emigrant* (1935), is suggestive of the obstacles that faced immigrants to Canada in this period. Baldwin, a 'stocky,' working-class 'boy from the Midlands' (3), may have had the requisite British ethnicity, but the first-person narrator laments that his agrarian ideal was elusive: 'I had come to Canada to practise the virtues of my race and escape the doom of industrialism. And there I was being drawn into factory work or at best the life of a roustabout pick and shovel stiff' (47). Only after a considerable series of initiations in the factories and farms of southern Ontario and Manitoba, the westbound freights, the lumber camps of northern Ontario, and the indomitable terrain of his homestead grant in Manitoba, does 'Harry' finally receive the patent on his quarter section.

If homesteading was not always an option for pre-war immigrants, seasonal work in the agricultural sector was; sometimes, as in the case of the seasonal Swedish labourers on the North Dakota Bonanza Farm in *A Search for America*, such temporary work was used to finance a homestead in its early years. Avery shows that in the period of high immigration between 1896 and 1914, the Canadian government particularly sought seasonal farmworkers for the grain fields of the prairies and the sugar beet and fruit farming operations of Ontario, Alberta, and British Columbia (19). As a result of the expanding agricultural sector in the first decade of the twentieth century, the number of such male, immigrant workers increased dramatically: in 1901, 20,000 harvesters were recruited through the agents employed by the Immigration Branch of the federal government; in 1914, the year after Grove took up his first teaching post in Manitoba, 50,000 such labourers were sought (Avery 21). Struthers notes that 'regular employment for the labourer was unusual' in the early decades of the twentieth century in Canada because the 'labour market for primary sector workers was dominated by an immigration policy shaped to suit the needs of Canada's agricultural and resource industry employers,' which meant that there was 'a constant tendency towards over-supply in order to keep wages down and to ensure that enough men were available' for peak seasons (*No Fault* 4). The seasonal industries – logging, mining, railway or other construction, and manufacturing industries – that formed the backbone of the young Canadian economy in the pre-1930 period relied on and subsequently lobbied the government for supplies of cheap, seasonal, immigrant labour.

Martin Allerdale Grainger's 1908 novel *Woodsmen of the West* documents the seasonal, mobile character of work in the early twentieth-century west coast logging industry and defends the way of life it represents:

> And if my balance-sheet for the year is no great affair, in your sophisticated eyes; if I spend, in idleness in bad winter weather or in wandering to fresh fields of effort, much of my yearly profit; if, in fact, my year's work has inevitable interruptions – still, is it not the best, most satisfying work that is intermittent, that gives one rest after toil, time for recuperation? Work such as that is a more buoyant affair than the deadly treadmill work that goes on, soogey-moogey, day in day out, for forty-nine perfunctory weeks of the year. (42)

Grainger's narrator critiques working conditions in the logging industry but nevertheless privileges the 'freedom' of seasonal labour. Writing against the Protestant, liberal values that suffused the best-selling fiction of Ralph Connor, whose *Black Rock: A Tale of the Selkirks* (1898) pits a muscular Christianity against the intemperate habits of itinerant miners in a British Columbia frontier town, Grainger's defence implies that the morality of the itinerant labourer was a source of concern for church and state authorities. A much greater, though often related, source of anxiety for immigration officials was the fact that a mobile workforce required a very porous immigration policy. By 1913, this led immigration officials to wonder if Canada was becoming 'increasingly committed to a guest-worker form of immigration' (Avery 29). The 1910 Immigration Act (which was in place until 1952) granted Cabinet the ability to regulate 'the volume, ethnic origin, or occupational composition' of immigration (Knowles 110), but industry nevertheless played a central role in immigration practices in this period. In the early twentieth century, the mining industry, like railway construction, required a mass of labourers who were willing to work for low wages in dangerous conditions. Along with the railway and logging sectors, mining interests lobbied the government for an 'open door' immigration policy, often ignoring statutes like the 1897 Alien Labour Act.[16] The vociferous demands of such corporations as the Canadian Pacific Railway were able to goad the government into abandoning its ideal of attracting settler agriculturalists. Early twentieth-century immigration thus reflected the need for workers 'willing to roam the country to take up whatever work was available – railroad construction in the Canadian Shield in the summer, harvesting in Saskatchewan in the fall, coal mining in Alberta in the winter, and lumbering in British Columbia in the spring' (Avery 17–18).

Many poetry collections and fictional and non-fictional narratives published in the interwar period, most of which have been more or less forgotten by contemporary readers and critics, unsettle the settler-pioneer ideal of *A Search for America* and speak to this history of transient labour. Such narratives of mobility may be read against any number of modern novels, such as Douglas Durkin's *The Magpie* (1923), Laura Goodman Salverson's *The Viking Heart* (1923), Robert Stead's *Grain* (1926), or Hubert Evans's *The New Front Line* (1927).[17] Most obviously, the radical poets of the teens and twenties, who generally expressed themselves in the popular ballad form, offer narratives of mobility. Poets such as Nova Scotia's Joe Wallace and Cape Breton's Dawn Fraser documented the lives of itinerant labours; indeed, these poets often lived this life of seasonal labour mobility. The poems of Dawn Fraser offer telling examples of the way in which a popular poet of the period both celebrated and queried the transient life that was necessary for the survival of so many working-class men in early twentieth-century North America.[18] Fraser's early ballads from the years preceding the First World War, many of which were later included in *Songs of Siberia and Rhymes of the Road* (1919?), record 'the excitement and exhilaration of a footloose working class youth on the roam through the Boston States, an experience shared by thousands of Maritimers of Fraser's generation' (Frank and Macgillivray 10). Although the experience of serving in the First World War modified Fraser's early poetic persona as a 'youthful drifter' (Frank and Macgillivray 12), the poems of pre-war work-camp life in *Songs of Siberia and Rhymes of the Road* embrace the concordance of transient mobility and the popular ballad form, but they are not simply idealizations of transient mobility in the way that Carman's and Hovey's vagabondia poems are. In 'Introduction,' Fraser's persona informs us that

> I offer the rhymes of a rover,
> Rhymes of the land and the sea,
> Oh! Give me the Wild the great simple child,
> Give me the open and free. (10)

Yet other poems in the collection are less sanguine about the rover's freedom. 'Shanghied,' for instance, narrates the price the itinerant, seasonal worker must pay for his brief periods of autonomy. In 'Shanghied,' the desperate position of the worker at the end of his 'hard earned summer's roll' leads him to join a crew heading for northern Maine (109). A profligate night en route to the work camp enables the speaker to dream 'I married Cleopatra and lived some-where in class, / While her Oriental servants poured my Boose out by the glass,' but the escape is temporary: 'I woke up in a Logging Camp, up on Mus-qua-cook Lake' (109). By contrast, the speaker of 'Marching Down the Tote Road,' who describes the end rather than the beginning of a work contract, willingly barters a three-month 'sentence' in the same Maine logging camp for the mobility the 'time slip' engenders (199). The author's comment on 'Marching Down the Tote Road,' however, suggests that its celebratory chorus, which figures the departure from the camp as a 'hike' that allows the transient labourer to return to his natural state, is the product of idealizing youth: 'Aint that just a grand "Pome"; we wrote that when we were very young' (199).

Narratives of mobility also appeared in the travel-writing genre. Elizabeth Waterston identifies numerous 'reports of wanderers in hungry search of work' as one component of the vogue for 'travel' narratives about Canada, many of which were authored by British writers, in the interwar period (108–10). Non-fictional narratives such as Baldwin's *A Farm for Two Pounds*; *Adventures and Misadventures, or, an Undergraduate's Experiences in Canada* (1922) by the pseudonymous 'Lofty'; G.H. Westbury's *Misadventures of a Working Hobo in Canada* (1930); and Edward Fitzgerald Fripp's *The Outcasts of Canada: Why Settlements Fail* (1932), for example, offer episodic accounts of itinerant life in the teens and twenties. The accounts of itinerant life in the latter decade, such as Fripp's, condemn the 1922 Empire Settlement Agreement, a scheme designed to place experienced British farm labourers and farmers and their families on Canadian land, to employ unemployed British women as domestics in Canada, and to supply 'juvenile immigrants' to the labour market (Kelley and Trebilcock 192–8). Split into two halves, Fripp's narrative follows two arcs: the buoyancy of the settler's hope when confronted with the potential rewards of farming in the Okanagan Valley and working as a 'clerk' in Vancouver, and the descent into utter despair as the promises of making a 'stake' become increasingly risible. If a common trope in these narratives is the English 'public-school' boy determined to show his prowess as a labourer, these texts also attempt to represent those itinerant labourers who were not writing in English about their experiences in this period. These labourers – Italian sojourners in *A Farm for Two Pounds* and Chinese market gardeners in *The Outcasts of Canada*, for example – create anxiety for the British-born narrators because they 'can accomplish an astonishing amount of work in a day' and so make the British would-be farmer's efforts look meagre (Fripp 117). In Fripp's account, however, we are told almost without irony that such efficacious workers cannot own the land they work, and are condemned to rent from British settlers.

In the realm of the novel, as well, the narrative of mobility appeared. Magnus Pyke's *Go West, Young Man, Go West* (1930) and Bernard J. Farmer's *Go West, Young Man* (1936), both first novels for their respective authors, adapt the frontier discourse of the nineteenth-century United States to Canada in the 1920s, but their ironic deployment of the imperative indicates the common bonds they share with the travel narratives of the period.[19] Like Dawn Fraser's ironic ballad 'Go West, Young Man, Go West' (reprinted in *Echoes from Labour's War*), which he wrote in the context of the labour strife and economic uncertainties of Cape Breton in the mid-1920s that led to an exodus of workers from the region, Pyke's and Farmer's novels overturn the celebratory mobility of the frontier settler. Pyke's is a satirical novel set, like Farmer's, in British Columbia, and if that location seems 'like England, only larger' upon the protagonist's arrival, his dream of escaping the tedium of city life on a Canadian farm is soon dashed, and he settles for life as a bank clerk in Vancouver (6). Farmer's protagonist, a naive and stiff young Englishman named Peter Cochrane, encounters the defensive prejudices of Canadian settlers and must learn to live with rough labour, the tyrannical foremen of lumber camps and section gangs, and unmannerly 'bohunks,' all of which link *Go West, Young Man* to the travel narratives of the 1920s and early 1930s. As R.S. Kennedy's review of the novel in the April 1936 issue of the cultural periodical *New Frontier* reveals, Farmer drew on his own experiences as an immigrant from Britain in the 1920s to pen his narrative:

> Bernard J. Farmer himself did most of the things which his hero does, – and suffered much greater privations. When working on a Northern Ontario construction gang, part of a crane fell on his shoulder and rendered his arm useless for many months. In hospital, this young man, – with no literary affiliations whatever, started writing stories – the only way he could think of to earn a living when he got out. He never gave up that attempt. In the end he succeeded, and this first promising novel is his first venture into the larger field. (34)

It is precisely such a happy ending that distinguishes Farmer's novel from its non-fictional predecessors, all of which refuse the romance ideal that concludes *Go West*: married to the woman he loves, working in the well-paying job he has earned, and watching over his newborn son, Peter reflects sanguinely on the setting sun, 'red and gold, startlingly vivid, splendid even in its dying – a Canadian sunset. Henceforth Canada's great star would be his' (309). In the conclusion to *A Farm for Two Pounds*, Baldwin expresses an analogous love for the land of his adoption – its 'over-arching sky that lifted the heart to its height whatever the weight of care' – but the price he has paid for such a sky has clearly been excessive (299). For 'Lofty,' who exploits the narrative potential of his middle-class, 'undergraduate' persona, the life of an itinerant labourer is appallingly ill-fitting, and he beetles back to England to enlist as soon as the First World War breaks out.

Another narrative of mobility appeared in the same year that Grove's *A Search for America* was published. *A Search for America* first appeared in print in October 1927, and Trevor Maguire's 'O Canada! A Tale of Canadian Workers' Life' was published serially in the weekly Toronto newspaper *The Worker* from February to September 1927.[20] *The Worker* was the 'official organ' of the Communist Party of Canada (CPC) between 1922 and 1936 and sold for five cents an issue. A cultural expression of both the structurally entrenched forms of mobility that characterized Canada's early twentieth-century labour market and the labour unrest and anti-union activity that marked the volatile period following the First World War, Maguire's serial novel first made its appearance in the pages of *The Worker* alongside an article that makes it clear that for many working-class Canadians, the Depression only aggravated existing problems for workers and their families. Adumbrating the protests that would filter into the discourse of social democracy in the 1930s, 'Calgary Unemployed Want Investigation' (19 February 1927) decries the characterization of Calgary's unemployed as criminal 'vagrants' and criticizes the inadequacy of provincial relief programs. Moreover, Maguire's novel attends to the ethnic and linguistic diversity of the mobile labour force of the period without collapsing into stereotypes. In this way, 'O Canada!' also offers a counter-narrative to those Depression-era periodical texts discussed in the next chapter that strategically confine unemployment to Anglo workers as a means of arguing for the necessity of state intervention.

Like *A Search for America*, Maguire's 'O Canada!' attempts to narrate the coming-of-age tale of the Bildungsroman. George Hawtrey is the young, adventure-loving son of a middle-class Methodist parson in the village of Cambridgeshire, England, in the first decade of the twentieth century. Unlike Phil Branden, he is not disinherited but rather rejects his bland inheritance – a clerical position in London and a meagre life at a desk in a stifling class system. Advertisements beckon George to the open west of Canada, and his family sends him off after convincing him that employment as a bank clerk in Toronto would be more fitting for a young man of his birth and upbringing than labour as a harvest hand. He leaves England 'equipped with fatherly advice, a trunk full of clothes packed by his mother, and letters of introduction from prominent Methodist ministers' (19 February 1927). With each weekly instalment, George sheds more of these middle-class appurtenances and advantages, until his dissatisfying work as a bank clerk, his experiences as a soldier in the First World War, and his exploitation as a seasonal worker in railway construction, road building, and harvesting leave him with nothing save a 'cheap, secondhand packsack' that he fills with rocks in order to be admitted to the various labour camps he secures employment at (2 July 1927). He must not be a shiftless tramp with no baggage if he wants to be hired; paradoxically, however, the mobile life of seasonal employment has made it impossible and undesirable for him to own anything, and his packsack functions as a powerful parody of liberal conceptions of property. Ultimately, like Phil Branden, Hawtrey abruptly dissolves his unhappiness in the chimera of an ideal, but unlike Branden's ideal, Hawtrey's is undercut by the narrative itself. In the case of the ironically entitled 'O Canada!' the ideal is the possibly greener pasture of the United States, where, as the narrator tells us with tongue firmly in cheek, 'fortune might again smile on him' (10 September 1927).

In his literary history of the communist left in Canada, Doyle lauds Maguire's 'innovative' deployment of social critique, which he situates on the vanguard of a communist cultural aesthetic in Canada that flowered more fully in the context of the Depression (75–9). While Doyle interprets the novel's didacticism as a feature of its anticipation of the conventions of proletarian fiction, he contends that such didacticism is better suited to the form that most fiction writers on the radical left came to favour in the 1930s – the short story (96). Yet Maguire's use of the form of the serialized novel complements rather than detracts from the central theme of 'O Canada!' Most obviously, the pattern of seeking work and finding long days, unsafe and unsanitary conditions, and low wages is echoed in the form of the weekly instalment, which appears to be taking the reader somewhere – often the instalments end at the hopeful beginning of the next journey – but, like the 'monotonous, jarring rumble' of the freight trains Hawtrey hops, leads only to more of the same (18 June 1927). There is another level on which this synonymity of form and content operates: there are some strange gaps and incongruities near the end of the novel that speak to the precarious conditions under which both George Hawtrey and Trevor Maguire labour(ed). During the summer of 1927, the novel undergoes two brief periods of silence and then resumes its regular weekly appearance in September before its final instalment appears on 10 September 1927. One of the summer instalments (16 July 1927) confuses the serial narrative trajectory and places George and his companion, Paddy Kehoe, in the west at threshing time rather than in North Bay in the early winter. As if Maguire himself could not keep pace with the dizzying requirements of seasonal labour migrations and becomes, like his characters, unable to connect with any broader history or cultural memory, this instalment makes it clear that one job is as good – or bad – as another. Doyle surmises that both Maguire's silences in the summer of 1927 and the 'abrupt, arbitrary, and mechanically introduced' conclusion could be attributed to 'external circumstances,' such as the waning commitment to literary material in *The Worker* under the editorship of Maurice Spector or the emerging Stalinist-Trotskyist split that was polarizing the ranks of the CPC in the last years of the 1920s (78–9). Yet the radical incompleteness of Maguire's Bildungsroman – its utter inability to merge self and space – also mediates a worker's alienation as it is produced within the Canadian labour market in the decades prior to the Depression. In this sense, Maguire's 'O Canada!' anticipates the crisis of form embodied in the open-ended road narrative of the Depression-era cultural left.

Like his analysis of Canada in the first decades of the twentieth century, Trevor Maguire's life as author and political activist has received little attention in Canadian cultural history. Indeed, very little is known about Maguire: he was born at Carleton Place, Ontario, in 1887 and fought in the First World War; he was a founding member of the CPC and proselytized energetically for the party until his arrest for sedition in 1922; and he laboured administratively and creatively for *The Worker* during the 1920s (Doyle 73–4). Given the nexus of political and creative work in Maguire's life, it is unlikely that he held the literary author in very high regard. Like many of his contemporaries, however, Frederick Philip Grove believed fervently in the romantic cult of literary genius, which he seamlessly and deliberately merged with his sedentarist ideal. Mobility's contest – the opposition of U.S.-American speed and its nefarious effects in the labour market to Canadian settlement and its salubrious moral, cultural, and artistic effects – is clearly a central theme of *A Search for America*. Complementing this dichotomy throughout the narrative is the anti-modernist opposition of mass-produced (American) and organic (Canadian) art.[21] The binary opposition of an urbanized United States and a pastoral Canada that is implicit in much of Grove's writing about a national literature was common in the cultural discourse of Canadian postwar nationalism. For example, Lionel Stevenson's 'Manifesto for a National Literature,' which appeared in the Canadian Authors' Association (CAA) periodical the *Canadian Bookman* in February 1924, contrasts U.S.-American and Canadian literatures by noting the 'pervasive' influence of industrialized, urban life – 'cities and factories and immigrating swarms' – on American letters, and urges Canadian poets to open themselves to the 'natural influences' of their nation (206).

As *A Search for America* tells us, books in the United States have ceased to retain unique value. As a door-to-door peddler of travelogues in New York, Grove's Phil Branden discovers that cheap, mass-produced books, such as 'Dr Elliott's Shelf of Best Books in the World,' are just one more product in the market rather than objects with unique value. Here the focus of Grove's anti-modernist critique is an anachronism: Charles W. Eliot's 'Five-Foot Shelf of Books,' also known as 'Harvard Classics' because Eliot had been president of Harvard University, was published in the United States by P.F. Collier and Son beginning in 1909 (and not the 1890s, as Grove suggests). Intended to 'furnish a liberal education to anyone willing to devote fifteen minutes per day to reading them,' these books anticipated the various forms of middlebrow culture that emerged in the three decades following the First World War (Rubin, *The Making* 27–8). If this middlebrow mass culture was feminized by the time Grove was writing *A Search for America*, the alternatives of organic art and open space are clearly masculinized. Although Branden's boss, appropriately named Mr Tinker, avers the democratizing influence of a book in every house, he discourages Branden from actually reading the books and insists that he sell them by means of a standard 'canvass' (170). Branden finds value in the experience only when he deviates from the canvass and, adumbrating his later decision to wander, ventures outside of the recommended sales territory and into the 'open country,' where an encounter with a farmer enables an honest sale. Before the sale can happen, we are reminded that Branden and the farmer are 'both men, face to face with Nature' (188). Yet this job ends when Branden finally reads the travelogues and discovers, to his horror, that 'the whole work was dead, lifeless, without a spark of genius. The author had seen what everybody sees; he had followed the beaten track of tourist-travel, even though he had gone far and wide' (202). Both the peddler of the travelogues and their author are confined to predictable, knowable mobile practices in order to achieve mass distribution.

Branden's second book-selling experience initially appears to offer him the opportunity of honestly representing the value of 'a very high-priced, limited edition de-luxe' encyclopedia (209–10), but he soon learns that the company he works for has neither limited production nor enabled artisanal book production. Instead, the 'de-luxe' edition is a scam: its 'Holland paper' is a 'machine-made' forgery, its numbered prints are a hoax, and its 'hand-painted illustrations' are made by 'some fifty young ladies sitting who colour the half-tones at the rate of twenty an hour, or the boss wants to know the reason why' (240). Moreover, the contents of the books offer evidence of the fact that 'scientific and liter-ary America did seem parasitic; it rooted in the millennia-old culture of Europe' (214). An industrial culture premised on mass production and middlebrow fakery, Branden concludes, cannot nourish an authentic ar-tistic genius that springs from contact with the soil. As Walter Benjamin ambivalently observed in 1936, modern conditions of production, which he dated to the turn of the nineteenth century, had rendered obsolete a number of concepts, such as 'creativity and genius, eternal value and mystery' (218), only to conserve them, in T.W. Adorno's words, in the 'foggy mist' of the 'decaying aura' (102). Grove's Branden shares none of Benjamin's celebration and all of his reservations about the age of mechanical reproduction. Grove later echoed this theme in his 'Na-tionhood' lecture, in which he characterizes the spiritual and intellec-tual corruption of the United States in terms of the nation's avowal of both 'mass-production,' which 'does away with artistic aspirations,' and 'standardization,' which renders the 'individuality' of the artist obsolete (143).

In Grove's 1928 novel *Our Daily Bread*, the aging farmer/patriarch/protagonist John Elliott Senior confronts the modernity he loathes in the sumptuous (but unpaid for) Winnipeg home of his daughter: while guests at a social gathering in the home complain that young men can no longer survive on the land, Elliott encounters a 'bold woman' dressed to 'underline her sex' who claims to want to write a novel 'about pio-neers,' although she has never met one (182–3)! Elliott is disgusted by the 'minx,' her rejection of her God-given womanly duties, and her ab-surd literary ambitions. Significantly, his response parallels Grove's deep conviction that life on the land was the only authentic ground for the nurturing of a national literature. As Grove asserts in 'Nationhood,' a society converted by the 'new gospel of economic success' looks after neither its arts nor its citizens, but an agrarian settler culture produces a national artistic spirit through its contact with the 'fundamental conditions of man's life on earth' (147, 155). Indeed, he claims that his departure from Europe, like Phil Branden's, entailed the search for 'an environment which would help me to express that individual, tragic reaction to life, the world, the universe – to God – which I felt to be alive within me.' If, says Grove, such a search came to nothing in the United States, it was realized in the Canadian west (154–5). Out of this encounter with the Canadian west will come not a 'parasitic' art but a grounded one – a European heritage respectfully transformed by a 'new hopefulness' that comes from 'the fact that here, in this country, [settlers] can own the soil on which they stand' (163). Grove thus implies that the production of *A Search for America* has only been possible because he crossed the border into Canada, where a true artistic culture – and the individual visionary with a European heritage who is the centre of that culture – may take root in ostensibly unoccupied space that is, crucially, owned by the European settler. In this way, Grove maps the colonizing discourse of settling blank space onto the romantic discourse of literary genius, which assumes that creation entails unique and original thought – new writing on a blank canvas. The convergence of genius with an Anglo-European pedigree, the Canadian west, and botanical figures of rootedness and growth is key here. Such a convergence is clearly operating in the dedication that appears in the first (Graphic) edition of *A Search for America*. The dedication echoes the romantic tropes of growth employed in 'Nationhood' to situate the book in humble relation to George Meredith, Algernon Swinburne, and Thomas Hardy: 'Canadian literature is a mere bud on the tree of the great Anglo-Saxon tradition.' The 'bud' of Grove's own literary production is both respectfully dependent upon and youthfully distinct from the tree that parents it, transformed by its contact with the Canadian west and his own, individual genius. Benedict Anderson locates in discourses of nationalism the 'Janus-faced' character of anti-modernism, which, in its appeal to 'roots' and 'authenticity,' paradoxically enables nationalism as a 'historically new consciousness' figured as a 'radical break with the past' (98). It is precisely this simultaneous appeal to authenticity and newness that is apparent in Grove's tropes of tradition.

Grove and his contemporaries urged the growth of a national literary spirit but wrote little of the conditions of authorship and publishing that were preventing the emergence of 'genius.' Indeed, Mazo de la Roche's novel *Jalna*, which was published in the same year as *A Search for America*, uses the troubled but visionary character of Finch to urge readers to believe in what Frye later called the 'romantic' 'notion' that literary '"genius" is a certain quantum that an individual is born with, as he might be born with red hair' ('Conclusion' 335). Despite Grove's predilection for botanical tropes and the notion of genius, his own well-made book did not emerge organically from the contact between a visionary individual and the 'fundamental' soil of the nation, but from the precarious network of relations that constituted Canadian publishing in the interwar years. The publication history of *A Search for America* offers an intriguing parallel to the view of art that Grove developed in *A Search* and then refined in his lectures for the Association of Canadian Clubs in the late 1920s.

In contrast to Mr Tinker's travelogues or the phony 'de-luxe' encyclopedias that Branden sells, The Graphic Publishers advertised themselves as producers of 'well-made Canadian literature' – a slogan that emphasizes the implicit connection between a well-wrought national literature and a considered process of book manufacturing. Graphic's unswerving dedication to Canadian writers and Canadian manufacturing was unique in a period when there was no state support for publishers and, consequently, most Canadian publishers relied on agency contracts with firms in Britain and the United States to stay afloat (Parker, 'The Agency System' 163–5). Graphic was nevertheless known for the 'remarkable quality' of its books (St John 10), and the president of the company, H.C. Miller, took pains in his correspondence with Grove to emphasize his desire to make *A Search for America* physically attractive. Production was delayed in late 1926 and early 1927, for example, because Miller wanted to 'use a new type face on this book,' and he also developed plans for a 'de luxe edition of this book using deckle edged paper, and a half leather binding, with a special numbered autographed page.' Miller proposed limiting this autographed edition to one thousand or fifteen hundred copies that would then be advertised to 'professors throughout America.' This 'beautiful book,' he hoped, 'will actually put us on the world's map as good book makers';[22] however, this limited edition never materialized, largely due to the financial difficulties in which The Graphic Publishers were beginning to be mired in the late 1920s and which ultimately brought the firm to bankruptcy in 1932 (St John 10). The attractive edition of *A Search for America* that Graphic did produce was a very good seller – Grove's best – and seemed to confirm Miller's belief that the Canadian market could support itself.[23] Yet Graphic's short-lived success indicates that the publisher's formula of combining nationalist sentiment with well-made books faced a host of structural challenges in the North American market, not least of which was the fact that the Canadian market could and did function as a site for the sale of books with U.S.-American copyright.[24] Grove's conflation of a sedentarist ideal, an undeveloped capitalist infrastructure, and individual vision is clearly not borne out by the publishing history of *A Search for America*.

Grove later repudiated his romantic view of art and the settler ideal, or at least denounced their possibility in Canada, in his 1942 'Postscript to *A Search for America*.' Published in *Queen's Quarterly*, this article wryly observes that the vocation of the Canadian writer is a doomed one, and that he had been obliged to 'return to the status of a labourer' in a pea-canning factory in order to 'make his daily bread' (198). What Grove tacitly recognizes here, but underestimated in the context of a heady 1920s nationalism that found in him an ideal representative (Stobie 126), was the crucial role that a healthy publishing industry would have to play in nourishing Canadian writing. Grove had been forced to seek 'employment inadequate and wasteful, in a national sense,' and he compares this waste to the 'extraordinarily inefficient' mechanized process of canning peas (199, 213). The nation, Grove charges, squandered his literary talent and placed him at the mercy of the periods of seasonal unemployment that had long plagued agricultural and other workers in Canada. It is this history of what Avery calls 'occupational pluralism and geographical mobility' that allows us to read against the grain of Grove's romantic, sedentarist ideal.

Chapter Two

The Politics of Unemployment in Leftist Periodical Cultures, 1930–1939

As the crash of the Wall Street stock exchange in October 1929 sent its shock waves out into the world, Canadian corporations and economic analysts sought to reassure consumers that all was well. In the *Globe and Mail's* 1930 Annual Financial Survey, Edward W. Beatty, the president of the Canadian Pacific Railway, predicted that current economic conditions represented only a 'passing phase' that would soon give way to 'a more vigorous and better balanced forward movement than has been experienced in the past' (21). Surrounding Beatty's prediction are equally sanguine headlines: D.C. Durland of the Canadian General Electric Company foresaw a 'Bright Outlook' for 1930, and Ross H. McMaster of the Steel Company of Canada confirmed that a 'Widening Demand for Steel is Made Evident Every Year.' Such optimism did not prevail. The facts of the economic slump known in Europe and North America as the Great Depression are well known: in Canada, the plummeting of the economy in 1929 was followed in 1933 by an uneven recovery that led into a severe recession in 1937–8. Historian Michiel Horn observes that of all Western nations, only the United States suffered greater economic decline than Canada in this period. The dependency of the Canadian economy on the export of raw and semi-processed goods, protectionism, overproduction in wheat and pulp and paper, excessive debt in public and private sectors, and government lassitude all contributed to a disastrous situation in Canada that lasted for almost ten years (Horn, *The Great* 5–7).

This chapter begins with an analysis of the anxious responses to the transient unemployed in Depression-era state discourse, and then turns to a discussion of a diverse group of leftist periodicals that span the shift from the Third Period of the Communist International (or Comintern)

(1929–34) to the Popular Front (1935–39) – the *Canadian Forum, Masses, The Worker, New Frontier*, and the *Daily Clarion* – in order to describe how contributors to these publications imagined unemployment and its potential solutions. The unlikely yoking together of periodicals that appear to have divergent political affiliations – from the social-democratic *Canadian Forum* to the CPC paper the *Daily Clarion* – is deliberate: despite their differing ideological commitments, these periodicals all contributed to the work of advocating for federal programs such as unemployment insurance, which became an important component of the postwar welfare state. In 'The Forum during the 1930s' (*Canadian Forum*, April/May 1970), Horn confines the 'influence' of the *Forum* to the 'field of literature and the arts,' claiming that 'it was not until the 1940s, 1950s and even 1960s that many of the welfarist assumptions and proposals which had found voice in the journal during the Depression gained widespread political acceptance and legislative enactment' (40). This is accurate, but the relation between Depression-era leftist periodical culture and the postwar welfare state is an understudied one.

Following McKay's non-sectarian designation of the periods of Canadian socialism, this chapter considers leftist interventions in the 1930s unemployment crisis as aspects of the overlapping second and third formations. Lasting from about 1935 to 1970, the third formation was shaped by the Depression as well as the advent of the anti-fascist Popular Front, and was characterized less by the sectarian revolutionary discourses of the second formation (with which it overlaps and which includes the radical Third Period) than by the language of planned economies and national management (*Rebels* 169–83). As McKay argues, this third formation led to the absorption of many leftist demands into the liberal welfare state's 'passive revolution' in the postwar period, a process that is abundantly evident in these periodicals in the tensions between discourses of revolution and reform and in the salience of the question of who should be the recipient of state protection. Gesturing toward the 'passive revolution' that followed the Depression, this chapter will thus consider theoretical issues that recur in all of the subsequent chapters: here and later I will call attention to the particular nuances of Gramsci's phrase that deserve emphasis – particularly his abandonment in 'Americanism and Fordism' of all 'instrumentalist' conceptions of the state, whereby the state is reduced to a 'monolithic repressive apparatus,' and a 'strictly superstructural' conception of the 'passive revolution' that would suggest a 'kind of dualist reformism between base and state, production and politics' (Buci-Glucksmann 218, 222). 'Passive revolution' is a useful concept for theorizing Canada's postwar period, but its deployment involves careful attention to the role of civil society in the making of the liberal order.

Governing Unemployment

The statistics are unreliable and variable, but it is estimated that at the lowest point of the Depression in 1933, the national income in Canada was 51 per cent of what it had been in 1929, and nearly one-third of wage earners (as opposed to salaried professionals) were out of work (Horn, *The Great* 3, 10).[1] The very fact that unemployment statistics from this period are unreliable indicates that 'unemployment' and the 'unemployed,' as categories that are measured by and linked to state programs, were only just emerging in the interwar period: during most of the 1930s, for example, there was no federal agency that collected unemployment statistics on a national basis, and women were generally not considered among the ranks of the unemployed.[2] Moreover, the concept of a national labour force under the jurisdiction of the federal government did not emerge until after the crises of the Depression with the 1940 passage of the Unemployment Insurance Act. Municipal, provincial, and federal wrangling over jurisdiction, as well as what Dennis Guest calls a 'residual approach to social security,' which privileged the maintenance of the work ethic and responded in an ad hoc fashion to emergencies, characterized debates about poor relief in the 1930s. However, the prospect of masses of unemployed veterans from the Second World War finally encouraged Mackenzie King's Liberal government in the late 1930s to obtain permission from the provinces to amend the constitution so that the federal government could enact a form of social insurance that would cover Canadians who were out of work (Guest 85–91, 106–7).[3]

The epidemic of unemployment has come to be a salient feature in subsequent writing about the 1930s in both the United States and Canada; however, just as social and political responses to the Depression differed in these two nations, so the problem of joblessness in Canada may be distinguished from the interwar situation south of the border. The structurally entrenched problem of seasonal unemployment discussed in the previous chapter was exacerbated during the Depression years, especially because the sectors that depended on export and which were the most vulnerable to changes in international markets, such as coal mining, logging, and fishing, also tended to depend on pools of unskilled, often immigrant, labourers for seasonal employment (Horn, *The*

Great 9; Brown, 'Unemployment' 523).[4] The export-dependent sectors that employed the unskilled were also concentrated in particular regions (e.g., coal mining in Cape Breton and on the BC-Alberta border), a fact that indicates that the effects of the Depression were not evenly experienced. Moreover, if unemployment varied by region, the situation of unemployed workers also varied by marital status, ethnicity, and gender.[5] It is clear that male workers who were not born in Canada and their dependents suffered greatly in the 1930s. Exacerbating the disproportionate effects of unemployment on this group was the spectre of deportation: approximately thirty thousand recent immigrants from Europe were deported during the first half of the 1930s, an unprecedented rate of deportation in Canadian history (Avery 133; Kelley and Trebilcock 221).[6] The seasonal, resource-based economy that had encouraged labour mobility and that had depended on immigrant labour in the pre-1930 period produced the central menace of the Depression in Canada – an unemployment crisis that was proportionately more concentrated on single, immigrant men than in the United States (Struthers, *No Fault* 97). Not surprisingly, the character of the labour mobility that had been a feature of the Canadian labour market for so long changed during the Depression, as immigration, a great source of mobile, seasonal workers, more or less halted.[7] Single, male, unskilled workers remained highly mobile in this period, but only because their options were few. Since married men could only apply for relief if they could prove stable residence, they were encouraged to remain still, although there was a significant level of public concern about desertion in 1930s Ontario, where many women whose husbands had opted for the road were left with no choice but to claim desertion in order to obtain relief (Campbell, *Respectable Citizens* 49, 79–82).[8]

Throughout the Depression years, local, provincial, and federal governments juggled financial and social responsibility for unemployed workers; all levels of government were reluctant to assume authority over, and responsibility for, this group. Under the Conservative government of R.B. Bennett (1930–5), municipalities and provinces administered federal relief, but when the temporary Relief Act expired in 1931, this meant that most programs denied relief to non-residents (Palmer, *Working-Class* 206–7). Transient men were the greatest victims of this restriction (Struthers, *No Fault* 51). Yet if the mobility of the transient unemployed was both a cause of and a response to their ineligibility for relief, the practice of cross-country rail riding and the visible presence of these men in cities across Canada provided evidence for those who argued for unemployment as a national responsibility, one that the Bennett government was reluctant to admit. Thus the transient unemployed became 'the symbolic battleground' of the contested issue of jurisdiction over unemployment and relief (Struthers, *No Fault* 55).

The fear of transients, and immigrant transients in particular, as potential radicals formed a crucial element of this battleground. In 1935, when more than one thousand transients undertook an eastward trek to Ottawa to demand, among other things, work for wages and insurance for the unemployed, Bennett responded by directing the RCMP to halt their progress at Regina but agreed to meet a delegation of eight men in Ottawa. In his report of this meeting to the House of Commons, Bennett emphasized that seven of the eight delegates 'were not born in Canada,' and proceeded to link this fact to the foreign menace embodied in the 'various Communist organizations throughout Canada,' which represented a movement 'neither national nor continental' but 'international' (Dominion of Canada, *Dominion of Canada* vol. 4: 3899–900). This discourse imbued Bennett's refusal to take responsibility for the trekkers' demands with a moral authority: if he could represent the eight delegates of the On-to-Ottawa trek as typical of the thousands of trekkers halted in Regina, then none of these men had any claim on the resources of the nation-state they were neither born into nor claimed allegiance to.

As immigrants from the rural prairies flocked to western cities like Winnipeg in search of work or relief, many municipal officials suggested that this exodus was in fact *responsible* for the unemployment crisis, and advocated a back-to-the-land panacea through programs like the 'Colonization at Home Movement' in 1930 or the federal-provincial Relief Land Settlement Agreement of 1932, which attempted to place qualified urban families on farms as a means of weaning them off direct relief. In 1932, Bennett's minister of immigration, W.A. Gordon, noted that the influx of immigration immediately prior to 1930

contributed largely to the unemployment problem which is facing this country today because if the figures are analysed it will be found that a large number of these people did not go into the open spaces of the country and engage in agriculture, where they could at least support themselves, but drifted into industry in the cities. (Dominion of Canada, *Dominion of Canada* vol. 1: 440)[9]

Gordon then notes that the 'Colonization at Home Movement,' under which government-owned land was given to those who could pay the related expenses of settlement, had gone some way to removing recent immigrants who had flocked to the cities from the unemployment lists (Dominion of Canada, *Dominion of Canada* vol. 1: 440).

In their 1936 play *You Can't Do That*, Co-operative Commonwealth Federation (CCF) politician William Irvine and Elsie Park Gowan satirize such programs by marooning the federal cabinet on a deserted island in the St Lawrence while the prime minister's niece engineers a reversal of federal policy regarding responsibility for unemployment relief.[10] Linda, the cunning niece, scoffs that the ministers need a 'chance to get back to primitive conditions, and wrestle with nature, as they're so good at telling other people to do' (7). Predictably, the ministers are hopeless in the wilderness, and Linda's plan to reform relief along the lines of the CCF platform is a spectacular success. Like analogous movements in late nineteenth-century Britain and the United States, back-to-the-land ideology was fuelled by the belief that Canada's western frontier could and should continue to absorb labourers who were willing to do honest work (Struthers, *No Fault* 8–9).[11] The programs had enthusiastic advocates in Canada, such as W.M. Jones, who reported in 1937 that the Relief Land Settlement Agreement had saved governments $200,000 in relief payments and that it had succeeded in turning ailing urban children into 'sturdy, ruddy youngsters' (271). Unsurprisingly, the beguiling appeal of these anti-modernist discourses gave the federal government an excuse to reject calls for unemployment insurance (Struthers, *No Fault* 8–9). However, as in *You Can't Do That*, back-to-the-land solutions proved to be less ideal than its advocates hoped because farmers – especially those on the drought-stricken prairies – suffered the most during the Depression (Grayson and Bliss xv). As the census analyst W.B. Hurd observes in a May 1936 article in the *Canadian Forum*, the approach also underestimated the fact that the late nineteenth- and early twentieth-century transformation of Canada into an urban-industrial society would not be easily reversed. This transformation had at least two significant and related consequences during the Depression: single, unemployed men were less likely to have sources of familial support to rely on in times of economic calamity, and the concentration of these men in cities and towns across the nation made it clear that an urbanized, national labour force had emerged in Canada.

Following immigration restrictions and deportation, the first sustained governmental strategy to contain the social threat embodied by transient men appeared in the form of relief camps. In 1932, the Bennett government established camps for single, unemployed, physically fit men across the country in an attempt to curtail the worrying, and illegal, transient practice of using railway infrastructure to move across the country in search of work and handouts. The Department of National Defence ran these camps, and, unlike comparable 'work for wages' programs under Roosevelt's New Deal administration, camps in Canada offered board, a daily twenty-cent allowance, and 'make-work jobs' instead of meaningful labour (Brown, 'Unemployment' 532). The institutionalized labour in the camps was meant to vitiate what the federal government increasingly viewed as the lassitude of the 'dole mentality' and preserve the work ethic of Canada's labourers, who were encouraged throughout the Depression to accept the lowest wage in lieu of worklessness (Struthers, 'Two Depressions' 74; Struthers, *No Fault* 100). General A.G.L. McNaughton, who oversaw these camps for the Bennett government, asserted their primary goal in a 1934 letter:

> The most important feature of our work is, of course, not reflected either in the financial figures or in the number of man days relief afforded. Projects have been directed to the breaking up of the congestion of single homeless men in the principal centres of population and if these had not been dispersed it is hardly conceivable that we would have escaped without having had recourse to the military forces to suppress disorder. (qtd in Horn, *The Dirty Thirties* 329)

Given that at least two transient strikes over the issue of federal responsibility – the On-to-Ottawa trek of 1935 (which culminated in the Dominion Day Riot at Regina) and the Vancouver Sit-Down Strike of 1938 – arose out of the context of these camps, McNaughton's appraisal seems somewhat sanguine in retrospect. These mobile strikes demonstrate the way in which mobility – its exercise and its limitation – lay at the core of the contest between the unemployed and the carceral strategies of government.[12] The federal government could compel single, homeless men to enter and remain in the camps only by wielding the threat of arrest for vagrancy or rail riding, a practice that the RCMP increasingly monitored as the decade wore on (Brown, 'Unemployment' 525).

Mackenzie King's Liberal Party rode to easy victory in 1935 on the path of Bennett's broken campaign promise to eradicate unemployment, although the Liberal victory was shared with the newly formed, social-democratic CCF and the Social Credit Party. Mobility was, of course, a factor in the election: inmates in the state-monitored relief camps were effectively disenfranchised because they did not meet the residence qualifications required under the electoral procedures (Brown 539). Such disenfranchisement offers a good example of the way in which transience and citizenship were viewed as mutually exclusive during the 1930s; similarly, naturalization, which in this period functioned like national citizenship and was available to immigrants who had resided in Canada for five years, was increasingly denied and revoked on 'racial grounds' or on the basis of reports attesting to 'bad character, as evidenced by unemployment, involvement in labour disputes, or support of communist or socialist organizations' (Kelley and Trebilcock 230–1). Ideally, in the 1930s the citizen was to be neither a member of any of the non-preferred categories of immigrants nor unemployed.

· The King government proceeded to abolish the unpopular relief camps, but his government's replacement program was equally unsuccessful, perhaps because it continued to place most of the responsibility for transients on local and provincial governments (Struthers, *No Fault* 192). As the decade unfolded, the belief that the federal government should be responsible for the welfare of what was a national labour force – employed or not – gained support from a number of key individuals and organizations. King's own National Employment Commission and his labour minisiter, Norman Rogers (Struthers, *No Fault* 168–76), espoused this view, as did the 1937–40 Royal Commission on Dominion-Provincial Relations, whose Rowell–Sirois Report concluded that urbanization and industrialization had forever altered the role of the federal government in the direction of 'increasing interference with a view to improving social and economic conditions' (Smiley 185). Although the King Liberals had proposed a system of unemployment insurance as early as 1921, they did not bring a national system to fruition until 1940.

Leftist Periodicals and the Emergence of the Unemployed

If Depression-era discourses of governance understood the male transient – and, in particular, the immigrant, radicalized, male transient – to embody a considerable threat to state authority, and if the federal government continually dodged demands for unemployment insurance as a right, the political and artistic cultures of the left in 1930s Canada sought to revise these positions as a means of making an incontrovertible case for a national system of unemployment insurance. Their agitation for direct relief in the form of federal unemployment insurance constitutes a 'largely unrecorded history of attempts to introduce "citizen participation" into policy making and administration' (Guest 85). One important, and often overlooked, site of agitation was the emergent leftist periodical culture that sought to intervene in debates regarding joblessness as a social crisis. From 1932 to 1944, Dorothy Livesay did not publish a poetry collection; instead, she devoted herself to her job as a social worker and to the writing of poems and short stories that appeared in the left-wing magazines of the period. Livesay's literary activity during the 1930s is certainly not representative of writers' experiences in Canada during this decade, but it does indicate the importance of periodical publishing to those writers who were actively concerned with the social crises of the Depression. As Irvine observes, the 1930s witnessed 'the emergence of an English Canadian leftist magazine culture' ('Among *Masses*' 185). Writers such as Livesay, Arthur S. Bourinot, A.M. Klein, Frederick Philip Grove, Oscar Ryan, and many others who either wrote anonymously or never forged careers as writers contributed to the *Canadian Forum*, *Masses*, *The Worker*, *New Frontier*, and the *Daily Clarion* and were thus part of a broad – if often agonistically divided – left political culture that probed the social problems of the Depression, the most salient of which was unemployment.

Given that the contemporary U.S.-American versions of the transient figure have cast such a long shadow on popular North American narratives of the Depression, it is worth noting how U.S.-American discourses of mobility differ from those employed by Canada's left. Novels such as Edward Dahlberg's *Bottom Dogs* were 'classics' of the U.S. proletarian avant-garde, a literature that celebrates life on the road in narratives of 'masculine rebellion' (Denning 187–9). The situation in Canada was somewhat different. If agitating for increased federal responsibility was one of the goals, broadly speaking, of writers on the left, then this clearly motivated figurations of the nation as a home from which the worker has been cast out. Whether imagining the female body as a 'home' that the male transient has lost or deploying the figure of the native son to argue for the transient's right to the resources of the nation-state, these texts mediate social anxiety about transient mobility to argue for the rights of the unemployed. While the Third Period writing from *Masses* is distinguished by its revolutionary call to transform tramping into marching, these radical texts were subsumed by a Popular Front culture that emphasized the state's responsibility for the unemployed.

Of course, conditions for literary labour also differed in the United States and Canada during the 1930s. In the U.S.-American context, broad, leftist coalitions formed through the Works Progress Administration (WPA) programs, which placed writers and other artists among the

ranks of other formerly jobless workers and allowed specialized conceptions of what Szalay calls 'literary labour' to emerge (5). The situation
in 1930s Canada was different because the state did not involve itself in
cultural production as a means of economic recovery. Although contributions to the publications of the Canadian radical left were frequently
drawn from the ranks of unions or radical political organizations and
so were often authored by unemployed workers who were literally writing from the road, many of the writers examined in this chapter were
not unemployed or even underemployed; indeed, contributors to mainstream publications like the *Canadian Forum* and novelists such as Irene
Baird practised professions in fields such as law, journalism, social work,
or teaching – relatively privileged occupations that were nonetheless
predisposed to the work of assessing social problems. It is clear that in
1930s Canada the 'exclusive concentration of artistic talent in particular individuals' that, for Marx, characterizes bourgeois society had not
yet congealed (*The German Ideology* 109). As Frank Davey demonstrates,
the Depression exacerbated the precarious status of authorship in Canada, and, in any case, the category of the professional author would not
emerge in this country until well after the Second World War ('Economics and the Writer' 107–10).[13] The effects of an emerging 'exclusive concentration of artistic talent' in the interwar period were moderated by
radicalizing politics *and* structural conditions within the interwar field of
cultural production. For example, radical leftist discourse in the 1930s
frequently subordinated cultural to political work, such that figures like
Livesay, Oscar Ryan, and Ed Cecil-Smith negotiated their commitment
to artistic labour through the political imperatives of the era. Moreover,
structural conditions in the interwar period required many literary labourers in the 1930s to engage in what Heather Murray calls 'piecework'
– an assemblage of literary and cultural activities, as in the case of Mc-
Clelland and Stewart editor Donald G. French or poet Alan Creighton,
who, in addition to his creative writing was hiring out what Murray calls
'criticism-by-the inch' to would-be poets in the 1930s ('The Canadian
Writers' 171, 173). Between the wars, such assemblages just as often comprised creative writing, political activity, and a 'day job,' as in the case of
figures such as Dorothy Livesay and F.R. Scott.

  The specifically political function of literary periodical culture has a
long history in Canada that precedes Confederation, and, of course, the
periodical press has been allied for centuries with forms of dissent.[14]
In the 1930s, small magazines in Canada were competing with popular
U.S. publications like the *Saturday Evening Post*, as well as the products of

J.B. MacLean and Company, which produced two of the most popular mass-consumer magazines in 1930s Canada – *Maclean's* and *Chatelaine*. Like the popular literature of the period, which included fiction and verse by Robert Service, L.M. Montgomery, Ralph Connor, and Mazo de la Roche, mass magazines offered romance and adventure as an escape from the economic crisis and the environmental disaster of drought (Harrison 84–6). While an eyewitness narrative of life 'on the bum' – Ronald F. Elliott's 'Low Road' – appeared in *Maclean's* in the 1 February 1934 issue, stories like this were uncommon in the magazine; moreover, the advertisements for Mobiloil Arctic ('It's an expensive walk to take'), Dr Scholl's Zino-Pads ('New or tight shoes stop hurting at once!'), and Chrysler, Plymouth, and Dodge that surround the margins of the story's text confirm the middle-class voyeurism that the story's rail-riding adventure was meant to titillate. Mass-market publications like *Maclean's* clearly reached a larger audience than leftist periodicals did: for example, while some consumer magazines in the interwar period had circulation numbers as high as ninety thousand subscribers, the left-leaning *Canadian Forum* had approximately nineteen hundred subscribers in 1929 (and sold for twenty-five cents per issue) (Djwa, 'The *Canadian Forum*' 8). The editorial for the final issue of the radical periodical *Masses* (March/April 1934) argues that the magazine's circulation had surpassed that of the *Forum*, making it 'the leading cultural magazine in Canada' (3); however, this seems a probable exaggeration, even if *Masses* was less expensive (ten cents per issue), and, in any case, radical publications tended to survive for only very brief periods.[15]

Writers and artists of the left had recourse to few publishing venues in Canada during the 1930s. Those periodicals that provided an outlet for leftist and progressive writing apparently faced significant economic challenges, and yet the 1930s witnessed an explosion of periodical and pamphlet publication. Many of these publications intervened in the fractious debate surrounding the issue of worklessness. In addition to the more culturally focused publications that are discussed in this chapter, short-lived undertakings such as the *Toronto Unemployed Worker* (1930), *Calgary's Unemployed Bulletin* (1931–2), the *B.C. Relief Camp Worker* (1933–5), Kingston's *Camp Worker* (1934), and the *Victoria Jobless Journal* (1938) testify to the ephemeral print culture that the crisis of unemployment engendered. Although the periodicals considered in this chapter diverge in significant ways – in their politics, their sources of funding, their physical formats – the term 'small press,' defined as 'the non-commercial production of books and periodicals with a literary orientation, is-

sued in limited runs for specialized readerships, and often dedicated
to experimental writing or identity-based perspectives' (McKnight 310),
encompasses all of the publications considered here.[16] Some of the party
organs discussed – the CPC's *Daily Clarion*, for example – stretch the
limits of this definition because they are more properly political newspapers, but their interest in cultural issues and their publication of stories,
poems, and literary reviews justifies their inclusion here. While these leftist and progressive periodicals might differ, they share comparable projects: their politics and aesthetics are often international in scope, but
they all aim to communicate with an audience in Canada; unlike coeval
U.S. periodicals, such as *New Masses* and *Partisan Review*, they attempted
to create (rather than simply disseminate) 'socialist culture' and were
committed to 'encouraging Canadian literary culture' (Irr 183); and
they all functioned as new forums for political dissent and as media
through which to evaluate the relations between state and culture. In
this sense, the writing found in these periodicals might be thought of as
what Raymond Williams calls 'emergent practices,' practices that may be
'oppositional' in their not yet fully articulated search for 'new forms or
adaptations of forms' to resist dominant, hegemonic traditions (*Marxism*
115–26).

Rejecting some aspects of Euro-American literary modernism but
adopting and adapting others, writers affiliated with diverse positions
on the left in 1930s Canada contributed to what is increasingly being
recognized as the aesthetically, geographically, and temporally unstable
category of modernist artistic production. Di Brandt, Brenda Carr Vellino, and Rifkind, for example, engage Barbara Foley's claim that, in the
United States, 'the charge that the majority of American literary prole-
tarians repudiated literary innovation simply does not stand up under
the evidence. The concept of "realism" guiding most literary radicals'
sense of their enterprise may not have been rigorously defined. But it
seems not to have precluded, but instead to have fostered, experimentation of various kinds' (57).[17] Moreover, as Rifkind argues, many of the
aesthetic practices of the literary left in 1930s Canada – the recycling of
older leftist forms such as choral repetition, for example – are forms of
innovation that have been overlooked by critics and writers influenced
by a dominant but limited understanding of modernist experimentation
(*Comrades* 13–14). With regard to the representation of the transient unemployed, who embodied much social anxiety about the open-endedness of the Depression, leftist writers almost never employ the crudest
or most prescriptive methods of socialist realism.[18] The transient texts

of leftist periodicals are less socialist realist – less politically prescriptive – than others have claimed them to be: their anxiety and uncertainty about the ameliorative methods that might be applied to the social and economic crises of the Depression often finds its corollary in the hybrid forms these writers used.

The *Canadian Forum*, the Unemployed Type, and the Planned Economy

Key to understanding the cultural politics of the *Canadian Forum* in the Depression years is the recognition of the magazine's association with the League for Social Reconstruction (LSR) in the latter half of the 1930s. The LSR promulgated social-democratic federalism and advocated a federal system of unemployment insurance. While long viewed as more progressive than its counterpart the *Canadian Bookman*, the political specificity and stridency of the culturally nationalist *Canadian Forum* increased when LSR and CCF member Graham Spry rescued the *Forum* from financial distress in 1935, making it the League's 'chief means of reaching Canadians' for six years (Horn, *The LSR* 129–31).[19] During this time, LSR and CCF members such as Spry, Frank Underhill, Irene Biss, King Gordon (son of Charles Gordon, otherwise known as Ralph Connor), Eugene Forsey, and F.R. Scott contributed as both editors and writers to the *Forum*. The LSR was a largely middle-class, intellectual, socialist organization composed of academics, clergy, teachers, and the like, many of whom had been educated in the United Kingdom and influenced by Fabian socialism and the Chicago School of sociologists.[20] Membership of the discussion and research group was never over one thousand, and members were 'overwhelmingly college-educated, urban, Anglophone, and central Canadian' (Horn, *The LSR* 14). Through pamphlet and book publications, initiatives like the Social Science Research Project at McGill University (led by Leonard Marsh) and social work education at the University of Toronto, and eventually through the *Canadian Forum*, the LSR advocated the creation of a socialist cooperative commonwealth through parliamentary means. The LSR's *Social Planning for Canada* (1935), for example, theorizes how a 'planned economy' based on the centralization of state powers could accommodate a federal system of insurance to replace unemployment relief and indicates how the federal government might use research into population, employment, housing, and sanitation as a guide for its social policy. LSR research was not without effect in Ottawa: the group had close ideological ties to the CCF, which sent seven members of Parliament to Ottawa in the 1935 election. Additionally, Leonard Marsh's broad-ranging study of employment and unemployment, *Canadians In and Out of Work* (1940), outlined the foundation of a national welfare policy, and his *Report on Social Security* (1943), which evolved out of his decade with the Social Science Research Project, became 'the basis of the Canadian social welfare system' in the postwar period (Shore 261, xviii).[21]

The federalism advocated by the LSR is also abundant in the *Forum* of the 1930s: there are countless articles and essays advocating public ownership of various Canadian industries and a federal system of unemployment insurance. The editorial page of the May 1936 issue, for example, decries the fact that 'after six years of depression the care of the unemployed is still a buck to be passed back and forth between Federal and Provincial and Municipal governments in accord with political expediency and without regard for the condition of the unemployed' and claims that the 'major share' of responsibility for this 'chaotic condition' rests with the federal government (3). Stories such as L.A. MacKay's 'Another Man's Poison' (October 1936) articulate a similar argument indirectly by exploring the utter powerlessness of individual actors to ameliorate structural problems in the labour market, and satirical poems such as David Stevenson's 'Three Ostriches' (December 1938) lampoon the political stasis that resulted from wrangling among the three levels of government:

Three wise Ostriches conferred
About the single unemployed;
The first, a Municipal bird,
Compelled by office to avoid
Commitments for the City Hall
Thought nothing could be done at all.

The second, of Provincial breed,
Skilled in the talents of his kind,
While fully realizing the need
That 'Unemployment' be defined,
Could not with honesty intrude
On tasks of Federal magnitude.

The Federal bird, more qualified
In Government and Constitution

Regretted from the legal side
There was no Federal solution,
Which proved to each sagacious bird
There were no single unemployed.

Each bent his scaly neck around
And stuck his fool head in the ground. (269)

Stevenson's satirical allegory was timely indeed, for it coincided with the work of the Royal Commission on Dominion-Provincial Relations, which held hearings across the country from 1937 to 1940 in an attempt to discern the appropriate roles for each level of government in the context of the social problems of the Depression.

Echoing the conclusions of his 1929–32 government-commissioned study of unemployment and relief in Ontario, LSR member and social-work educator H.M. Cassidy's article 'Is Unemployment Relief Enough?' (January 1934) calls for the immediate implementation of a federal system of unemployment insurance, arguing that state inaction had already unwittingly nurtured a socially threatening kind of mobility:

> Imagine the effect of a year or two roaming across the country as a transient upon a young man of 19 or 20, who has not yet settled down to a very disciplined existence. He becomes a 'bum' in the process, becomes unreliable, incapable, indolent, unemployable – whereas he never would have developed in such a way if he had had a regular job and a reasonable scale of living. (132)

Moreover, Cassidy argues, 'unemployment contaminates family life,' resulting in 'broken homes,' 'desertion,' working mothers (who necessarily 'neglect' their homes and their children), working children, and children born out of wedlock (132). Anticipating Marsh's emphasis in *Report on Social Security for Canada* on the necessity of a 'family wage' that would enable men to support dependents (Pierson 82–3), and positing the male-dominated family and the potential of the working male at the centre of the nation's survival, Cassidy insists that the federal government must take the lead in preserving the social fabric of the nation. Cassidy's argument exemplifies the ways in which unemployment has been posed as a problem for liberal governance and patriarchy. According to Foucault, the family, 'considered as an element internal to population, and as a fundamental instrument in its governance,' is crucial to the modern art of government (99), and, as Walters points out, unemployment 'undermines the assumption of the (ideally) self-governing household, of the male breadwinner supporting a family, and of the wage being a sufficient basis to support the life of the wage-earner' (3). The 'indignity of the Depression,' from this perspective, was 'the transformation of male breadwinners into breadliners' that was thematized in *Forum* stories such as Maurice Lesser's 'Bread Line' (September 1933) (Rifkind, 'The Hungry Thirties' 177).

Recalling Cassidy's argument, Arthur S. Bourinot's poem 'Outcasts' (January 1939) (later included in his 1939 Governor General's Award–winning collection *Under the Sun*) represents the 'sodden bulging boots' and 'furtive shifty glance' that made the unemployed such a menace to the middle-class residents of towns and cities. Using the form of the mass chant that is more common to radical poetry, Bourinot suggests a kind of collective threat. Yet the poem neatly contains this possibility: these 'outcasts' are not footloose wanderers who relish the freedom of the road – they are headed only for 'the final lurch / And thrust of impetuous crime / To a barren grave' (216). The almost elegiac repetition of 'We are the outcasts' in the first line of each of the four stanzas, and the ponderous, trochaic strings of plodding adjectives in the second line of each stanza convey the joylessness of enforced mobility: 'hungry empty hearts' and 'furtive shifty glance' thud that much more listlessly because of the lack of punctuation and the final stressed syllable. Such men are not to be feared; they are to be pitied.

Another 'transient' poem in Bourinot's *Under the Sun* is 'Transients,' a poem in alternating monometer/dimeter couplets that similarly assumes the voice of all the wandering unemployed. The world to which these men have been cast is homeless and grim; they yearn for

> some love
> a woman's breast
> our heads to rest
> for we are dead
> half dead. (21)

Like the grave-ward 'thrust' in 'Outcasts,' these short lines create an eerily inevitable forward momentum, as if the lurching men can no longer control their own bodies. The synecdoche of the 'woman's breast' becomes a metaphor for home, a well-worn figure that aligns female corporeality with the domestic sphere, as well as arguing for the perversity of the life of the single male on the road. As Brian Atkinson's story 'The Transient's Return' (September 1939) indicates, such perversity is an unavoidable characteristic of transient life, which nourishes a casual approach to sexuality and ingrains distaste for 'being in love and going to shows or walking hand-in-hand in the moonlight' (183). The ballad 'Unemployed' (November 1933), written by Nova Scotian poet Alan Creighton, similarly invokes this perversity by placing the virility of the unemployed ('pulses clear and strong') and the paradox of the young, male 'living-dead' in ironic juxtaposition (71), thus lamenting the lost opportunity of the idle male body.[22] The immobilization of the unemployed male body is followed to a horrific conclusion in Yvonne Firkins's short story 'The Wheels Squeaked' (January 1937), which draws a parallel between the 'walk weary, talk weary' body of an unemployed man, Janek, and the inefficient squeaking of the baby pram that he must push around the city while his wife works in a box factory (25). When a 'man had no work his hands or brains must do' save the care of an infant, he loses all orientation in and agency over the urban space he moves in and steps off a curb into a speeding car (25). Given that court records, oral histories, and reminiscences indicate that male unemployment in Ontario, for example, rarely led to 'men doing anything connected with women's work in the domestic sphere such as shopping, cooking, sewing, or even looking after children' (Campbell, *Respectable Citizens* 66), Firkins's story plays on a very palpable fear in the period – that the loss of work would entail a breakdown of the patriarchal family.

Despite the salience of the emasculated male figure who gains his symbolic power through his relation to the threatened patriarchal home, *Forum* contributors in this period did not altogether fail to acknowledge the plight of workless women. In a November 1936 editorial, state planning for unemployed women is called for, but the writer admits that these women must not displace men (5). A March 1937 editorial announces that a CCF member of Parliament, C.G. MacNeil, has taken up the cause of unemployed single women, whose meagre relief earnings oblige them to 'live only in the most disreputable parts of the city' and render them 'ready material for prostitution in its most sordid forms' (5). An inherent fragility and feminine morality, rather than a wasted virility, is at stake here, and state protection is embodied in the fatherly care that the minister of labour is called upon to exercise. However, in addition to CCF members of Parliament J.S. Woodsworth and A.A.

Heaps and Labour MP Agnes MacPhail, MacNeil was one of the few MPs in the House of Commons to raise the issue of women's unemployment during the 1930s (Pierson 77).

Simon Marcson's short story 'Dream Train' (November 1933) is an interesting if somewhat unique example of the open-ended transient narrative that appeared in leftist periodicals in the 1930s. Marcson's protagonist is a rail rider who is sweeping through the prairie evening on a swiftly moving freight train. The mobile or open-ended form of Marcson's story conveys great anxiety about the unanswerable questions that loomed over North American society during the nadir of the Depression. The economic crisis becomes a 'structure of feeling' in open-ended rail riding and road narratives that mimic the mobility of the transient through, for example, experimentation with narrative voice. Like George Abbe's short story 'A Stranger Here' (July 1935), 'Dream Train' attempts a stream-of-consciousness narration: Marcson employs a third-person narrator whose voice is focused through a rail rider who is conjuring a disjointed montage of memories that are rendered in sentence fragments joined by dashes. Such fragmentation indicates the story's anti-realist aesthetic, one that has more in common with Brechtian expressionism than Lukácsian objective realism. The tension here is between the character's attempts to tell the story of his political conversion in a cogent way (his 'dream' for a socialist future), and the capitalist logic for which the moving train is a figure. The train's speed induces a 'dream'-like bafflement that is analogous to the effects produced by the apparently magical processes of capitalism, and the physical dislocation literally imposed by the movement of the train conjures capitalism's power to dislocate labourers.

The symbology of the train is underscored in 1931 issues of the *Canadian Forum*, in which advertisements for the fiftieth anniversary of the Canadian Pacific celebrate the 'teamwork' that enabled 'railway and settlers' to go 'forward side by side for the final conquest of the country.' In these advertisements, it is not the workers who built the railway who are commemorated but the 'pioneers' and the personified railway, whose combined force equals economic and social progress. Such language forcefully urges the reader to forget the 'ground' of the train's value – the immigrant workers, including the Chinese, who built it. To suggest that this move is analogous to the apparent magic of the early twentieth-century system of exchange, in which everything depended on the 'reader' (or consumer) forgetting the 'ground' of value (gold) and trusting the signifier (paper money, cheque) is not inconceivable. The

Canadian government finally abandoned the gold standard for good in 1929, ten months before the Wall Street crash, and both events affected the consumer's ability to trust money's narrative – the convention of trust that had previously allowed paper money and other paper forms of credit to represent value. Such a crisis of representation is precisely what 'Dream Train' embodies.[23]

In Marcson's story, the transient passenger initially appears to subvert the capitalist logic of the train by imagining an entirely different purpose for it. As the train wends its way through the night, it becomes a parallel for his growing consciousness of the need for social change: 'The train had taken the curve, it was gathering speed. Jolting increased. Train passing through night. Yes, the phrase, out of an ocean of darkness. His dream train. Taking him on. Must go on' (71). The impending revolution, which will come out of 'an ocean of darkness,' is inherent in the structures of capitalism, which the train's movement represents. In this way, Marcson's story echoes the strategies of many writers on the literary left in 1930s Canada insofar as they used representations of the infrastructure of capitalism – steel mills, for example – to express both workers' oppression and their ability to turn the raw materials of production to their own subversive use. Marcson's 'dream' train is shooting through the 'Canadian grain fields' and crossing the nation; it thus metamorphoses into a symbol of the emergent, socialist Canada and indicates the future end point of the train's journey.

Yet this possibility is ambivalently positioned in relation to another, less utopian one. The lack of plot and the rankling open-endedness of 'Dream Train' indicate a crisis of representation, a crisis in which the mobile form of the narrative – whose 'jolts' echo the movement of the train – will ineluctably continue even as the narrator fades off the page: 'His dream train. Taking him on. Must go on. But – Ocean of darkness …' (71). This is less a story that represents the inexorability of revolution than one that worries the crucial conjunction 'but': the train is 'gathering speed' as the story careers to its conclusion, and it is not in any way clear that the velocity will hurdle the rail raider into a world of social change. Michael Denning reads the open-ended road/rail narrative as a crisis of representation that responds to the dissolution of the 'knowable communities and settled social relations that provide the underpinning for realist narrative[s]' (119). In the U.S.-American context, such dissolution took the form of the 'Okie' exodus, which was represented in narratives of 'mass migration,' such as John Steinbeck's 1939 novel *The Grapes of Wrath*, which contains the crisis of representation by reducing political struggles to a story of 'natural' disaster (Denning 266). In 'Dream Train,' the unsettling juxtaposition of two irreconcilable 'dreams' suggests that the future is frighteningly indeterminate.

In 'Dream Train,' the anxiety generated by such indeterminacy is controlled through a white, male worker figure who embodies the claims of all the unemployed to a home, wages, and a family. Marcson posits a societal model of collective, participatory action by glancing at the possibility of a new national socialist order, but this work is realized through the strategy of typicality, which was common to much leftist writing from the 1930s and which appears in other *Forum* stories of the period, such as Frederick Philip Grove's 'Riders' (February 1934) and P.W. Thompson's 'Man without Work' (December 1936). Although 'Dream Train' has a strong expressionist aesthetic, it also draws on the notion of the type that was developed by Georg Lukács in the late 1930s. In his 1948 study of realism, Lukács describes the type as 'a peculiar synthesis which organically binds together the general and the particular both in characters and situations' (*Studies in European Realism* 6). As film historian Zoë Druick points out, such realist typicality also characterizes the modern documentary in Canada and has much in common with the social-scientific study that emerged in the interwar period. Marlene Shore's research demonstrates that many LSR members, such as Leonard Marsh, were involved in these years in early sociological studies that advocated the use of economics and actuarial science (statistics derived from population samples) in order to assess typical employment, housing, and health needs, such that the needs of the entire national population could be predicted and managed.

'Riders,' 'Man without Work,' and 'Dream Train' all employ types who stand in for the workers of the nation. Like Henry Paul's reportage piece 'I Am a Transient' (May 1939), these stories emphasize the 'strong uniformity' of the transient experience (Paul 47), and both 'Riders' and 'Dream Train' anticipate Paul's strategic emphasis on the middle-class background of the transient unemployed. Grove's 'Riders,' for example, figures the male transient as an average guy who is deserving but unlucky. The roadside transient Reg Gardiner, a figure for the masses of unemployed men who traverse the nation, is introduced as 'a member of the huge army of workless men who were tramping the roads' (177). He is differentiated from Archibald Langford, the travelling life-insurance salesman who picks him up in his car, only by virtue of the way that they experience the road:

One thing, and one only, betrayed him to be a member of the huge army of workless men who were tramping the roads: he carried a bundle neatly rolled up in black oil-cloth and slung, by a leather strap, over his shoulders. Apart from that, he might be mistaken for a clerk with a modest but comfortable salary, or for an agent who was out canvassing like Langford himself. (177)

Gardiner and Langford are also former classmates who share similar backgrounds, a doubling that urges the reader to consider the transient as a figure for all working – and not just working-class – people. Grove thus urges the educated, middle-class *Forum* reader to witness his or her own proximity to the unemployed. He also anticipates the vociferous defences of ostensibly fraudulent relief claimants that appeared in the *Forum* in mid-1936 in the wake of the Ontario government's decision to purge the relief rolls of so-called 'chisellers.' For instance, Martin M. Cohn's 'A Defence of Chisellers' (June 1936) contends that North American social workers identified the unemployed as an 'average cross section of the community, no worse, and no better, than those of us who happen to be fortunate enough to have held our jobs' (19).

As the conclusion of the previous chapter indicates, Grove's fortunes as a writer seriously declined in the 1930s, and his own precarious existence in this period adds poignancy to 'Riders' and its demystification of the settler ideal that concludes *A Search for America*. Grove's deployment of the doppelgänger motif – the well-to-do Archibald Langford confronts his poorer self in a man who, like Grove, was an elementary teacher in the rural west – operates as a figure for Grove's anxiety regarding both his identity and his changing economic fortunes. Furthermore, Grove's alignment with the native-born transient Reg Gardiner bolsters his claims to the nation. Although Gardiner was once a 'star pupil' in 'the little school north of Carvil,' he knows that he will now be refused work in a neighbouring community. Like Grove, who moved his family from Manitoba to Ontario in the early 1930s, Gardiner has moved across the country – from Saskatoon to Sudbury – in search of 'any kind of work' and so is no longer considered a resident of the area. 'Riders' thus tacitly suggests that Gardiner's (and Grove's) stake in his nation is, in fact, more valid than Langford's because he has worked and lived in more of it and is thus a more typical Canadian male. Although mobility is not to be desired – the point of the story is that Gardiner should be able to settle and work somewhere – it creates claims on the nation that cannot be dismissed.

The rail-riding protagonist of Marcson's story 'Dream Train' is a young, bourgeois convert who has renounced his 'fairy castle' life of 'blackboards and teachers,' 'dances,' and 'rugby' in order to ally himself with the 'brotherhood of unemployed' (70–1). This character's background is assured by the cues of his former life: his world of 'knights, beautiful damsels, and dragons' suggests an upper-class gentility that also connotes, in this period, the Anglo society of the dominant class. But he has given up this ease for a life of social struggle. This young man of privileged background is clearly one of the transient unemployed, but he is not an individual character; the third-person narrator does not describe the character physically, nor is his name given, which suggests that he is a metonym for the unemployed masses. That the masses the young man stands in for stretch across the country is reinforced by the speeding train, which travels swiftly across the 'Canadian grain fields' and deftly sews the prairie region into the fabric of the Canadian nation (70). By subsuming all of the transient unemployed under the sign of this figure, the story elides the ethnic diversity of those who were set adrift by the economic crises of the Depression, while suggesting that a white, Anglo-Canadian male *is* the unemployed of the nation.

Grove's and Marcson's protagonists are clearly in dialogue with the figure of the typical proletarian of socialist realism, a universal worker figure whose positive characteristics herald the coming social revolution. Writing about this figure in U.S.-American proletarian literature, Irr argues that the left 'did not always adequately appreciate the history of ethnic, racial, or gendered antagonisms of the working class,' but she insists that a preoccupation with 'an ideal citizen, the well-muscled and committed proletarian' was less about 'a supposedly totalitarian drive to reduce human diversity to a single master narrative than with a quite contrary impulse to make a mark on North American culture by foregrounding "new" or poorly represented social categories and spaces' (3, 99). While Grove's and Marcson's attention to the experiences of those marginalized by the Depression corroborates Irr's claim, it is also true that writers in leftist periodicals used the reduction of human diversity strategically, as a means of making an argument for a national labour force whose right to national resources could not be disputed on grounds of ethnicity, or, for that matter, gender. In other words, the representation of a national labour force depends upon the homogeneity of that group; the national labour force must look like the dominant class in order for the argument to be effective. There are some exceptions to this typology of unemployment in the pages of the *Canadian Forum*, the most striking of which is Paul D. Anderson's short story 'The County Line' (October 1938); however, because it is set in the United States, Anderson's narrative fails to make an explicit commentary on the correlation of immigrant status and transient unemployment in Depression-era Canada.

Representations of the relation between the homeless transient and the home of the nation in *Forum* stories are intriguing when read in the context of the LSR vision of native socialism, which distinguished Canadian and international socialisms by aligning the former with northern vigour and the latter with the trope of the ailing foreigner. In the interwar period, both the LSR and the CCF believed in the need for a native socialism. At the 1933 Regina convention, CCF Party leader J.S. Woodsworth championed a specifically Canadian socialism, a position that grew in the interwar period out of his anti-capitalist and anti-imperialist nationalism (Penner, *The Canadian Left* 210). Likewise, a 1935 LSR pamphlet calls pre-Depression socialism in Canada a 'European growth.' The pamphlet's rhetoric asserts that both the LSR and the CCF will encourage a home-grown socialism: 'It is no longer a somewhat sickly immigrant; it is a vigorous infant, native to the soil' (*Canada and Socialism*). The metaphor of the immigrant is telling; even after the Comintern's 1935 declaration of a united front with liberals and social democrats against fascism, many CCF and LSR members continued to use the pages of the *Forum* to align the CPC with a Soviet tradition of radical socialism that they figured as alien to North American and British traditions of democracy and liberalism.[24] In his history of the CCF, Walter D. Young describes the problems that the CCF confronted in attempting to distinguish itself from the CPC and its affiliated 'front organizations,' which, particularly during the 1930s, pursued causes that reflected the work of the CCF in government. The CCF thus had to 'wage war on two fronts,' against 'enemies' on the right and on the far left, with whom social democrats were often confused (Young, *The Anatomy* 226). However, if the CCF and the LSR made few overtures, at least in the 1930s, to the unskilled, largely immigrant working class, CCF MPs in this decade 'consistently challenged' the federal government's deportation practices, which, as I argue above, linked recent immigrant status to the problem of unemployment (Kelley and Trebilcock 223, 235–6). In 1937, Eugene Forsey's LSR pamphlet 'Does Canada Need Immigrants?' responds to the ongoing unemployment crisis in Canada with a rejection of the government's suggestion that immigration for agricultural jobs might be reopened. While Forsey is making an argument that was very common in all political camps in the 1930s, his specific reference to the potential displacement of the 'native Canadian' who will end up on relief is telling: in the context of their campaign to urge the federal government to adopt the centralizing powers accorded to it in the British North America Act and to assume responsibility for national unemployment, LSR members wanted to make their case for the 'deserving' unemployed as compelling as possible.

The concept of the national labour force that was emerging during the Depression is linked to ideas about citizenship, or, more broadly, membership in the state. As one *Forum* editorialist put it in June 1938, 'Who but the federal government can make the unemployed Canadian citizens?' (70). Artists on the cultural left in this period were involved in the process of imagining and negotiating what came to be the social rights of citizenship in the postwar period – what Janine Brodie describes as the 'social entitlements' 'embodied in the social policy regimes of postwar welfare states' that 'advanced the bargain between individual citizens and the state beyond formal legal and political rights to include access to a minimum level of economic security for every member of the national state' (377–8). Citizenship as a legal concept did not appear in Canada until 1947, but the relationship between activist cultures and the emergent welfare state in this period indicate its importance as a historical moment during which citizenship was being defined from below – against and through the concept of class. There is a paradox here: while opposing the defining characteristics of what McKay calls the nation's liberal 'project of rule' ('The Liberal Order Framework' 620), *Forum* contributors anticipated what British sociologist T.H. Marshall later called the 'social rights of citizenship' – a concept that Marshall used to describe what he viewed as the basis of the worker's necessary compact with the liberal welfare state. Marshall's theory of social rights incorporates working-class members into a given society without necessarily changing the capitalist structure of that society (Turner 8). Importantly, the social rights of citizenship are bound to what Richard Falk calls the 'modern idea' of citizenship – the twentieth-century notion of 'individuals endowed with entitlements or rights in relation to the governments of territorial sovereign states' (5). While denouncing individualism in favour of collective action and the 'social good' and using the unemployed type to argue for the social rights of many, writers like Grove and Marcson consolidate the binary upon which liberal citizenship has come to depend – the binary of the individual outside the state and the individual inside.

When the King government finally introduced a federal program of unemployment insurance in 1940, it had long been a social welfare

measure that CCF members had been agitating for in Parliament and
that LSR members had been calling for in publications like the *Forum*.
Despite their resistance to CPC efforts to establish a united front in the
period after 1933, when the leaders of the CPC were imprisoned under
the infamous Section 98 of the Criminal Code and the party was forced
to do its work through front organizations like the Canadian Labor Defense League, social democratic bodies shared with the CPC and its affiliated organizations and publications an interest in a federal program
of unemployment insurance.[25]

Masses: Revolution or Reform?

Third Period social radicalism found an outlet in the early 1930s in the
little Toronto-based magazine *Masses* (1932–4), which was developed
and funded by the Progressive Arts Club (PAC), a cultural group with
branches across the country that had connections to the CPC.[26] The unsigned editorial in the first issue of *Masses* (April 1932) boldly announces
that the magazine's goal, like that of its U.S.-American counterpart, is
to 'provide the basis for the development of a militant working class art
and literature' (2). The Toronto branch of the PAC comprised members
such as Dorothy Livesay; playwright, poet, political activist, and journalist
Oscar Ryan; and writer/actor Toby Gordon, all of whom also had ties to
the PAC Workers' Experimental Theatre, which produced the notorious
play *Eight Men Speak* in 1933. The agitprop produced by the Workers' Experimental Theatre in the early 1930s, much of which was featured in the
pages of *Masses*, is an intriguing example of art and protest being combined to produce a solution to unemployment: unemployed men and
women often participated in these collaborative dramas. Moreover, the
agitprops of the Workers' Experimental Theatre were often used as elements in the pageant of protest undertaken in the context of the CPC's
unemployed movement. Frank Love's one-act agitprop *Looking Forward*
provides a good example of this: a member of the Toronto PAC and
an unemployed electrician, Love was 'assigned' to write a 'propaganda
play' that would be performed 'at each night stop' of the 1932 Hunger
March to Ottawa, a national protest of the unemployed organized by local branches of the CPC-affiliated National Unemployed Workers' Association (NUWA) (Wright and Endres 15–16). *Looking Forward* articulates
the issue of relief to unemployed men and their families in the typically
polarized terms of the early 1930s, but, significantly, the play's dialectic
of passivity and protest is enacted not through the feminine-masculine

binary that permeates Third Period discourse, but rather through the opposition of a 'disheartened' older generation that accepts its fate and a younger, radicalized generation that includes men as well as women who 'refuse to be sitting at home mopping' (Wright and Endres 17). Oscar Ryan's one-act play *Unity*, which appeared in the May/June 1933 issue of *Masses*, offers similar evidence of the deep connections between the Workers' Experimental Theatre and the unemployed movement. Performed on May Day in 1933 at Toronto's Hygeia Hall, *Unity* relied on non-professional actors who were 'for the most part unemployed' (Wright and Endres 97). Ryan's play exploits a visual opposition between four 'capitalist' types in top hats and four 'workers' in black workers' theatre uniforms, and elaborates the opposition by contrasting the capitalists' jejune disarray and the workers' collective power, deliberateness, and choral and ideological unity.

Doyle describes *Masses* as a small, experimental monthly magazine whose sporadic publication (it ultimately appeared about six times a year) and 'homemade appearance' were 'offset by the contributors' enthusiasm for experiment and controversy' (89–90). Although its form differed greatly from the *Forum*, many of its commitments did not, a fact that is somewhat surprising given the magazine's explicit rejection of the 'pink' *Forum* – a rejection that was typical of the communist sectarianism of the Third Period.[27] Ambivalence between 'bourgeois nationalism' and international allegiances also plagued communists and fellow travellers throughout the 1920s and 1930s, and this tension is played out in contributions to *Masses*. CPC leader Tim Buck supported Canadian independence and shared many of J.S. Woodsworth's ideas in this regard, but the official position of the party had, by the early 1930s, been disciplined into the more properly international (i.e., Stalinist) perspective of the Third Period (Penner, *The Canadian Left* 94–9). Yet Irr argues that despite the officially internationalist perspective of the magazine, it located and nurtured a Canadian proletarian literature (183), and Irvine demonstrates that *Masses* was aimed at a specifically Canadian audience (*Editing* 33). L.F. Edwards's 'Authorship and Canadiana' (April 1932) and Maurice Granite's (possibly a pseudonym for Oscar Ryan) 'On Canadian Poetry' (July/August 1932), in particular, call for cultural revolution in national terms.[28]

Because it employs stridently revolutionary rhetoric, the conceptualization of the nation in *Masses* is more radically socialist than the critical nationalism of the *Canadian Forum*, yet like the *Forum* in the 1930s, the articles in *Masses* are influenced by attempts to goad the federal government into acting on the issue of unemployment insurance, among other measures, to deal with the impact of the Depression. Indeed, unemployment was one of the defining issues of Third Period politics: in 1928, the Comintern pronounced that capitalism had entered a 'Third Period' of postwar development during which mass unemployment would instigate a profound political crisis (Manley, '"Starve, Be Damned!"' 467). As historian John Manley has documented, the Third Period activities of the CPC – which included the formation of the NUWA in 1930, a mass petition in 1931 that called for 'state non-contributory unemployment insurance,' the creation of a non-sectarian and reformist National Council of Unemployed Councils (NCUC) in 1932, a National Unemployment Conference in Ottawa in 1932, and a National Hunger March to Ottawa in 1933 – were focused almost exclusively on the issue of unemployment ('"Starve, Be Damned!"' 467, 471, 473, 478–9; Penner, *The Canadian Left* 156).[29]

In the inaugural April 1932 issue of *Masses*, the founding editor of the magazine (and prominent CPC member) Ed Cecil-Smith made his opinion regarding the crisis of joblessness clear. 'Unemployment' decries government inaction with regard to the unemployed and sharply observes the contradiction between the state's deportation of thousands of jobless immigrants in 1931 and Minister of Immigration W.A. Gordon's 1932 plan to increase immigration in order to pay for debt incurred by the building of Canada's railways (3).[30] Cecil-Smith's article anticipates the kind of statistical analysis of unemployment that social democrats such as Leonard Marsh later called for in their studies of joblessness:

> To frontier states, such as Canada and the U.S., the realization that unemployment is a permanent concommitant [*sic*] to industrial capitalism is new. European countries, lately industrialized, also have learned of it only since the war. In Great Britain, however, where a fairly accurate estimate of the unemployed has existed relatively longer, one finds that close to 10% of workers are always out of work. That figure has been gradually raised since the war, and now stands at nearly 25%. Last year, unemployment figures in four leading capitalist countries were, in round figures: U.S.A., 8,000,000; Germany, 5,000,000; France, 2,800,000; Britain, 2,600,000. In each case this represented a large increase over the previous year ... All these figures are taken from the records of the International Labor Office, Geneva, and are certainly most conservative. (3)

While Cecil-Smith uses these figures to call for the death of capitalism and not, as social democrats did, a system of unemployment insurance, by December 1932 an unsigned editorial urges workers to demand 'non-contributory unemployment insurance, to be paid for by the capitalist state and the coupon clipping class' (3). Such a demand should be made through the democratic channel of municipal elections, the editorialist contends; professional and non-professional members of the working class are thus directed to join forces to elect 'real working class candidates' (3). An editorial in the September 1933 issue similarly calls on workers to demand state protection collectively: 'Only the pressure of a united front of all workers, organized and unorganized, employed and unemployed, can compel the rulers to grant unemployment and social insurance' (4). The moderate political work of the editorials and articles in *Masses* that treat the issue of unemployment exists in tension with the revolutionary cultural work of many of the poems that appeared in the periodical; the revolutionary claims in this poetry must therefore be read with a sense of this contradiction. After the Comintern's declaration of a Popular Front in 1935, the CPC and its front organizations turned more openly to parliamentary and legislative solutions (Manley, '"Communists Love Canada!"' 72–3), and the non-fictional contributions to *Masses* anticipate this shift.

Instead of focusing on the single, male transient who is ubiquitous in the pages of the Depression-era *Forum*, Maurice Granite's – possibly Oscar Ryan's – poem 'This Is the Road' (November 1932) represents the slow but sure radicalization of the men, women, and children of the working-class family as they take to the road in order to join the 'swing of drumming hearts' (4). In this sense, the poem uses the road as a metaphor for workers' unity, but it simultaneously literalizes the effects of unemployment on women and children: they too must take to the road if there is no work and no adequate system of relief. Although, as is typical of internationalist Third Period poetry, the poem does not refer to a specific geographic location, it suggests that the end result of mass unemployment in Canada and elsewhere will be the homeless family. Yet enforced mobility has actually created a new community of workers, all of whom share the 'gray, foot-worn' road as a new kind of home:

Hey!
Cry, cry, cry.
Voices waking in the night;
Stealing the softness of whispered lullabies;
Voices hard as the mountain;

Voices twisted and blasted with dynamite.
Voices in the swing of drumming hearts.
Drum, drum, drum.
THIS IS THE ROAD. (4)

'This Is the Road' shows how the 'homeless' workers that the capitalist system creates can in fact use their common homelessness and mobility to unite. The chant's simple refrains of single, stressed syllables – 'cry, cry, cry' and 'drum, drum, drum' – suggest deliberate marching rather than the listless plodding of Bourinot's 'Outcasts.' The dawning sun is no naive figure for utopian ideals here; it is a compromised figure, 'all hard and barefisted / and eaten with rough seeds of harsh / cruelties' (4). Instead of looking to an always-delayed future, Granite's poem suggests the urgency of revolution in the moment, on the road, with whatever materials are at hand. This is an inclusive revolution: rather than privileging a single, male proletarian figure, the chant encompasses men, women, and children in its broken rhythms and, crucially, uses the 'hey!' of the workers' chant to call the reader to join the 'voices waking in the night.' While contributions to the *Forum* tend to privilege the sanctity of home as a place to which the transient must be returned, Granite's poem challenges such arguments, contrasting the 'walls of empty shanties' to the community of 'heads singing in the twilight' (4).

One of the issues that creative contributions such as Maurice Granite's probe is the question of what the unemployed population of Canada looks like. As the first part of this chapter indicates, those who were affected most by the initial wave of Depression unemployment were recent immigrants, many of whom had emigrated from central Europe in massive numbers throughout the late 1920s (Avery 114). It is important to note that unlike the LSR or the CCF, which eschewed ties with organized labour until the postwar period, the CPC was committed to organizing among the immigrant working classes. Indeed, its Workers' Unity League (WUL), which was established in 1930 and quickly affiliated with NUWA, was the only labour organization in Canada that reached out to the unemployed – a largely immigrant population – even if a Comintern directive to eliminate sectarianism in 'semi-autonomous language federations' within the CPC proved divisive in this period (Avery 128–32).[31] Indeed, as Manley observes, one of the obstacles faced by the numerous communist bodies organizing the unemployed in the early 1930s was the fact that 'many Anglo-Celtic workers gravitated towards non-Communist groups because the Communist-led movement was identifiably "foreign" and "dangerous"'; nonetheless, the unemployed movement did succeed in attracting Anglo-Celts to the party in increasing numbers during the early 1930s, and 'ethnic rivalries by no means dissolved' ('"Starve, Be Damned!"' 479–80).

Dan Faro's short story 'Colonist Freight' (November 1932) offers an intriguing example of how racial politics functioned on the communist left in this period. It focalizes its representation of the racial conflict between Italian and British immigrant workers through David, a British immigrant. David contrasts the 'naive and childlike' Italians with the anemic appearance of an English family, who remind him of 'a family of white mice' (5, 6). The ethnic particularity of both groups – the Italians and the British – fills David with distaste; his response is to emphasize their common class. The groups share the same car on a train, the same powerless relationship to state and capital; working-class solidarity, 'Colonist Freight' tells its reader, must transcend ethnic divisions. Writing under the pseudonym 'H. Francis,' Frank Love makes a similar argument in his story 'Madeline Street' (January 1934). The third-person narrator in Love's story (which claims to be an excerpt from the 'forthcoming novel' *The Road to Bitterness*) urges the reader to understand the principle of solidarity that undergirds an unemployed council: 'Down here there was no room for individual troubles; they had to be thought of collectively and worked on in the larger sense' (8). Love then directs this didacticism into exemplification as the story follows Mitch, an organizer for the unemployed council, in his efforts to defend a black worker and his family from eviction. While Buck Jones, the black worker in question, is stereotypically represented as an Uncle Tom – stoic, cheerful, and submissive – Mitch rejects this role playing, calling Buck's habit of referring to Mitch as 'Mistah Mitch' instead of 'Comrade Mitch' a 'bourgeois habit' that he will have to 'get over' (9). This insistence on workers' equality and the importance of interracial solidarity is reinforced in the story's conclusion. Mitch is not the saviour of the Jones family; rather, the cheerful 'fighting spirit' he encounters in their house reinforces his commitment to his labours on behalf of the unemployed (9).

Masses contributors also drew attention to and challenged the enmeshment of racism and anti-red sentiment. Maurice Granite's story 'Fellow Workers' (June 1932), for instance, links the anti-Communism of the police to racism. This same issue displays a linocut print of hulking, proletarian figures in coffins with the words 'DEPORTED' stamped diagonally across their bodies, and contains a review of *Deported*, the Workers' Experimental Theatre production about a family of foreign-born workers who are to be deported 'as charges on the state' (8), as well as a vitriolic dissection and condemnation of the 1932 Scottsboro (Alabama) case, in which nine black 'hobos' were lynched for allegedly raping white prostitutes (4). Recalling the martyrdom of immigrant radicals often mobilized by the international left in this period, *Masses* contributors incorporated the persecution of the immigrant unemployed into their wider cause. *Masses* also dealt with the problem of racism as it emerged in other ways from the unemployment crisis. As the letters sent to R.B. Bennett during the Depression reveal (collected in Grayson and Bliss's *The Wretched of Canada*), resentment bubbled throughout the 1930s over immigrants – or those, such as Japanese and Chinese workers in BC, who were perceived as foreign – who were accused of usurping the jobs of native-born Canadians. Maurice Zigler's story 'Four Cents a Bread' (April 1932) directly confronts this prejudice. The narrator in Zigler's story emphasizes that the 'small, plump' baker who denies a steaming, fresh loaf of bread to a hungry male transient is of indeterminate ethnicity: 'His nationality was hard to tell. He might be an Irishman, a Jew, or an Italian' (6). Refusing to name the ethnicity of the story's petit-bourgeois figure, Zigler's brief narrative insists that the conflict between these men results from their class rather than their ethnic differences.

Dorothy Livesay's poems, which appeared regularly in *Masses*, are evidence of her commitment to the internationalism of the CPC in this period and also indicate her attempts to negotiate the relation of working- and middle-class women to the unemployed. Livesay was exposed in these years to the worst effects of the Depression through the fieldwork placements that she completed in order to earn her social work diploma. Her participation in *Masses* was embedded in a turn to radical politics that informed all aspects of her life, including her rejection in this period of the state solutions that Harry Cassidy (a professor in the department of social service at the University of Toronto where Livesay studied) proposed in the pages of the *Forum* and elsewhere. Ken Moffat situates Livesay's dialectical 'politics of engagement' against the more 'rigorous social-scientific' models of social work that prevailed in this period and that emphasized the importance of theorizing the social ideal *before* moving into social work practice (68, 51). Complicating this opposition is the fact that, in the 1930s, new forms of feminized social work that attempted to place unemployment in broad social and familial contexts were also increasingly devalued against the more 'scientific study of unemployment' undertaken, for example, by Leonard Marsh and his colleagues at the Social Science Research Project (Campbell, *Respectable Citizens* 63).

In accordance with her internationalist commitments in the early 1930s, Livesay's 'A Girl Sees It!' (March/April 1933) makes no reference to any particular geographical setting or political context; however, one sees in it the poet's attempt to grapple with the relation between 'unmarried mothers,' whom she so regularly encountered in her fieldwork, and the political commitments that she was exploring though her involvement with the PAC, the Young Communist League, and, eventually, the CPC (*Right Hand* 59). As Livesay describes in her memoir of the 1930s, the complementary ends of these pursuits were not always evident (*Right Hand* 59). In 'A Girl Sees It!' Livesay uses the solitary figure of the male transient as a vehicle through which the misguided speaker of the poem, a young female domestic servant named Annie, comes to political consciousness. Annie, who has just given birth to a 'bastard' fathered by her former employer's son, rejects all the discourses that purport to 'save' a 'girl' in her situation, and so the poem offers a sharp-edged critique of the collusion of patriarchal and class systems. Yet if Annie understands this collusion, she nonetheless comes to her understanding of revolution through the figure of the male transient. The transient, who is unnamed and who stands for all the men 'out there tramping, / Looking for work,' tells Annie, '"You've got to know what you're fighting against, and then / You've got to show others the way. Together you'll swing / Out onto the road. That's solidarity"' (6). The poem therefore juxtaposes the bourgeois 'green solariums,' which are private (and, as Rifkind points out, highly feminized [*Comrades* 61]) places of passive contemplation, with the public, urban space 'down near the waterfront' where Annie first encounters the unemployed (6). As in Granite's 'This Is the Road' and Livesay's pantomime 'Joe Derry' (September 1933), it is in this public space that the enforced mobility of tramping will be transformed into the 'onrush of our feet,' which will signal another kind of birth – the coming of the 'International' (6). While Annie counts herself as one of the 'we' who will 'march up past green solariums / With no more fear, with no more words of scorn,' she comes to her understanding of solidarity and to her new mobility through her male teacher, who condescendingly addresses her as 'kid.' Moreover, she describes her political enlightenment by reference to her newborn son: 'And more than once I listened to him. / Till after a while it was I myself who cried: / "I have a son who'll be a fighter yet!"' (6). If Livesay's 'A Girl Sees It!' pronounces the female speaker's radicalization in its title, the poem itself tempers such feminist claims and brings them more in line with the masculinist aesthetics and politics of *Masses* and the radical left, more generally.[32]

Nevertheless, the poem echoes the discourse of militant, maternal feminism that Manley identifies as a feature of the communist unemployed movement in this period ('"Starve, Be Damned!"' 471).

In insisting in the final lines of the poem that Annie's feet will join the marching workers whose steps will herald the coming 'International,' Livesay transmutes *all* of the forms of work in the poem – the private isolation of Annie's labour as a domestic servant, as well as the public 'tramping' of the unemployed – into a slightly menacing and certainly hopeful 'onrush' of feet. In this respect, the poem's feminist argument anticipates later debates, insofar as Depression-era agitation for unemployment insurance produced a system of insurance that excluded the sector that women worked in almost exclusively – private domestic service (Palmer, *Working-Class* 207). A poem such as A. Nesbitt's 'Workless Sister' (June 1932) accomplishes a similar end. The speaker of the poem, whose gender is not identified, addresses a 'gentle, quiet, workless sister' and urges her out of physical and mental confinement:

> Do not weep in silence, sister!
> Bring your tears and bitter sighs
> As a message in the open,
> That will reach the very skies!
>
> And replace the sickly pallor
> Of your cheeks, with burning rage!
> And demand your rightful sharing
> In the riches of the age. (11)

Contrasting the indoor 'pallor' of the addressee with an outdoor vigour, the poem sets up women's class emancipation as a matter of verbal and spatial transgression: the 'workless sister' must speak her oppression boldly and must enter new, public spaces where her voice has not been heard. Significantly and uniquely, Nesbitt's poem represents women as members of the unemployed, as did the CPC, which affiliated the NUWA with its Women's Labour Leagues (WLL) in 1931 in an effort to combat contemporary resistance to women's waged employment (Manley, '"Starve, Be Damned!"' 470).

Between the folding of *Masses* and Livesay's involvement with the Popular Front cultural magazine *New Frontier* (1936–7), she published her poem 'An Immigrant' in the Toronto-based CPC newspaper *The Worker* (1922–36) in the 14 March 1936 issue. Unlike the *Forum*, *Masses*, and *New*

Frontier, but like the CPC paper the *Daily Clarion* that replaced it in 1936, *The Worker* privileged political reporting over cultural production. Following the example of the Soviet Proletarian Cultural and Educational Organization ('Proletcult'), the first editor of *The Worker*, Maurice Spector, was 'prepared to acknowledge the promotion of literary culture as part of the paper's responsibilities' (Doyle 62); however, short stories and poems did not appear in every issue and, when they did appear, were relegated to the third or fourth page alongside 'With Our Women,' a column that solicited and reprinted letters from women readers about politics, family life, food preparation, and fashion.[33] If this arrangement suggests the feminizing of literary work on the radical left, it also echoes the man-on-the-road / woman-at-home structure of the transient narratives in *The Worker*, such as J.W. Toronto's 'Transient Youth' (13 July 1935), which represents a young transient on the 'front lines' of the Depression crisis who sends missives to his sister indicating that he has tested her radical ideas in the real world and that they do indeed hold water. The polemics of *The Worker*, however, did not fail to notice occasionally that the exclusion of women from the category of the unemployed, by the state and the left alike, had terrible consequences for working-class women. An unsigned editorial entitled 'About Women Jobless' in the 17 October 1931 issue complains that this short-sighted interpretation of unemployment should be tackled by local Unemployed Councils in order to challenge the 'brazen, hard-bitten bourgeois demand that married women shall withdraw into that place in which God and bourgeois morality see fit to shove them – the home' (2).

Livesay's 'An Immigrant' is an elegy that embodies a call to action: it is a lament for an unemployed Polish immigrant named Nick Zynchuk whom the RCMP killed in the process of evicting him from his home in Montreal in 1933. The poem's original date of composition is unclear, but both its occasional subject and its Third Period call for revolution indicate that it was first written in the early 1930s.[34] As Livesay makes clear in her memoir of the 1930s, she struggled in the early years of this decade to renounce her bourgeois background, and her time in Montreal in 1933–4 offered her the further challenge of understanding the working class in all of its cultural and linguistic diversity – a challenge that she undertook with alacrity in organizing 'Ukranian, Russian, Latvian, Swedish, Finnish, and French labour organizations and getting them to send their singers, dancers, and actors' to an 'ethnic festival of working-class plays and songs' that she was organizing for the CPC (*Right Hand* 74). In the sense that it draws on an actual event situated in a specific time and place, St Louis Ward in Montreal, 'An Immigrant' also testifies to the tensions between Livesay's commitment to the internationalism of the Third Period and her desire to represent local conditions in Montreal, where she was working and living when she likely composed this poem. Indeed, when it first appeared in the pages of *The Worker*, Livesay's poem was accompanied by both a subtitle indicating its occasion – 'Commemoration: Montreal, March 6, 1933' – and a gloss, which explained that 'on March 6, 1933, Nick Zynchuk, an unemployed worker, was shot dead by Constable Zappa at an eviction in Montreal' (4).[35] Insofar as it seeks to integrate Zynchuk, a recently arrived immigrant, into the 'ground' of a Canadian working-class movement, 'An Immigrant' also thematizes the party's emphasis in this period on the importance of naturalization (Manley, '"Starve, Be Damned!"' 480). Earlier narratives of unemployment in *The Worker*, such as the hobo 'diary' of a 'worker correspondent' (17 October 1931), provide context here: the diary, entitled 'Impressions of a Jungle Tour through Canada,' emphasizes how the non-violent discipline of the CPC's unemployment movement guides the energies of a restless, agitated 'group of hobos of all nationalities' who are intent on 'blowing up a few railway bridges' (3).

Drawing on the actual events surrounding Zynchuk's death and using a pastiche of contrasting voices to show how power is exercised over the marginalized, 'An Immigrant' anticipates the modernist documentary aesthetic that Livesay developed throughout the 1930s – an aesthetic that she later put to work in her long poem 'Day and Night,' which, like 'An Immigrant,' emphasizes the importance of inter-ethnic, working-class solidarity. Analysing Livesay's 'Day and Night,' which was first published in the CAA's *Canadian Poetry Magazine* in 1936, Dennis Cooley contrasts 'the private stable self' of the lyric 'I' that Livesay favoured in her early collections, *Green Pitchers* (1926) and *Signpost* (1930), with the 'rude babble' of 'sub-literary or anti-literary' voices that, like the discordant voices of 'An Immigrant,' jingle, exhort, narrate, sing, and instruct in 'Day and Night' (246–7). Yet 'An Immigrant' also demonstrates how Livesay's political poetry returns to the romantic, lyric elements of an early poem like 'Green Rain' in order to put them to work in a politicized context.

What makes this poem so fascinating is its interest in the moment at which the homeless become homed – its transference to an immigrant subject of the tropes of rootedness so common to romantic-nationalist literary discourse in Canada. The desire to root national cultural forms in the soil from which they ostensibly spring is a central preoccupation of both German and British romantic nationalisms, and, as Jonathan

Kertzer demonstrates, the botanical tropes that ensue from this philosophical tradition profoundly influenced late nineteenth- and early
twentieth-century discourses of Canadian nationalism (41–7). While 'An
Immigrant' initially presents a distance between the speaker's second-
person address of Nick Zynchuk (and the 'newcomers' he stands for)
and the collective 'our' who possess Canada's idealized 'golden stretch
of wheat,' its concluding stanza enacts the process by which the martyred
Zynchuk becomes the soil in which the seed of revolution is planted:

> Alert and quick,
> New voices take command; thin children grow:
> As willows stiffen in the sun their arms
> Stretch out to life; and Zynchuk, smiling quietly
> Is part of moving green along the hills;
> Is garden for their seed. His breath is blown
> Stronger than this March wind upon their lungs. (4)

Like 'A Girl Sees It!' this poem channels its vision of social change
through a homeless male, but by figuring the 'unknown and unob-
served' immigrant as the 'garden' in which Canadian children might
grow revolution, Livesay directly challenges social fears about immigrant
radicals. Zynchuk is not menacing: his quiet smile is sewn into the pastoral image of the 'moving green along the hills.' Moreover, as an element of the very landscape, Zynchuk's 'alien' politics become native.
Such uses of the pastoral call to mind the back-to-the-land panacea that
some municipal officials favoured in the early years of the Depression.
That Livesay began to favour pastoral images on the advent of the Popular Front is perhaps surprising, given that the ravages of drought on the
western Canadian prairies had by the middle of the decade made the
anti-pastoral a more common mode on the left. Rifkind, for example,
reads such anti-pastoralism in Anne Marriott's 1939 documentary poem
The Wind Our Enemy (*Comrades* 107). Yet there are other significant examples of the pastoral in Livesay's Popular Front poetry. The February 1937
issue of *New Frontier*, for example, pairs two Livesay poems about the unemployed – 'The Dispossessed' and 'In Praise of Evening' – in order that
the latter poem's pastoral imagery may resolve the state of urban limbo
evoked by the former poem's 'burning street' and 'sooty walls' (7).[36]

   Cooley describes the meeting of the romantic and the political in Livesay's Depression-era poetry as a radical pastoral mode that resists and re-
vises some important lyric conventions (266). Rather than serving as the

external stimulus to personal introspection, as in Livesay's earlier poem 'Green Rain,' the 'moving green' of the natural world in 'An Immigrant' incorporates Nick Zynchuk, and together they signal a transformation to come. Yet the transformation is tentative, a seedling only, and, crucially, it relies on Zynchuk's strong 'breath,' which is both identical with the wind (its metaphorical vehicle) and stronger than it. In its specific evocation of a Canadian 'ground' in which the unemployed might metaphorically take root, 'An Immigrant' marks a shift in Livesay's poetics of the unemployed. Particularly after the advent of the non-sectarian Popular Front, Livesay situates many of her poems more explicitly within Canada and eschews the revolutionary march of 'A Girl Sees It!' in favour of a more conciliatory engagement with the Canadian state.

New Frontier and the Coalitional Politics and Aesthetics of the Popular Front

In 1936, *New Frontier: A Canadian Monthly Magazine of Literature and Social Criticism* emerged from the ashes of the militant *Masses*. Slightly more expensive than *Masses* – twenty-five cents per issue rather than ten – but also longer and more polished in its layout and design, the Toronto-based *New Frontier* endured until October of 1937.[37] The initial editorial board of this new journal included Margaret Gould, Leo Kennedy, Dorothy Livesay, and LSR member and *Forum* editor J.F. White. Indeed, many writers and thinkers who contributed to *New Frontier*, including Livesay, Graham Spry, and Mary Quayle Innis, had long-standing associations with the *Forum*. Committed to a united front and to the cause of the Spanish Civil War, especially from late 1936 onward, *New Frontier* brought together a diverse body of leftist opinion. Although the voice of communism was muted in the magazine, prominent CPC leader and *Masses* editor Ed Cecil-Smith – who later went on the lead the Mackenzie-Papineau battalion in the Spanish Civil War – appeared in its pages (in the September 1936 issue), and on the inside cover of the April 1937 issue there is an advertisement for the CPC's Popular Front newspaper the *Daily Clarion*. The editorial of the inaugural (April 1936) issue of *New Frontier* declares a commitment to the front defending 'democratic liberties' threatened by fascism: 'It is the hope of the editors of *New Frontier* that the ominous uniting of forces of reaction will be opposed by a drawing together of the forces for progress' (3). While aimed at furthering the causes of the Popular Front in Canada, *New Frontier* 'attempted to facilitate communication among members of working and middle classes, among leftists and fellow-travellers, and among an international bloc of sympathetic authors and readers leaning toward the political left' (Irvine, *Editing* 58). This broad political front is also revealed in the funding sources of the magazine: 'intellectuals and artists of broad political persuasion and class orientation,' such as Jean 'Jim' Watts, who possessed a private fortune, kept *New Frontier* financially solvent (Irvine, 'Among *Masses*' 206). The internationalism of *New Frontier*, and the politics of anti-fascism that fuelled it, led to a diminished focus on ostensibly national issues such as joblessness; nevertheless, the writers of the 'Ottawa Notes' column that was a regular feature in each issue, as well as the creative contributors to *New Frontier* did comment on unemployment, often fashioning it as a non-sectarian issue that invited state intervention.

The inaugural issue of *New Frontier* in April 1936 includes three stories – Mary Quayle Innis's 'Staver,' Katherine Bligh's (Dorothy Livesay's) 'Six Years,' and A.M. Klein's 'Friends, Romans, Hungrymen.' Each story probes, in Morley Callaghan's words in this same first issue, the theme of the 'man out of work' (24). The issue also features a lithograph by Ernst Neumann entitled 'Unemployed No. 5' (part of a series of unemployed figures that Neumann executed in the early 1930s), which renders in stark lines the idle body of an unemployed male. Seated close the ground, the figure fingers a cane that is suggestive of premature aging, while alluding to the debate about transient mobility that raged in the 1930s. Callaghan's appraisal of the first issue of *New Frontier*, which the editors of the periodical solicited, treats unemployment as a distinctly anti-aesthetic subject, and also clearly indicates a growing satiety on the part of middle-class readers with the diet of unemployment. Although from the late 1930s Callaghan famously struggled with the challenges of earning a living by writing, in the early part of the decade he was afloat in the continental success of his Depression-era novels; as Gary Boire puts it, Callaghan was in the first half of the 1930s still nurturing his 'literati' persona, but he would soon be transformed into a 'professional scribe' (170). It is unsurprising, in this context, to read his 'criticism':

> It is odd that these three pieces should have been on the one theme – the man out of work. The editors tell me that this was not a deliberate selection, but that nearly all the stories they received were about men who were out of work. If this keeps on it will appear that either all the young writers of the country are out of work, or that they feel a little frustrated, a little cynical, or even defeated, and that living in this country doesn't leave one with a strong feeling. (24)

Although Callaghan's critique targets a decided lack of realism – a dearth of 'good feeling' 'sharply' evoked, an absence of the 'juicy racy flavour' of 'colloquial speech' (24) – it simultaneously resists the notion that the most typical experience of everyday life in 1930s Canada *was* joblessness. The appraisal is striking for its bland assessment of unemployment as a lack of artistic imagination, and is a good signal of the way that unemployment lost its discursive urgency as the 1930s drew to a close and other threats loomed more vividly.

A notable irony here is the way in which both Livesay's 'Six Years' and Innis's 'Staver' dismantle the comfort of a detached middle class that is given voice in Callaghan's 'A Criticism.' Although Mr Dakin in Livesay's story appears to his working-class neighbours to be making 'good money where he clerked, somewhere in the city, shot up flight after flight each morning by the elevators,' his daily walk to the trolley turns out to be a ruse: the ironically named 'Reliable Insurance Company' has fired its male employees 'because they have to be paid more than the girls' (13). Mr Dakin has been pretending to go to work in order to maintain a fragile middle-class identity.[38] Innis's story 'Staver' thematizes (and genders) the process by which a female, middle-class observer uses the 'powerful' body of an unemployed male as a means of heightening the aesthetic experience of her own groomed body: 'In her new blue dress and hat, walking in her shining white shoes over the crisp, sharp-smelling grass she wished childishly that Staver would notice her' (19–20). If Innis offers a steady gaze at the problem of cross-class relations, particularly as they cut across gendered lines, Callaghan unwittingly assumes the middle-class perspective she is trying to unsettle. However, as a judge for the 1936 *New Frontier* play contest (sponsored by the New Theatre Groups of Canada and co-judged by Garfield King of the Vancouver PAC), Callaghan demonstrated sympathy with the theme of cross-class relations and the issue of unemployment. The winning play, Mary Reynolds's *And the Answer Is ...* (February 1937), recalls Innis's 'Staver' insofar as it asks its middle-class audience to confront its hypocrisy and blindness with regard to the poverty and unemployment that remained common experiences in the latter half of the 1930s.

Also in the first issue, Klein's story 'Friends, Romans, Hungrymen' is a satire of the process by which capitalism renders some workers part of what Marx called the surplus population. Unusual for its use of satirical humour to estrange the ubiquitous experience of unemployment, 'Friends, Romans, Hungrymen' anticipates the approach used by James Hinton in his short story 'Meat!,' which appeared in *New Frontier* in the

July/August 1937 issue. Ironically alluding to the mystifications of fairy tales, Klein's first-person narrator describes how he lost his job:

> So one day, back in the time of the fairytales, the boss called me into his cave and said that he was sorry but he was going to lay me off. He said it nicely, like an ogre elocuting fee-fi-fo-fum. He grabbed me, wrapped me up in a little package, and laid me down upon a dusty shelf. Then he stuck out a long tongue, licked the gluey side of a strip of paper, pasted it on me, and read it over: Unemployed. (16)

This opening paragraph introduces the ironically intimate paternalism of 'the boss,' who has the power to label some workers – in a process that mimics the labelling of products and the assembly line of the Fordist economy – unemployed. Throughout Klein's story, the unnamed narrator (known only to the reader as 'Unemployed') emphasizes the nightmarish quality of his condition through an experimental, anti-realist aesthetic: he lives in a city park and applies for membership at the zoo; meets God and asks for 'a dime for a cup of coffee,' but is directed to a 'swell flophouse on the Milky Way' (16); and has another encounter with his boss, who tells him that he is only a 'ghost' with a wind-up heart (16). Indeed, much of the story's oneiric quality comes from the way Klein presents the gap between the signifier and the signified: the narrator attempts to engage the world through lawn signs, the symbols on coinage, and newspapers, but all of these encounters fail because the signifiers have no stable referent in the world. The job ad the narrator finds in the newspaper, for example, refers to no actual job. Significantly, the title's allusion to Mark Antony's famous speech from Shakespeare's *Julius Caesar*, in which Antony manages to suggest to a crowd of mourners that Brutus is responsible for Caesar's death, fails to offer the kind of resolution that is so typical of high-modernist deployments of allusion. Instead, Klein undercuts this allusion by placing it in the mouth of an agitator, one of the many who offer bombast rather than actual social change to the unemployed. 'Friends, Romans, Hungrymen' thus interrogates both high modernism's view of art as restorative and socialism's predilection for the utopian, offering instead an estranged reality that seeks to motivate social change.

Given the Popular Front politics of *New Frontier*, it is not surprising that Klein, who was associated with the CCF and the cause of ant-fascism throughout the 1930s and '40s, appeared in its first issue. Klein, like the poets with whom he was associated, embraced the aesthetics of modernism and sought, in the spirit of the Popular Front, to ally those aesthetics with a recognition of the social and political crises around him. Denning contends that an experimental coalition of socialism and modernism characterized the aesthetics of the Popular Front period in the United States and that the 'inability to imagine a completed narrative' paradoxically energized the 'contradictory fusions' that emerged in this period (118–22). Drawing on Kenneth Burke, Denning reads what he calls the 'proletarian grotesque' as the 'poetic form most appropriate to moments of crisis and transition' and points to how the strange mixtures and defamiliarization strategies of many Popular Front texts function as an 'attempt to wrench us out of the repose and distance of the "aesthetic"' (122–3). Although this argument applies in a more limited way to the unfolding of the Popular Front in Canada, it is helpful for understanding the literary experimentation of a writer like Klein, whose aesthetic of the grotesque functions not as humour but as discomfiting agitation.

Concerned specifically with the possibility of the rise of fascism in Canada, contributors to *New Frontier* made much of the social alternative embodied in the motley group of men who crossed the nation in search of work. The 1935 On-to-Ottawa trek, a mobile strike of relief camp workers with diverse political affiliations who hoped to reach Ottawa in order to publicize their plight, was an important symbol for Popular Front politics in Canada. A June 1936 *New Frontier* editorial, for example, uses the strike to claim 'the necessity for the unity of all progressive forces to uphold the right of free speech and freedom of organization in Canada' (3). In the September 1936 issue, the periodical also responded to King's announcement of the closing of the federal relief camps. Suggesting that the Bennett government might be blamed for almost succeeding in turning the desperate transient population toward fascism, Burnett A. Ward insists that the 1935 trek represents a strong anti-fascist sensibility among the unemployed:

> The credit for this complete disillusionment of the boys must not, however, be granted entirely to our singularly obtuse rulers. That would be an injustice indeed to the earnest band of organizers and teachers, Communists, I.W.W.'s, Socialists, and others, who for five years have wandered from camp to camp, advising, instructing, restraining, and leading. Their desire was not to agitate for the sake of agitation. They were impelled by fear, and they fought against time; a fear that the rulers of Canada would realize their mistake and build on the despair of youth a Fascist psychology and movement. (13)

Through his appeal to a seemingly homogeneous group – 'the boys' – Ward silences the very real rifts between the CPC and the CCF in this period and emphasizes a united front.

Despite the importance of the On-to-Ottawa trek as a rallying symbol for the Popular Front, Dorothy Livesay did not publish her 1936 poem dealing with the Regina riot that ended the trek in the pages of *New Frontier*. 'Dominion Day at Regina,' written in July of 1936 when Livesay was participating in a *New Frontier* promotional tour in the western provinces, takes as its subject the riot that occurred in that city one year earlier – on 1 July 1935 – when the joint forces of the RCMP and the Regina police attempted to arrest the leaders of the On-to-Ottawa trek on charges of sedition.[39] In the poem, Livesay shifts away from the sectarian revolutionary discourse of 'A Girl Sees It!' and elides all particularity in favour of a united left. The 'we' of the poem is prominently positioned at the beginning of the first, third, and fifth stanzas, effectively opening and closing the poem with a collective assertion of belonging and common cause. In the first stanza, the 'we' identify themselves as

> from the prairie's sweep
> reared with the wheatfields
> who followed the gopher
> home to his mating   (*Right Hand* 186)

Raised like grain out of the earth, these men assert their natural right to the 'home' they share with the animals of the prairie. In the next stanza, the meaning of 'home' grows geographically wider, as the trekkers claim to be 'Kin to the pine tree / tossed with sea foam' (*Right Hand* 186). Mimicking the trajectory of the eastward trek, the poem's 'we' encompasses the nation. Livesay's romantic tropes recall the figuration of Nick Zynchuk in 'An Immigrant,' while contesting the technological symbol of nationhood represented by the train, which carried the trekkers east but which is simultaneously symbolic of their plight. The 'home' in the first stanza is contrasted to the dubious home that the trekkers have found through their labour, which is owned by others:

> in rusty rock's heart
> blasting a home
>
> We from a mining town
> seared with black dust

suckled on bosses' oath
schooled by our struggles   (*Right Hand* 186)

The last two stanzas turn to a more regular rhyme scheme (abcb; defe) to emphasize the collective voice behind the imperative that concludes the poem: 'Give us the work / and it shall be done!' (*Right Hand* 186). Despite the imperative, the verbs employed in the two final stanzas lack the militance of much Third Period art: addressing the capitalist state, the trekkers 'ask' for bread and 'offer' their 'hands,' 'sinew and bone' (*Right Hand* 186). Responding perhaps to the state's characterization of the trekkers as foreign and potentially violent agitators, Livesay's 'Dominion Day at Regina' figures them instead as native sons of the soil who ask only for the work that will allow them to reassert their claims to the land.

The *Daily Clarion* and the Popular Front Politics of Conciliation

Unlike *Masses* and *New Frontier*, the *Daily Clarion* (1936–9) was an official CPC publication and, as such, had a much closer affiliation with party directives, but like *New Frontier*, it was a manifestation of Popular Front ideologies. The shift to Popular Front tactics and the worsening of the economic situation improved the stature of the Canadian communist movement and led to its increased involvement in publishing ventures in the latter half of the 1930s (Doyle 102–3), as well as its renewal as a more public, less 'bohemian,' less 'foreign,' less radical party that attempted to attract progressives of all stripes and adopted a more conciliatory attitude to parliamentary reform (Manley, '"Communists Love Canada!"'). Additionally, the election of a Liberal government in 1935 and the subsequent repeal of Section 98, the anti-sedition law that had made the CPC illegal throughout the first half of the 1930s, temporarily improved the party's fortunes (Avery 139).[40] Although after 1935 the party shifted away from its Third Period work of building a national unemployed movement and moved toward an emphasis on its anti-fascist campaigns, it did continue to act on the former issue, while privileging 'electoralism and faith in the state' (Manley, '"Starve, Be Damned!"' 488).

In 1936, the Toronto-based CPC organ *The Worker* was replaced by the less sectarian *Daily Clarion*, which 'in its size and format and even in some of its contents (comics pages, sports sections), attempted to compete with the bourgeois papers' (Doyle 103). A daily paper, the *Daily Clarion* was delivered to homes in Toronto for the price of twelve cents per week (other rates were available on request). An advertisement for the newspaper that appeared in the April 1937 issue of *New Frontier* provides good evidence that the CPC sought a broadened audience for its Popular Front organ; the simple design of the advertisement and the tone of its prose, which offers the *Daily Clarion* to readers as 'the one dependable, steady guide in a mass of muddled printed matter,' suggests that the paper was cultivating moderation and restraint. Readers were treated in a manner that does not differ substantially from the techniques of the contemporary mass media; for example, they were provided with regular features that instructed them how to assume their proper roles within the patriarchal family. A regular women's page included culinary advice, recipes, and fashion tips; the children's section featured didactic stories about social injustices; and the men had their choice of news, a sports section, and generously if incongruously placed photographs of beauty contestants and stunning Soviet women. In 1937, the paper instituted a weekly book page (with William Lawson, formerly of *New Frontier*, as literary editor), but this section favoured reviews over original contributions. Despite its mimicry of bourgeois papers, creative contributors to the *Daily Clarion*, most of whom were party members, were able to disseminate ideas through the periodical that were not palatable to mainstream publishers (Doyle 96).

As a Popular Front publication, the function of the *Daily Clarion* was to give voice to the rallying cry of international socialism against fascism, and as an official organ of the CPC, the paper also participated in the party's attempts to launch proposals for parliamentary reform, particularly with regard to the unemployed. On 10 June 1938, the *Daily Clarion* reprinted a parliamentary address given by CCF member of Parliament C.G. MacNeil in which he argues that, contrary to the beliefs of many, at least half of the transients who were involved in the 1938 Vancouver Sit-Down Strike were in fact residents of British Columbia. Echoing the standard *Forum* argument of the period, MacNeil insists on federal responsibility for the unemployed based on the inability of the province to protect its own workers. MacNeil's attempt to convince the government that the strikers were in fact residents with rights is related to the government's fear that many transients in BC camps were organized by the communist-led Relief Project Workers' Union – an affiliation that often led to suspicion of so-called foreign agitation (Struthers, *No Fault* 192). This article's appearance in the *Daily Clarion* indicates the CPC's desire to support the cause of the unemployed in a politically non-sectarian manner and also offers an example of how the Popular Front

CPC worked through the legitimating reputation of the CCF in order to dispel their own image as foreign agitators preying on Canada's innocent sons. Echoing the *Forum*, an editorial on 15 October 1936 entitled 'Homeless at Home' decries the lack of federal solutions for unemployment in the wake of the dissolution of Bennett's 'slave camps' (4). Drawing on its title's irony, the editorial insists that the federal government must assume responsibility for 'young Canadians, homeless in Canada!' (4) Like the treatment of the issue of unemployment in the *Canadian Forum* and by the CCF, the *Daily Clarion* uses the transient's nativity – his inalienable claim to the nation of his birth – as grounds for his right to the resources of the nation-state.

The transient narratives in the *Daily Clarion* likewise resist the stereotype of the foreign radical. In keeping with the CPC's self-image as a nationalist party of the Canadian 'people' after the advent of the Popular Front, and with the party's desire to participate in the parliamentary reform that would bring about unemployment insurance (Manley, '"Communists Love Canada!"' 63–9), the transient figures in the *Clarion*'s short fiction are clearly marked as native sons. Many of the transient stories that appeared in the books section of the *Daily Clarion* are of the 'bottom dogs' type: popular in U.S. proletarian literature from the Depression, the 'bottom dogs' narrative is marked by a weak, unemployed, transient protagonist who, in contrast to the positive worker-hero, enlists the sympathy of a middle-class audience and thus 'expose[s] the social conditions of the nation during the Depression' (Irr 110). Bert Whyte, a *Daily Clarion* staff writer who had also spent time in various relief camps across the country, is the author of many such narratives. His documentary stories 'Night Freight: Canada's Youth on the Move' (1 July 1936) and 'Hell on Wheels: Young Canada on the Road' (18 November 1936) use an authorial persona as a metonym for 'Canada's Youth.' This first-person narrator establishes a generous rapport with the reader, which is based on male camaraderie, a hobo idiom, and a strong implication that the men he meets on the road are all like him. In 'Hell on Wheels,' for example, the narrator's feet begin to freeze as he travels on the roof of a boxcar until a 'chap from back east, from Cobalt, rubbed my feet until they began to burn.' The narrator thanks his 'comrade,' who replies: 'Okay pal, maybe you can do the same for me some day' (4). This exchange becomes particularly significant if one examines the representation of the relief camp foreman in Whyte's non-fictional article 'What I Know about Relief Camps' (23 May 1936). The foreman, Holst, is sourly described as 'a drunken Norwegian ... one-time engineer of sorts, [who] tried to drive us as though it were a contract job, all the while feeding us the poorest grade of cheap foods' (3). The dichotomy of the good transient and the evil foreman functions partly by means of the specific ethnic marking of Holst and, conversely, the deliberate unmarking of the young man from Cobalt. Whyte therefore suggests that work and wages are surely owed to 'Canada's Youth' if they are owed to a drunken, aging Norwegian immigrant.

Recalling the social-democratic argument that privileges the reinstallation of the male in the home, *Clarion* stories draw on a narrative structure of homecoming to demonstrate that identity should be connected to place but that the effects of capitalism have sundered this crucial link. In Lee Hendricks's '... and Bill Came Home' (13 December 1938), a third-person narrator describes the thwarted homecoming of the unemployed rail rider Bill Wayne. The outcome is adumbrated in Bill's ungainly arrival: 'When he finally let go [of the box car] completely, he tried vainly to catch up with himself for an instant, then fell flat on his face in the cinders' (6). This awkward dismount demonstrates that Bill, who has been wandering for many years, cannot fully arrive at home; he has become unnaturally mobile, and so the arrest of a homecoming manifests itself as physical pain. Despite the awkwardness of the arrival, Bill's visceral craving for home is evident: 'Home! Home! Home! He didn't say it. It just rose up inside him from somewhere' (6). As he soon discovers, however, the ravages of the Depression have destroyed his hometown, and there is no longer anything for him to claim. Bill ends up back at the train depot, where he collects the mobile home – a coffee pot and cooking pans – that he had optimistically discarded upon arriving. The life he is returning to knows no rest; he will have to catch the westbound freight 'on the fly' (6). Hendricks's story and another, Marc Bliss's 'Home to Uncle Ollie's' (5 December 1938), seem timed to capitalize on the homecoming nostalgia of the holiday season as a means of emphasizing the injustice of enforced mobility. Significantly, this injustice is based on the transient's claim to a small, rural Canadian town where his extended family lives. The transient has a right to return to this rural home because an identity based on place has been lost and should be recovered. The young man who returns yearns not just to reclaim the safety of his settled life, but also to restore the family and its concomitant gender roles. In Bliss's 'Home to Uncle Ollie's,' for example, the male first-person narrator describes with relish the homecoming meal his Aunt Lonie will fix for him. Indeed, the prevalence of the man-on-the-bum stories in the *Daily Clarion* seems to respond not only to the large number of men actually roaming the country, but also to the gender politics of the periodical generally. The roaming men and stable women of the 'bottom dogs' stories complement the structure and content of the paper; while the paper is overwhelmingly targeted at the man in the family, the women's section corrals the woman of the family into the tidy space of a page devoted to cooking, sewing, and other such gendered activities. The pages for men literally roam about this section and, indeed, cover a much more spatially and temporally diverse range of issues than the women's section.

In conclusion, I suggest that reading these diverse periodicals of the cultural left comparatively and across the divided political terrain of the 1930s offers a picture of how a broad range of dissenting voices imagined similar ideals – state protection for workers and the right to unemployment insurance. If these periodicals sometimes exhibit a strategically narrowed vision of Canada's thousands of unemployed, they nevertheless agitate for profound kinds of social transformation. Indeed, the protest work of the cultural left and the political parties with which it was affiliated brought national attention to this issue of unemployment during the 1930s and ultimately, if indirectly, contributed to the passage of the Unemployment Insurance Act in 1940.

While a form of unemployment insurance was a primary goal of Depression-era leftists, it is important to note that this program was severely limited in its application: its system of graded benefits avoided federal responsibility for guaranteeing a national minimum standard of health and decency, and although it was intended to cover 75 per cent of the Canadian workforce, less than half of the workforce qualified for benefits in its first decade of implementation. For example, seasonal and casual workers and anyone earning over $2,000 annually were excluded from the scheme (Struthers, 'Shadows' 5; Struthers, No Fault 200–1). Moreover, between 30 and 40 per cent of women in the paid labour force in the interwar period worked as nurses (hospital or private) or domestics in private homes, and these occupations were similarly excluded from coverage (Pierson 99). Single and married women also experienced an array of 'indirect limits' on their access to unemployment insurance, including the act's failure to acknowledge that women were 'disproportionately concentrated in low-paying and irregular or intermittent jobs' and would thus have 'difficulty fulfilling the statutory conditions for eligibility' (Pierson 102). Indeed, it is clear that male 'breadwinners' were given priority in the policy discourse of the postwar period: for example, the 1945 *White Paper on Employment and Income* professed the state's commitment to 'high and stable' levels of employment, and this commitment referred primarily to male workers (Keck 65). Guest also points to the fact that the passage of the Unemployment Insurance Act marked the beginning of 'one of the more enduring myths of the welfare state in Canada' – the notion that 'benefits as of right are inseparably linked to contributions' (107).

Despite its limited application, unemployment insurance functioned as a crucial component of the state's postwar compact with labour, allowing the state to absorb dissent and maintain a functioning capitalist society. Other state programs and initiatives from the postwar period had similar effects. In the 1940s, the National Film Board (NFB), for example, became almost synonymous with the documentary form, which played a vital 'institutional role in representing the population in order to help predict and manage it' (Druick 5). Wartime collaborations between the NFB and the Dominion Department of Labour worked to identify, as members of the cultural left had done in the 1930s, the 'typical' unemployed. These collaborative documentary films staged the encounter of that universalized and abstracted individual with the nascent welfare state's program of unemployment insurance. For example, the first documentary produced by the NFB, *The Case of Charlie Gordon* (1939), identifies a typical 'Canadian community' and its equally typical unemployed – a single, white, male youth who is on relief and who, having come of age in the 1930s, has never held a job. The booming voice-over informs us that community-generated apprenticeship programs, and not federal relief, are the answer to the problem of unemployment: 'Like any other industrialized country, Canada must face the task of absorbing her surplus youthful energy into the working life of the nation.' *The Case of Charlie Gordon* insists on the important role that benevolent employers will play in the recovery of the nation and encourages workers to cooperate. Later films like *A Man and His Job* (1943) introduced the Canadian population, interpellated through the figure of the average unemployed male, to the new program of unemployment insurance and the new regime of state protection.

If the arrival of a social right like unemployment insurance, and the more general arrival of the welfare reforms of the postwar period, did not signal the radical change in Canadian society that many on the cultural left sought in the 1930s, their appearance marked an uneasy compact between workers and the state that improved the lives of many

workers – men and women, native-born and immigrant – in the years following the Second World War. Throughout the turbulent decade of the
1930s, leftist artists, activists, and intellectuals of all varieties in Canada
were negotiating the terms of this fraught compact between workers and
the state.

Chapter Three

Novel Protest in the 1930s

As the previous chapter argues, the cultural left articulated a crisis of joblessness in the periodicals that circulated in 1930s Canada. Yet for reasons I will explore in this chapter, few authors or activists in this period published novels that directly engaged Depression conditions or that criticized the federal government's inability or unwillingness to deal with the unemployed. The two novels published in the 1930s that do risk direct engagement of the state – Claudius Gregory's *Forgotten Men* (1933) and Irene Baird's *Waste Heritage* (1939) – are therefore crucially important texts for the theorization of the relations among the state, publishers, literary authors, and leftist or reform politics during the turbulent Depression years. These novels interrogate mobility's contest – the relation of the state to the worker that condensed around the transient unemployed in this decade – and also offer sites for an analysis of the ways in which this contest filtered into the material and symbolic production of texts and, indeed, into Depression-era conditions of authorship. If both novels remain distinctly distanced from radical politics, conditions of constraint in the interwar field of cultural production in Canada help to explain this distance.

Pierre Bourdieu's distinction between the field of large-scale production (producers who produce for a generalized public) and the field of restricted cultural production (producers producing only for other producers), as well as his assertion that the latter 'characterizes most systems of literature' (29), may be usefully adapted to the context of interwar Canada, a period during which a field of restricted cultural production was emerging. Rifkind makes the convincing claim that, like writers of popular adventure and romance, the literary left in 1930s English Canada sought to reach a mass audience – 'the people' – and thus challenged the prevailing conceptions of audience in the field of restricted cultural production (*Comrades* 29). While Rifkind's Bourdieuxian reading illuminates much, it must be added that writers with leftist sympathies and affiliations in this period and place were not always neatly opposed to the values of the national field of restricted cultural production. The publishing history of Baird's *Waste Heritage*, for example, reveals how Baird's anxious negotiation of political interestedness within the national field of restricted cultural production produced a highly ambivalent novel. *Waste Heritage* self-consciously thematizes the author's fears about libel charges, and the novel's critique of war as the state's solution to the problem of joblessness was subject to state censorship on the eve of the Second World War. Its publishing history thus suggests that Canadian novelists of social protest were subject to constraint during the Depression. Moreover, as Bourdieu notes, the autonomy of the field of cultural production 'varies considerably from one period and one national tradition to another' (40), and the fragility of an emerging national literature in 1930s Canada makes it imperative to consider how so-called autonomous principles were subject to standards created elsewhere, mostly in Britain and the United States. Significantly, such a tenuously defined literary field did little to nourish cultural producers' sense of themselves as workers who were entitled to make particular claims on the state through their art.

Although *Forgotten Men* offers a direct and unambiguous political message, that message is ultimately a conservative one of business-friendly reform. This particular form of political interestedness must be understood in the context of the novel's production and reception. The story of its production and the history of its intersections with the Conservative politics of reform and reconstruction that emerged in the latter half of the 1930s suggest that while *Forgotten Men* may be a novel of social protest produced for 'the people,' it is also the complicated product of the kind of coercion that can exist between an employer – Thomas Lisson, whose company printed the novel – and an employee – Claudius Gregory, who was that company's sales manager. *Forgotten Men* is a text that indicates a set of specific – and very rare – conditions that enabled the privileging of didacticism and political interestedness in the novel form – a form more commonly associated in interwar Canada with either the literary (i.e., the field of restricted cultural production) or the popular (i.e., the field of large-scale production). This case study demonstrates how a pro-business message of reform gained access to print because a small industrialist, Thomas Lisson, financed its publication and, arguably, influenced its content. This chapter thus expands the history of Depression-era literary production and social protest in Canada, arguing that the few novels of protest that do exist must be read from a thoroughly materialist perspective in order to appreciate what Bourdieu calls the complex 'position-takings' of their authors within the field of cultural production (30).

The Depression and the Novel

Before proceeding to a discussion of Gregory's and Baird's novels, it is crucial to analyse the wider conditions of constraint governing the production of novels in Depression-era Canada. As the preceding chapter makes clear, leftist magazines flourished, albeit in limited circulation, during the Depression years; however, while it appears that the economic crisis of this period did not affect the publication of poetry in Canada, it did undoubtedly have an adverse effect on the publication of original Canadian fiction.[1] The prosperity and nationalist spirit of the 1920s encouraged Canadian houses such as Ryerson Press and subsidiaries such as Macmillan of Canada to publish Canadian writers, but this trend more or less dissolved in the 1930s, as local houses relied almost exclusively on their agency profits or, in the case of some houses, on Canadian educational publishing, to buoy them through difficult financial times (Parker, 'Trade and Regional' 168; Young, 'The Macmillan' 119–20). In 1937 McClelland and Stewart rejected the manuscript of *Dry Water*, Robert Stead's novel about the social and economic conditions that adumbrated the Depression, because a publisher in the United States could not be found (Querengesser and Horton xxxii–iii); such co-publication arrangements were standard in the period because they allowed publishers in Canada to offload the cost of manufacturing books to publishers in the United States (Young, 'The Macmillan' 120). At Macmillan of Canada, president Hugh Eayrs's nationalism and inexperience led him, perhaps unwisely, to continue publishing considerable numbers of Canadian trade books well into the Depression years. Eventually, two factors caused Eayrs to retreat from Canadian trade titles in the late 1930s: the increasing popularity of U.S.-American textbooks (particularly in the context of the provincial curriculum reforms that occurred throughout Canada in the late 1930s) and the dampening effect that continental 'blockbusters' such as Margaret Mitchell's *Gone With the Wind* (1936) had on the sales of Canadian and other trade publications (Young, 'The Macmillan' 125–8). Eayrs received over two thousand manuscripts in 1939 but published only forty-three books, of which only fourteen were Canadian trade titles (Parker, 'Trade and Regional' 171; Young, 'The Macmillan' 123). In this context, Eayrs's decision in this same year to publish Baird's strike novel *Waste Heritage* is significant, especially because it was not writers who documented Depression conditions but internationally popular Canadian authors like romance novelist Mazo de la Roche and the exoticized Grey Owl, who kept Macmillan 'in the black' during the 1930s (Parker, 'Trade and Regional' 171–2).[2] Canadian houses were devastated in the Depression years by a number of other factors, as well, including the arrival of inexpensive British and U.S. mass-market paperbacks. By the late 1930s, both the Penguin series from Britain and Pocket Books from the U.S. had made their debuts in the Canadian market, 'captivating Canadian readers and heralding the arrival of the paperback revolution in Canada' (Parker, 'Trade and Regional' 171). As the next chapter discusses, the mass-market paperback eventually absorbed at least one Depression-era narrative of protest – Garner's *Cabbagetown* – which initially appeared in the 1930s as a series of reportage pieces in the *Canadian Forum* but was transformed by Collins into sensational genre fiction for a 1950 White Circle paperback.

Many of the Canadian novels that did find their way into print during the Depression are imbued with a sense of social crisis even if they do not specifically acknowledge the prolonged economic downturn and its social effects. Sinclair Ross's *As for Me and My House*, first published by the U.S.-American firm Reynal and Hitchcock in 1941, represents isolation and poverty without ever explicitly referring to the Depression and, as many commentators have observed, uses the drought-starved prairie dustbowl to thematize the arid conditions in which Canadian writers and artists were producing in this period. Irr contends that many Canadian novels from the 1930s – such as Ringuet's *Trente arpents* (1938), Gwethalyn Graham's *Swiss Sonata* (1938), and Ted Allan's *This Time a Better Earth* (1939) – gauge the explosive class and ethnic conflict that characterized the decade (142–68). Morley Callaghan's *Such Is My Beloved* (1934), *They Shall Inherit the Earth* (1935), and *More Joy in Heaven* (1937) probe the causes and effects of urban unemployment on young men and women but, unlike *Waste Heritage* or *Forgotten Men*, do not derive all their narrative action from the problem of unemployment and its potential political solutions. Indeed, the ironic symbolism of Callaghan's Depression-era fiction, which thematizes, according to Malcolm Ross, 'the ambivalence of the human act within the fence of time,' directs the reader away from the secular possibility of meaningful social change within human time

(Introduction viii). Tellingly, Callaghan dropped the issue of unemployment almost entirely from *The Season of the Witch*, his 1976 dramatic adaptation of *They Shall Inherit the Earth*, suggesting that unemployment is an element of the Depression-era setting of his 1935 novel rather than a central component of its theme of betrayal.[3]

Despite the fact that modern realists in Canada explored the conflicts that arose from the Depression, it has long been observed that the proletarian or socialist-realist novel, so prevalent in U.S. fiction of the period, was virtually non-existent in Canada. Writing in the *Dalhousie Review* in 1939, Ruth I. McKenzie was the first to make this claim, and it has been reiterated in contemporary literary histories of the left. Irr notes that in the U.S.-American context of the 1930s, the proletarian novel was diversely construed, but she admits that a plot of political conversion is usually present, although it is not always resolved with a utopian closure (110, 117–18). According to Irr, neither the proletarian novel nor its subcategories – the strike novel, the conversion narrative, or the 'bottom dogs' narrative of 'life on the bum' – were prevalent in the Canadian field of cultural production in this period (145). Irr suggests that a preoccupation in Canada with the 'thematics of geography and survival' might explain the lack she identifies (142), and Doyle points out that the influence of U.S.-American social realism and the moderate politics of the *Canadian Forum* tempered the politics of Depression-era short fiction in Canada and prevented much experimentation with the revolutionary aesthetics of socialist realism (99).

If neither the proletarian novel nor its variants were common forms in Canada in the 1930s, however, an expanded, more thoroughly materialized history is necessary for theorizing this absence. As the previous chapter contends, most progressive agitation around the crisis of the unemployed in Canada was shaped by and helped to create the dominant discourses of the third socialist formation, which can be identified with the state management and economic planning that characterized the postwar welfare state. That is to say that many of the writers who protested state lassitude with respect to the unemployed sought a rapprochement between the figure of the transient and the ideally benevolent state and thus eschewed those forms of proletarian and socialist-realist fiction that enacted a necessary gap between the unemployed worker and the liberal state. Moreover, as I mention above, novelists who felt compelled to document the dire conditions of the unemployed had few publishing venues to turn to during the Depression, and, as the example of *Waste Heritage* suggests, the relations between mainstream publishers and authors who had ideological sympathies with the left could be fraught with compromise, producing, in the case of *Waste Heritage*, an anxious and politically ambivalent novel. *Forgotten Men* certainly narrates a political conversion, but its message is inspired less by Marx than by Christianity and small capitalism. How and why did *Forgotten Men* – a novel exceptional in terms of its direct agitation for social reform and its unabashed political message about the problem of unemployment – appear in print?

Forgotten Men: The Production and Reception of Conservative Reform

As I argue in chapter 1, modern realist novels are often overlaid with strong romance elements. The persistence of idealizing romance elements in modern fiction – documented, for example, by Dennis Duffy and Willmott – helps to account for the significant differences between Baird's and Gregory's novels. It is true that both narratives contain strong elements of urban realism, which, as Hill notes, investigates the 'modern urban experience' ('The Modern' 222); however, if the frank treatment of sexuality, journalistic style, psychological realism, and experimentation with point of view in *Waste Heritage* mark Baird as a 'vital and important originator' of the modern-realist novel in Canada (Hill, 'Critical Introduction' xxxii–vii), *Forgotten Men* draws on a decidedly nineteenth-century form – the social-gospel novel – in order to witness Depression conditions. Like late nineteenth- and early twentieth-century examples of what Donna Bennett calls 'idealized realism,' such as Nellie McClung's *Sowing Seeds in Danny* (1908) or the novels of Ralph Connor, *Forgotten Men* subordinates aesthetics to the imperative of the ethical lecture (143).[4] *Waste Heritage* and *Forgotten* Men may also be compared using the terms modernism and anti-modernism. Literary modernism and anti-modernism share a profound discomfort with historical modernity. In Willmott's view, anti-modernism is 'that element of literary modernism that would, with a turn of the screw, recontain modern discontent, formal and thematic, in the accessibility of generic and popular forms' (164). Read in this way, anti-modernism is a constitutive element of modernism, or what Anderson calls its enabling 'dark-moon side' (103). Indeed, according to Rifkind, this expression of 'modern discontent' in 'generic and popular forms' was a 'widespread' response to the 'perceived disintegration in social relations' during the Depression years, and anti-modernism thus deserves recognition as a 'constituent element of modernism,' even if modernist and leftist critical discourses alike have excluded much of this literature as 'feminine' and 'sentimental' ('Too Close to Home' 96, 111). Moreover, if the idealizing conventions sometimes present in the social-gospel novel are often *anti-modernist*, these conventions enable a social-gospel argument that is *modernist* insofar as it insists on the inextricability of the sacred and the secular that constituted the 'essence of the modernist liberal impulse in Protestantism' (Cook 175). Thus, there is in this 'modernist liberal impulse' much that is modernist in the broader historical, less narrowly literary, sense of the term.

Forgotten Men is the 'earliest published English-Canadian novel dealing in detail with Depression problems' (Doyle 114), yet like the unemployed men evoked in its title and like its own fate in Canadian literary canons, which have (until very recently) privileged texts that have accrued symbolic and cultural capital, the novel remains a silent chapter in cultural history. Its title draws on a phrase that wielded a powerful discursive function in political and popular culture in Depression-era North America: employed by Franklin Delano Roosevelt in a 1932 campaign speech that lambasted the Hoover administration for failing to create 'permanent relief from the bottom up' and that called for 'the building of plans that put their faith once more in the forgotten man at the bottom of the economic pyramid' (qtd in Smith, *FDR* 263), the phrase inspired one of the most popular songs of the 1930s, 'Remember My Forgotten Man,' which was performed in Busby Berkeley's 1933 musical film *Gold Diggers of 1933*. The phrase is clearly situated within the U.S.-American cultural politics of the New Deal; however, the narrative of Gregory's novel puts the phrase to much different political and cultural use. If the title of *Forgotten Men* alludes to the New Deal, its physical appearance (disingenuously) suggests more radical affiliations. The dust jacket of the first (and only) edition of Gregory's novel, which was designed by Stuart Wallace, plays on the radical iconography of the decade through an image that is strongly reminiscent of the graphic arts featured in the pages of *Masses* and *New Frontier* and of the lino and woodcut prints that Hamilton artist Leonard Hutchinson began making in the late 1920s. Although Wallace's image boasts bold olive and turquoise colours against a black background (instead of the *Masses*-style black and white), this linocut or colour woodcut print is characterized by strong, simple lines that achieve an abstract rendering of the face of the 'typical' forgotten man (see figure 3.1).[5]

In Desmond Pacey's 1965 assessment of the novel in the *Literary History of Canada*, he derides its 'transparent' allegory but, in keeping with the then-canonical privileging of realist fiction, notes that its attention to so-

3.1 Stuart Wallace's dust jacket for Claudius Gregory's 1933 novel *Forgotten Men*.
Image courtesy of the author (private collection).

cial conditions sets it apart from the 'mass of romances being turned out in Canada at this time' ('Fiction 1920–1940' 197).[6] Yet in a period when a forward-looking realism was coming to define fictional prose in Canada, this largely backward-looking novel seemed to have little to say. Not surprisingly, leftist literary histories have also largely ignored *Forgotten Men*. For literary historians of the radical left, the novel's nostalgic retreat has proved an unpalatable alternative to the future-oriented utopianism of art influenced by socialism.[7] Other scholars of the cultural left have situated *Forgotten Men* within the social-gospel tradition – given voice in English-Canadian novels such as Agnes Maule Machar's *Roland Graeme: Knight* (1892), Ralph Connor's *Black Rock*, and Albert R. Carman's *The Preparation of Ryerson Embury* (1900) – that eventually influenced the CCF.[8] It is accurate to read *Forgotten Men* in the context of the history of the social gospel, but, as historians such as Ramsay Cook and Richard Allan have demonstrated, the social gospel was a diverse intellectual, cultural, and political movement that attracted conservatives, progressives, and radicals alike. This novel is indebted to the more conservative elements of social-gospel discourse, but it is only an examination of its publishing and reception histories that makes this clear.

In an initial dedication and a concluding note of acknowledgment, Gregory humbly honours his employer and political mentor, Thomas Dyson Lisson, 'through whose sympathetic and understanding collaboration has been made possible the weaving into the tale some constructive thought, which if put into practice would immediately relieve the present world crisis.' Gregory thus attributes the novel's basic social-gospel argument – its insistence on a Christian sociology that locates in the actions of Jesus Christ an ideal example of the fair distribution of earthly resources – to Lisson, one of the owners of Davis-Lisson Limited, the Hamilton, Ontario, printer that published *Forgotten Men* and that employed Gregory as a sales manager. This commercial or 'jobbing' printer did not regularly function as a publisher of novels, but rather produced advertising brochures, house organs, window displays, catalogues, and commercial stationery. Yet Gregory insists that Lisson's support of *Forgotten Men* was no caprice: as the final note of acknowledgment in the novel informs us, Lisson spent the fifteen years prior to 1933

> endeavouring to prove to humanity, and to business men in particular, where the conditions they were making were leading them. There has been an unselfish motive behind this work, for the cost of producing the numerous booklets he has written and distributed has been paid out of his own pocket. (442)

According to Gregory, these 'numerous booklets' include *Birth Control or Scrap Labor-Saving Devices* (1919) – a warning that the advent of new automatic printing presses would have to be coupled with a reduction in the birth rate lest massive unemployment result; *Five-Day Week* (1920); the prescient *Where Is Credit Leading Us?* (1926); and *Employment during 1931*.[9] Many of the surviving publications from the 1930s bearing the Davis-Lisson imprint are generally political in character. They include, for example, Peter L. Robinson's 1932 book *World Reorganization or Downfall, and the Remedy*, which echoes the political philosophy of *Forgotten Men* – and, apparently, Lisson – insofar as it founds its solution to the world economic crisis on a reform principle that takes its cues from the more equal distribution of nature's supposedly endless plenty.

Given Lisson's involvement with the politics of reform and Gregory's insistence that his novel's social-gospel argument is inspired by Lisson, it is intriguing to note that Hamilton, the city in which Lisson lived and worked, had a strong social-gospel tradition of labour reform by the early twentieth century. In the late nineteenth century, the Hamilton Knights of Labor published a weekly newspaper, *The Palladium of Labor*, which was a key site in the emergence of Canada's social-gospel movement (Cook 107). Like many of their progressive contemporaries, the Hamilton Knights of Labor believed in the regeneration of Christian faith through social criticism, but for the Knights, agitation for trade unionism formed an essential component of that critique (Cook 163). More than two decades later, Lisson also called for labour reform, but the Hamilton tradition of trade unionism did not appeal to him, and it is this difference that suggests how Lisson's position as a small industrialist influenced his politics, which were reformist but never radical, progressive but deeply liberal. During the 1920s and '30s, Lisson was involved in local organizations that sought, in an era of labour strife, to reform business practices and labour-management relations. He belonged, for example, to the Master Printers' Guild of Hamilton, which was formed in the late 1920s to advocate 'fair wage scales and hours of labor in all printing establishments in Ontario and eventually throughout Canada' and the 'establishment of conciliation and arbitration through which employees and employers may negotiate agreements with a maximum of industrial responsibility and a minimum of expense.'[10] Yet Lisson's politics of reform railed against union leaders, who, in his view, thrived unnecessarily on conflict and refused to loosen their self-serving 'hold upon the contributor employee.'[11]

In its note of acknowledgment, *Forgotten Men* gives voice to this aspect of Lisson's ideology of reform – the notion that the benevolent employer, if nudged by the state, is capable of easing the worst effects of the capitalist system. Gregory insists that his employer is no 'mouthing malcontent' – he is no labour agitator – but rather a reputable man of business who successfully applies his political ideals to the profit motive: 'The fact that his own business continues to thrive and increase in spite of business depression, is evidence in itself of the soundness of his thought' (442). In 1938, Gregory authored a promotional brochure for Davis-Lisson entitled *The Printed Word*, which repeats this notion that the employer is capable of treating his employees well without the interference of unions. In this attractive booklet, Gregory claims the commercial services of Davis-Lisson might bear profitable fruit for any number of groups, ranging from manufacturers to churches to management wishing 'to overcome the influence of demoralizing agitation among their employees' (8). Although authored by Gregory, *The Printed Word* is clearly an advertisement for Davis-Lisson that Gregory wrote at the request of his employer.

Significantly, *Forgotten Men* appears to have been produced under similar conditions. The narrative of *Forgotten Men* is so faithful in its echoing of Lisson's political thought that one may very reasonably speculate that Gregory wrote the novel at the request of and under the supervision of his employer. Jerome McGann's argument regarding the 'polyvocality' of literary texts is useful here: he posits that such texts are 'thick' with both figurative language and the 'textual presence and activities of many non-authorial agents' (42). Gregory was an 'author' insofar as that category is capacious enough to include the presence of the 'non-authorial agents' that produced 'his' novel (and the particular employer-employee power dynamic informing the political interestedness of the novel).

Echoing the 1932 Davis-Lisson publication *World Reorganization or Downfall*, the Christ figure of *Forgotten Men*, Christopher Worth, hinges his proposals for social reform on the redistribution of 'the earth's abundance' (411). Recalling his turn-of-the-century fictional counterparts Roland Graeme and Ryerson Embury, Christopher Worth is a convert to the causes of the working class and progressive Christianity who hails from the upper class and who transforms his sympathy into leadership. Contemporary middle- and upper-class readers, such as the reviewer of the novel in the July 1933 issue of the *Canadian Magazine*, found this trope of conversion attractive: 'To a Depression-ridden world – and especially to Canada – "Forgotten Men" brings a stirring message, designed to rouse those who still know nothing first-hand of the catastrophe to a realization of their brothers' predicament' (42). Christopher's dalliance with a deeply anti-liberal conception of property at the beginning of the novel is explicitly inspired by the story of Genesis and implicitly alludes to the ideas of the nineteenth-century political economist Henry George, whose ideas about land nationalization in *Progress and Poverty* (1879) fuelled the social-gospel movement (Cook 107). Yet Christopher's activist Society of Forgotten Men ultimately embraces a more moderate theory of reform.

Drawing on Lisson's concerns about the social effects of labour-saving devices, the Society of Forgotten Men eventually calls for full employment, which they argue can be achieved through the implementation of a globally uniform work week whose length is calibrated to employ every worker under the age of fifty-five. Christopher also embraces state controls on wealth accumulation – he insists that industrial enterprises that 'control assets in excess of ten million dollars' must be nationalized – in order to protect the 'small industrialist' (407). Indeed, small capitalism – an economic system based on networks of small industrialists like Lisson who cannot be threatened by the processes of vertical integration that transformed North American industry in the late nineteenth and early twentieth centuries – is the novel's key to social reform. Many nineteenth-century social reformers called attention to the disappearance of small industry and the nefarious effects of unrestricted competition on workers, and while the more radical of these reformers, such as Phillips Thompson, tended to view labour as the source of all economic value, the more moderate, such as John Clark Murray, argued that in the relation of capital to labour, each was entitled to a share of the product based on contribution to the effort (Cook 182). Allen's history of the social-gospel movement similarly identifies differences among radical, progressive, and conservative early twentieth-century reformers, noting, for example, that conservative reformers focused their energies on 'personal-ethical issues, tending to identify sin with individual acts' and thus worked for 'legislative reform of the environment' (17). In its advocacy of the benevolence of the small capitalist, rather than a state-imposed regulation of that capitalist, *Forgotten Men* takes up the more moderate version of the social gospel that does not challenge the core of the capitalist system and, indeed, allows it to flourish under new constraints.

Late nineteenth-century deployments of the social gospel, especially those penned by male writers, resisted the pervasive conflation of Christianity with sentimentality and femininity, and instead sought a renewed faith in a 'robust, muscular Christ,' a carpenter and fisherman who was 'not unlike the toiling workmen of industrial America' and whose 'activism and reforming spirit' embodied a 'radical populism' (Curtis, 'The Son of Man' 74–5). Like the popular novels of Ralph Connor, *Forgotten Men* takes up this masculinist version of social gospelism, critiquing the effects of industrialization on the spirit and intellect of men. Although Christopher Worth's program of reform clearly enables small capitalism, the novel yokes this system of production to idealized, pre-industrial forms of work and implies equivalence between them. The pivot of social change in *Forgotten Men* is Lee Hansen's printing shop, where the activist Society of Forgotten Men meets and begins to print its political pamphlets. Initially, the wood-panelled meeting room above Hansen's shop is intended as the home of his 'short lived' 'Authors' Club,' a literary group that he hoped would generate the 'thought that eventually would become writings that his type fonts and presses would give expression' to in the form of 'beautifully bound books' (142). The transformation of the room under the leadership of Christopher Worth is represented in a way that aligns the work of the Society with the work of leftist activists in the 1930s, for whom art became politics and politics became art. As a character in *Forgotten Men* phrases it, a benign 'stick of type' might become a 'wicked' tool requiring 'asbestos paper' in times of social upheaval (139). Also borrowing from leftist and anti-modernist critiques of mass culture, Christopher Worth observes that transformational uses of printing technology are urgent in a North American society saturated with the 'sensational copy' of newspapers and the distorted social norms of Hollywood films (217).

As a means of resisting the encroachments of technology, Gregory's novel offers a specific response to the threats posed to homosocial communities of labour. While the novel's elevation of the intellectual work of discussion, analysis, and writing is literalized in the fact that the meeting room is on the top floor of Hansen's shop, Gregory consistently emphasizes the organic interdependency between cerebral and physical labour. The important work of printing and disseminating reform pamphlets provides the Society with the almost magical opportunity to 'repeat the message as often as they desired' in order to 'reach the masses' (140), and yet the novel's representation of the technology of printing is a thoroughly materialized one. Like Davis-Lisson, Hansen is a 'jobbing printer,' a species of small, commercial printer that evolved out of the increasing specialization of printing work that accompanied the arrival of the machine-press period in the nineteenth century (Gaskell 252). While Hansen's shop prints using the machines typical of early twentieth-century 'jobbers,' such as the platen jobber, a small press operated by one worker who simultaneously worked a treadle and laid and delivered the paper, his shop lacks some of the more common technologies of the period, such as the composing machinery that had largely replaced the composing sticks of the hand-press period by the early twentieth century (Gaskell 265, 274). This is significant because the collective labour of the men in the shop functions as a figure for full employment – the autonomous labour of each individual contributes to a whole over which each asserts authorship and ownership. The reader of *Forgotten Men* is informed about each stage of the production process, from the pulling of the damp proof from the type form on an imposing stone to the small compartments of the case that hold the type that is expertly selected by hand and placed on the composing stick. Significantly, this instruction of the reader parallels the education of each member of the Society: as the group begins to coalesce around a solidly defined reform program, each member assumes a place in the print shop. Hansen, the expert, continues to work as compositor, and other members learn to tie up type, proofread, and feed the automatic press. This collaborative physical work extends the intellectual work that preceded it because it prompts further collective discussion and debate among the Society members. Executed to the whistled tune of 'Onward Christian Soldiers,' this is also labour with God on its side (262). The novel thus idealizes pre-industrial life and its local, homosocial forms of labour organization, such as the craft guild. While the platen jobber offers evidence of an encroaching mechanization – a shift that Lisson worried about in his 1919 pamphlet *Birth Control or Scrap Labor-Saving Devices* – the organization of the shop nonetheless provides work for all, unlike the large steel mill owned by Christopher Worth's father, which must periodically lay off workers in order to stay in business.

If the Society of Forgotten Men has God on its side, this does not guarantee protection from fallible human law, as the raiding and subsequent confiscation of Hansen's shop by the police later makes clear. Robbed of this means of production, Christopher Worth's movement loses its most potent worldly weapon. Worth's Christ-like martyrdom is fuelled by the print evidence of his so-called 'communistic' thought (336), and his subsequent imprisonment and death suggest the failure of print to mobilize social change in a corrupt world. Yet the cause of the Society of Forgotten Men is ultimately rescued when Barlow Worth, Christopher's industrialist father, reads the notes his son made for his unfinished book and is persuaded that he must lend his millions to the work of Hansen and the other remaining activists. It is thus the potential merger of benevolently redistributed capital and the modest technology of Hansen's print shop that will spread Christopher's reformist philosophy 'like the gospel of the man of Galilee' (393). If there is a palpable threat to the future in this novel, it is dissolved in this resolution, which simultaneously guarantees the dismantling of a large industrial concern, the continuance of the homosocial work community represented by the Society of Forgotten Men, and the engagement of Christ's work on earth. The conclusion would thus seem to do away with the necessity of the small industrialist and favour the decentralized form of labour idealized by the Society of Forgotten Men, but the reader must not forget that the program of reform that the Society is now able to print and disseminate is one that privileges the small industrialist and his caretaking role within small capitalism. The parallel between the thesis of *Forgotten Men* and its own production history is fascinating: the inside flap of the novel's original dust jacket represents *Forgotten Men* as a 'constructive' intervention in the crisis of the Depression that marks a 'new epoch' in the 'business progress' of Davis-Lisson. Moving 'forward in our business endeavours' is thus equated with the publication of a novel that argues for reform.

This concept of small capitalism is certainly one that Thomas Lisson held dear, and, by the mid-1930s, the printer was bringing his commitment to this idea to the federal level of party politics. Along with him, he brought *Forgotten Men*, and the story of his political activism in the latter half of the 1930s reveals much about the reception history of Gregory's now-forgotten novel. This reception history is intriguing particularly because it allows a view of the ways in which art was taken up in the political field in the 1930s, rather than telling the more well-known story of how art attempted to engage the political in this period. During the 1935 federal election, Lisson served as the first vice-chairman and national publicity manager for the newly born Reconstruction Party, and Davis-Lisson printed a Reconstruction manifesto, a speaker's handbook, and a weekly campaign newspaper. Less well-known than the other Canadian political parties that emerged from the ideological cauldron of the 1930s, H.H. Stevens's Reconstruction Party was a splinter party that captivated many disgruntled Conservatives, particularly those who, like Lisson, were independent retailers and manufacturers. Stevens was the minister of trade and commerce in Bennett's cabinet from 1930 to 1934 and may be most familiar to readers of modern poetry as one of the targets of F.R. Scott's satirical 'An Anthology of Up-to-Date Canadian Poetry' (first published in the *Forum* in May 1932), the epilogue of which quotes from 'My

Creed,' Stevens's 1931 statement to Canadian manufacturers. Scott uses this 'found' text to pillory a government beholden to industry rather than to its people and the promises of its constitution:

> I believe in Canada.
> I love her as my home.
> I honour her institutions.
> I rejoice in the abundance of her resources
> *****
> To her products I pledge my patronage,
> And to the cause of her producers
> I pledge my devotion. (291)

Stevens did not remain in Bennett's government: in October of 1934, in the wake of his controversial leadership of the Select Committee on Price Spreads and Mass Buying, which investigated the detrimental effects of big business practices on independent producers and retailers (and which, somewhat ironically, had been informed by F.R. Scott's and Harry Cassidy's 1932 exposé of conditions in the men's clothing industry), Stevens resigned from government (Djwa, *The Politics* 148–9; Wilbur, 'H.H. Stevens' 6–12). The schism that developed in the Conservative Party and in Bennett's cabinet as a result of Stevens's discourse of reform led to the creation of the Reconstruction Party.

Lisson corresponded regularly with Stevens after the latter's resignation from the Bennett cabinet in October 1934, repeatedly offering the rogue Conservative ideological as well as financial support. Lisson was so enchanted with Stevens's controversial leadership of the Select Committee on Price Spreads and Mass Buying that he compared the politician, as Claudius Gregory had done with his protagonist, to Christ. In turn, Stevens, who was always somewhat reticent in his replies to Lisson's exuberant hyperbole, indicated that he greatly admired Gregory's novel *Forgotten Men.*[12] In June 1935, while Stevens was still officially denying the possibility of leading a new party, he sent one of Lisson's recent letters to Warren Cook, asking him to comment on Lisson's ideas for a 'Stevens National Party' that would have what the printer called his 'Youth Movement' behind it. Cook's report of a subsequent meeting with Lisson indicated that the Hamilton printer could potentially make a valuable contribution to a new party and that he would also likely 'be very helpful in forming "Stevens Youth Clubs."'[13]

While Lisson promised to print Stevens's 'personal publicity' materials at no charge, in May of 1935 he boldly requested that Stevens send some 'party election printing' his way, which Stevens promptly arranged.[14] Yet it appears that once Lisson assumed his role on the national executive of the Reconstruction Party, his firm printed literature for the 1935 election campaign at no charge (Wilbur, *H.H. Stevens* 193). Lisson was certainly a shrewd small-business operator who sought some financial benefits from his political alliances; unsurprisingly, he committed his modest company – and his livelihood – to the politics of Reconstruction during the 1930s, a politics that championed the rights of small manufacturers and retailers. If Lisson's work with the Reconstruction Party is suggestive of the often ambiguous distinction between political and business interests, Gregory's novel attenuates such ambiguities to imagine the potential embedded in the collaboration of a small, commercial printer and political work for social change. He thus paints a very attractive and somewhat heroic picture of his employer, Thomas Dyson Lisson, who appears in the novel as Lee Hansen, the printer with a strong moral and political conscience who more or less turns his business over to the Society of Forgotten Men. Particularly if one takes account of the paratextual references to Lisson and his printing firm, *Forgotten Men* thus functions as a sort of advertisement for Lisson, who by the mid-1930s was making frequent if somewhat mercurial references to political ambitions that he had likely been entertaining for some time. Ultimately, however, Lisson's poor health convinced him to choose a behind-the-scenes role in the 1935 federal election.[15]

At a Hamilton meeting organized by Lisson and other disenchanted Conservatives on 5 July 1935, a petition requesting Stevens to form a new party to 'reestablish Canada's industrial, economic, and social life to the benefit of the great majority' was drafted and signed by the thirty-one people in attendance. Recalling the social-gospel discourse of *Forgotten Men*, the petition casts the would-be leader Stevens as one whom 'Providence has loaned' to 'Canada for this time and task.'[16] The next day, Lisson and Warren Cook, who eventually became the party's chairman and treasurer, took the petition to Stevens in Ottawa, and Stevens announced his leadership of the new Reconstruction Party (Wilbur, *H.H. Stevens* 181). According to a *Hamilton Spectator* clipping appended to Lisson's letter to Stevens of 18 June 1935, young reform advocates who supported Stevens were shaking up the Hamilton Conservative Association, and, clearly taking a cue from this source of support, when Stevens announced his new party in early July, he declared its commitment to

jobless youth. Later that month, when the party unveiled its manifesto
– printed by Davis-Lisson – Stevens spoke from a podium at Toronto's
Royal York Hotel with more evidence of his sympathy for unemployed
youth – a copy of *Forgotten Men* – displayed on the desk beside him (Wilbur, *H.H. Stevens* 181, 184).[17] The party's slogan, which appeared on its
letterhead in the summer of 1935, exhorted Canadian voters to 'Give
Youth It's [*sic*] Chance!'

There is a strong parallel between the intellectual heritage of the Reconstruction Party and the social-gospel thesis of *Forgotten Men*. J.R.H.
Wilbur attributes Stevens's daring break from the Conservatives to the
'old crusading Methodist zeal' he learned as a Methodist preacher (his
career before he turned to politics in 1911) (*H.H. Stevens* 202). As a
'Methodist Tory,' Stevens joined the 'progressive social creed' of Canadian Methodism with political conservatism; that is to say, like many 'red
Tories,' he affirmed the basic structure of the economic system while taking 'issue with its weaknesses and with those unscrupulous citizens taking
advantage of their fellows' (Wilbur, *H.H. Stevens* 14, 16–17); however,
if the 'red Tory' tradition famously permitted Gad Horowitz to postu-
late the link between conservatism and socialism in Canadian political
and intellectual history, the turn more recently to a 'liberal order framework' insists on the fact that Canadian conservatism shares with liberalism, among other values, a commitment to 'private property and social
inequality' (Constant and Ducharme, 'Introduction' 11–12). This point
is crucial to my reading of the production and reception of *Forgotten Men*:
while this social-gospel novel may appear to have more in common with
social-democratic discourses of the 1930s than with the liberal order that
prevailed in this period, I contend that the opposite is true.

The Reconstruction Party's manifesto called for reforms that were considerably more moderate than the already moderate proposals of Christopher Worth: a public works program, a national housing program, a
public marketing board for agricultural products, liquidation of the national debt through the development of Canadian resources, increased
taxes on higher incomes, and a federal tax scheme that would assess
each unit of large corporations; however, with regard to one significant
issue – youth unemployment – the party echoed the Society of Forgotten
Men. The Reconstruction Party called for an end to youth unemployment (but no unemployment insurance) and promised full employment, although the proposed means of achieving this – a public works
program – is significantly more moderate than Christopher Worth's
globally calibrated work week.[18] The Reconstruction Party's deployment

of *Forgotten Men* as a kind of manifestary text thus clearly drew on the novel's message of reform and its representation of the lost economic opportunities embodied in unemployed youth; yet if we recall that many of the reforms proposed in *Forgotten Men* go further than anything the Reconstruction Party was considering in the mid-1930s, it becomes clear that the novel was taken up strategically as a kind of political shorthand for the party's commitment to jobless youth. The Reconstruction platform was not, as Wilbur has pointed out, a radical one, and the party did not fare well in its attempt to carve out a niche of support between what the party's speaker's handbook called the 'dubious socialistic benefits' of the CCF's proposals for public ownership and the traditional politics of the Conservatives:

> [Stevens] had always upheld the basic features of the capitalist system, and even now, when an economic paralysis gripped the nation, Stevens believed that the system could be made to work if the people at large and the financial institutions would cooperate with a sympathetic federal government. Yet, because of his attacks on big business, Stevens could not expect much sympathy from some of the institutions, notably from the Montreal financial community. (*H.H. Stevens* 186)

Although Stevens's party ran candidates in 174 ridings (including Hamilton East and West), only Stevens himself gained a seat (Penner, *From Protest* 64), despite the fact that the party's candidates garnered almost 9 per cent of the popular vote (the CCF, which gained seven seats, attracted just over 9 per cent) ('History of Federal Ridings'). However, this short-lived party did manage to pose a considerable challenge to a Conservative Party that had waited too long to propose economic and social reform measures.

Forgotten Men insists on the mutually beneficial cooperation of small capitalist enterprise and political reformists, and this is clearly the vision that Lisson nurtured through his social-reform printing and, later, through his affiliation with the Reconstruction Party. The publishing and reception histories of *Forgotten Men* suggest links between essentially liberal discourses of reform in the interwar period and the earlier social-gospel movement, and attentiveness to this history is crucial to the work of reading the complex category of the protest novel in 1930s Canada. The nexus of power around protest and print in Depression-era Canada demands nuanced analysis, and Irene Baird's novel *Waste Heritage* offers a second intriguing site for the development of such work.

Waste Heritage and the Politics of Ambivalence

Like much Depression-era writing in Canada, Irene Baird's 1939 novel *Waste Heritage* was out of print for many years and, perhaps as a consequence, did not garner much critical or scholarly attention. Fortunately, University of Ottawa Press published a new edition of the novel in 2007, which is already bringing the attention of a new generation of scholars to bear on women's writing during the interwar period in Canada. Existing criticism of the novel is influenced by the New Left's project of recuperating it as an example of Canada's socialist literary tradition, a project that included its reappearance as part of Macmillan's Laurentian Library reprint series in 1973.[19] Leftist nationalist Robin Mathews, for example, has argued that Baird's novel should be heralded as a classic of proletarian literature in Canada – a novel that sympathetically represents the inevitability of class revolution. Critics who have rejected Mathews's reading have tended to adopt a polarized position. Doyle, for example, notes the 'atmosphere of futility' that hovers over the strikers' collective efforts and argues that the novel 'questions the effectiveness of strikes, demonstrations, and other efforts of the alienated men to relieve the crisis' (120–1).[20] Archival evidence regarding the publishing history of the novel has allowed me to reconsider the political interestedness of *Waste Heritage*. Although Baird has no author's papers and although the original manuscript for *Waste Heritage* is no longer extant, her correspondence with her Canadian and American publishers, as well as her articles on the writing of *Waste Heritage*, are integral to the process of interpreting the novel's conflicted position within the field of cultural production.

Baird's novel does decry the situation of those men who were cut adrift by the Depression and largely ignored by the federal government, but the narrative reinforces the social hierarchies and relations of power that the thousands of transient unemployed threatened to undo in the mass demonstrations and strikes they engaged in throughout the 1930s. As her communication with Macmillan of Canada and Random House in New York demonstrates, Baird's work was constrained – and influenced – by numerous factors, including her class and gender, the demands of her publishers, the influence of U.S.-American literary standards, and state censorship that resulted from the 1939 invocation of the War Measures Act, all of which led her to feel deeply ambivalent about writing a 'strike novel.' Baird possessed little symbolic capital in this early period of her career, and both she and her publishers were clearly uneasy about the influence of political interestedness on her literary text. Like other writers with leftist sympathies in Depression-era Canada, such as Dorothy Livesay, Baird articulates the importance of federal intervention in the crisis of mobility that had beset the nation, but her hesitancy regarding the politics of her project indicates that interwar leftist literary cultures in Canada (and the literature that has been incorporated into its marginal canon by, for example, leftist nationalists) were striated by tensions between revolution and reform. As Rifkind contends, the 'documentary referent' in Baird's novel is less the 1938 Vancouver Sit-Down Strike of unemployed transients than it is the postwar compact (*Comrades* 168) – what McKay calls Canada's 'passive revolution' ('For a New Kind of History' 71).

Waste Heritage represents an explosive event, the troubling effects of which remained fresh in the minds of Canadians in 1939, when the novel was first published. The Vancouver Sit-Down Strike involved more than one thousand transients who were protesting the fact that provincial and federal governments had been unable to formulate a permanent strategy for dealing with the unemployment that had ravaged the country for the better part of a decade.[21] The strikers inhabited the symbolically significant public sites of the Vancouver Post Office and Art Gallery for a month before the RCMP forcibly evicted them in late June; the men then proceeded to Victoria to make their voices heard in the provincial capital, and the strike ended in early July when the strikers accepted Mackenzie King's offer 'to pay the cost of relief for all non-resident transients ... pending their return home or an offer to them of employment' (Struthers, *No Fault* 192–4). Baird's fictional narrative responds to this labour crisis with a depiction of a typical unemployed transient, allegorically named Matt Striker, who comes to Vancouver by train to join the strike just after the evictions. There, he befriends a fellow striker named Eddy, falls for a young woman named Hazel, struggles with his sense of loyalty to the cause, and finds himself back where he started when the government settlement sends him out onto the road without hope of work or relief. Faced with so few options, Matt has a violent altercation with a police officer, kills the officer, and is arrested; Eddy, grieved by his role in Matt's arrest, stumbles onto the train tracks and is killed by an oncoming train.

Waste Heritage shares the ideological project of many of the stories and poems that appeared in leftist periodicals in Canada in the 1930s: through the figure of Matt Striker the novel argues for the existence of a national labour force that deserves the attention of federal coffers. As

I discuss in chapter 2, the possibility that Canada had a national labour force and, consequently, that the federal government was responsible for it, was an issue that formed the crux of much political debate in Canada in the 1930s. Insofar as *Waste Heritage* is sympathetic to this issue, it shares the commitments of both the social-democratic and communist movements in Depression-era Canada. As for contributors to leftist periodicals during the Depression, the transient unemployed became, for Baird, the symbolic battleground of the contested issue of jurisdiction over unemployment and relief. Baird hoped that her novel's 'protest' would create political change in Ottawa, as she noted in a letter to publisher Hugh Eayrs in 1939: 'There seems to be no doubt that this subject will be the ace election issue. I hope that this may redound to the benefit of all of us.'[22] The novel also makes its argument with regard to federal responsibility clear. The reader, for example, is meant to credit the one newspaper account of the sit-down that the strikers deem accurate and which calls the issue of unemployment 'a national responsibility demanding action by national authority and on a nation-wide scale' (66–7).[23]

In a description of *Waste Heritage* that Baird wrote for Macmillan's sales catalogue, she called the novel a 'protest against the stupidity, irony and menace of a policy that allows the country's richest asset to drift from coast to coast, homeless, unskilled, undisciplined and unwanted, its one hope of steady employment the next great European war.'[24] As this statement indicates, Baird also clearly objected to war as a substitution for structural change within the state, as did many of her contemporaries. Both 'To a Generation Unemployed' – the *Canadian Forum*'s 1936 parody of 'In Flander's Fields' – and Gabrielle Roy's novel *Bonheur d'occasion* (1945) represent analogous concerns. Roy's historical vantage point allowed her to dissect a problem that was rendered largely invisible during the crisis of joblessness of the 1930s, when male unemployment wielded particular discursive power. Set in wartime Montreal, *Bonheur d'occasion* critiques the phenomenon of the transient-cum-soldier and his newly respectable mobility. Even the young and self-engrossed protagonist, Florentine, is disturbed by the sight of formerly unemployed men 'qui marchaient déjà au pas militaire dans leurs vêtements flottants de gueux,' and experiences a vague but troubling impression that it is ultimately dire poverty that has created these new recruits (21). If 'le bruit des souliers cloutés' belonging to the unemployed-cum-soldiers echoes through *Bonheur d'occasion*, this inexorable march of war contrasts with the steps of the women of working-class Montreal who 'marchaient lentement,' and who, war or no war, must find new lodgings for their impoverished families each spring (395, 98). Francophone, working-class women, Roy tells us, will not pay the price of their lives for a new mobility, but neither will they actively participate in a public compact with the state that will alter their class identities. Baird's novel similarly critiques the apparently seamless transformation of unemployed transient to soldier but, written in the context of an ongoing crisis of joblessness that was frequently represented as a crisis of masculinity, focuses the force of its argument on the plight of workless men.

While *Waste Heritage* empathizes with the strikers' claims for work and wages and protests war as a solution to joblessness, it simultaneously assures its readers that the strikers cannot seriously challenge the prevailing social order. To gain public sympathy for the plight of the unemployed, Baird clearly felt that she needed her readers on her side but was also evidently aware that this posed a considerable challenge. Despite the rise of the New Left in the 1960s and a political climate that was newly receptive to leftist sympathies, Baird emphatically distinguishes herself from communism and radical politics and defends the novel's perspective in a 1976 article in which she reflects on the process of writing *Waste Heritage*:

> There will be questions, I suppose, about my politics then, especially as the years draw away from the events my novel is written about. To begin, I have never been connected with Communism and I have never thought of myself as a radical if being a radical means wanting to overthrow the system we live in in favour of another political system. I think a reader of the novel will find, however, that I don't praise or condemn some of the most important people in the novel who are obviously connected with radical politics ... The times were too bad to say 'I won't talk about that because I don't like the label you put on it.' ('Sidown, Brothers' 82)[25]

The 'you' in the final sentence is clearly not the unemployed themselves but rather those who would be offended by or suspicious of radicalism. Baird identifies strongly with this sceptical reader; she deliberately places herself among the politically moderate and emphasizes her position above the fray. This is perhaps unsurprising, given that Baird lived through a postwar political climate that was less than friendly to the CPC, a key player in the Vancouver Sit-Down Strike.[26] The corollary of this in the novel is Baird's deliberate refusal to name the CPC. The unemployed strikers of the Vancouver Sit-Down posed a particular threat to the provincial and federal governments because they were organized in the CPC-led Relief Project Workers' Union, an 'organization' that Baird does not directly name in her novel, although contemporary readers would likely have recognized the strike leaders as communists.[27]

Yet analysing Baird's position vis-à-vis the cause of the unemployed strikers is a vexed pursuit, as the novel's contested position within critical discourse reveals. Such analysis inevitably courts the reductionism of Stalinist demands for the writer's commitment to reflecting 'reality' – that is, the Marxist view that class struggle is the essential dynamic of society. Doyle's otherwise admirable study of the relations between political radicalisms and literary cultures in Canada often adopts versions of this Old Left theoretical stance, reducing, for example, Baird's *Waste Heritage* to a reflection of her (arguably moderate) political allegiances. Examining the play of material and ideological forces reveals that Baird's novel is deeply conflicted and fundamentally ambivalent about its own act of social critique. Consideration of what Williams calls the 'whole social material process' (*Marxism* 138) involved in the production of *Waste Heritage* demonstrates that the constraints within which Baird wrote – namely, her subject position as an Anglo, middle-class woman with little symbolic capital and the cultural politics of North America on the cusp of a world war – are key factors in the novel's political ambivalence. While close reading of *Waste Heritage* offers some evidence of this ambivalence, it is only an investigation of the material conditions of the book's production that reveals how its tensions are embedded in the larger field of cultural production.

Since no major plot changes were made to the manuscript that Baird initially submitted to Macmillan of Canada in early 1939, it is fair to assume that the novel's uneasiness, which is evident upon close reading, emerged prior to her dealings with her publishers. For example, as a means of anticipating criticisms of the strikers' political affiliations, the narrative not only refuses to name a political organization, it also disarticulates the common connection between so-called foreigners and leftist political activity. To this end, the novel strives to rearrange the terms of one of the central dichotomies of the 1930s – citizen vs transient. Matt Striker, who was born and grew up in Saskatchewan but who has crisscrossed the country in search of work for six long years, regrets that the 'authorities' of every province have warned him and other transients to 'get the hell out before we citizens has to call out the police to protect ourselves' (6). Citizenship, space, and power are articulated together, and Matt's response is to claim that he has 'bummed around so long even the country don't own me no more' (5).Significantly, however, the novel's advocacy of the transient's right to settlement and citizenship is articulated through the creation of another binary – the transients become the deserving if neglected native sons of Canada and are opposed to those who are labelled as foreign.[28] In other words, the notion of citizenship in the novel is articulated through an appeal to one's status as 'native' to a particular nation-state. As the previous chapter argues, there was much fear of so-called foreign agitation in the 1930s in Canada, particularly with regard to organizations that were or were perceived to be communist. *Waste Heritage* acknowledges this fear through its employment of a version of what Denning calls the 'proletarian sublime' – 'the aesthetic of awe and fear provoked by the emergence of a class of despised laborers, a social Other.' According to Denning, in the interwar period in the United States, this 'Other' was frequently racialized and opposed to the figure of the 'clean American' (194). Not all labourers in *Waste Heritage*, however, belong to this class of 'despised other.' The so-called foreigners in *Waste Heritage* – the 'Chinks,' the 'kike' junk dealer, the Greek café owner, the 'shrivelled old Chinaman' who 'looked like death' – constitute the panoply of workers who are, in Denning's terms, the novel's 'Other.' These figures are not labourers but rather small-business owners, and their avaricious, self-interested financial success stands as a counterpoint to the plight of the unemployed. Rather than a 'proletarian sublime,' therefore, one might read Baird's aesthetic as a 'petit-bourgeois sublime' in which awe and fear are provoked by the upwardly mobile, racialized 'Other.' While these foreign figures are distinctly racialized, most of the strikers are given no specific racial markings, save perhaps a Jewish tin-canner, Saul, a 'Slavic' looking man who abandons the cause in favour of a job, and Sklar, the 'Red' agitator whose attempts to rally the dispirited strikers at the end of the novel seem pathetic. The enforced mobility of the native sons contrasts with the settled security of the novel's foreigners, a security that is gained, the novel argues, through self-interested and therefore invalid means. When Matt and Eddy find themselves in an altercation with a prostitute, for example, they are observed by a 'shrivelled old Chinaman' who owns the local Chinese laundry:

> He looked like death watching. Then as the woman fell he made a high gabbling sound and a second Chink came out from behind and they stood together in the doorway watching ... From the other side of the street the two Chinks watched them disappear. They did not go across to pick the woman up. They went back inside the laundry, locked the door and turned off the light. (115)

In this scene, Matt and Eddy are represented as victims of the prostitute's wiles and, more generally, of the indifference of those who have a measure of social and economic security. That this indifference is consistently aligned with the novel's racial 'Others' demonstrates its use of a version of the 'proletarian sublime.' By turning to this aesthetic, the novel demonizes the racial 'Other' and vitiates the fears of those who would presume to find foreigners leading the agitation and who would thus withhold sympathy for the cause.

Waste Heritage also exhibits a pattern of entrapment that signals anxiety about the conflict engendered by the strike and, more specifically, about the mobile threat of the strikers. While a few of the more radical periodical contributions from the 1930s, such as Simon Marcson's 'Dream Train,' Maurice Granite's 'This Is the Road,' and Dorothy Livesay's 'A Girl Sees It!' open out onto a world transformed by the mobile politics of revolution, patterns of entrapment and claustrophobia were common in interwar social-realist short fiction (Doyle 98). Similarly, in novels such as Callaghan's They Shall Inherit the Earth, joblessness and immobility are explicitly coupled together as the narrator describes the downfall of Anna Prychoda, for whom the space of the city becomes 'smaller' and more alienating as she moves from work as fashion designer to part-time work as a salesgirl and, finally, to unemployment (106). Waste Heritage offers a stark choice between precisely this kind of immobility and settled, bourgeois existence. The novel is divided into four parts: 'Aschelon,' 'Transit,' 'Gath,' and 'Transit.' The allegorical city names of the first and third parts are meant to represent Vancouver and Victoria, respectively. The Old Testament names imply that the transients, who are aligned with the Israelites, have the right to settle in the cities conquered by the Philistines.[29] Yet the enforced mobility that the transients experience denies them the right of settlement. Paradoxically, the novel expresses this enforced mobility in terms of immobility, a condition of entrapment that lacks the security and agency of settlement. Although the intervening parts, both called 'Transit,' suggest spatial mobility, the novel demonstrates no concomitant narrative mobility, a fact that ironically undermines the implication of movement in the titles. The strikers physically move from town to town on their way from Aschelon to Gath, but, as one of the strike leaders comments dryly, their story would not make a good novel because 'you got nothing to make a book out of ... no plot, nothing' (247). Indeed, Matt Striker's response to the settlement that ends the strike emphasizes this lack of plot: 'All we freight car cowboys know for sure is that we are right back where we started. About the only way we know we are alive is that we are liable to get locked up for trying to prove it' (259).

Many early reviews of Baird's novel compared it to John Steinbeck's social protest novel *Of Mice and Men* (1937) because the relationship between Matt Striker and his helpless companion, Eddy, is so similar to George and Lennie's; however, while George's murder of Lennie is meant to convey his love for his companion, Matt is not able to maintain his role as protector of Eddy.[30] At the conclusion of Baird's novel, both men are equally victimized and immobilized by forces they can neither comprehend nor command. *Waste Heritage* might therefore be considered an example of what Irr calls the 'bottom dogs' novel, which partakes of a kind of 'slumming' because it makes the proletarian novel available to 'refugees from the middle class' by displacing the strong worker symbol with 'various forms of weak and mobile subjects' (110). If the transient's mobility threatens settled bourgeois life under capitalism, this threat is mitigated by Baird's representation of mobility as entrapment. These 'weak and mobile' figures allow the reader to enter the story and, perhaps, to sympathize with its narrative, but the potential threat of an army of jobless, hungry, angry men is utterly diffused as the novel develops.

The fates of Matt and Eddy are echoed in the narrative's circularity: the novel opens and closes with the image of a train, a symbol of capitalism's harnessing of mobility, inexorably charging across the nation. As Doyle observes, the cyclical form of the novel is especially apparent in the parallel structure of the scenes that open and close the narrative, both of which are set in the railway yards (121). The ineluctable movement of the train that is represented in the final lines of the novel serves as a counterpoint to Eddy's limp form: his 'doll-like arms' are 'jerked flat like semaphore blades' (275). Significantly, Eddy's frustrated attempts to purchase new shoes indirectly cause his death and Matt's arrest. These shoes would aid him, as Zhongming Chen observes, 'in his trek and perhaps, in his later hunt for a job' (232). Solid walking shoes therefore function as a symbol of motility; however, the symbolic possession of such agency consistently eludes both Eddy and Matt.

Trains in *Waste Heritage* certainly do symbolize, as Doyle argues, 'violent, meaningless death,' but they are also symbols of the capitalist logic that Simon Marcson's short story 'Dream Train' gestures to. Their constant forward mobility becomes modernity's narrative of economic progress from which the transient unemployed are excluded. W.H. Cole compares the symbology of the train in *Waste Heritage* to earlier social-realist novels in which the train is 'a menace' and a 'symbol of evil' (127). I would add that the train serves to emphasize the utter stillness of the lives of the strikers, who spend most of the novel waiting for something to happen. Hep, one of the strike leaders, observes the 'horse-power' that can be generated by a sit-down, but Matt is incredulous: "What d'you mean "horse-power"?' he asked. 'Where's the horse-power in a bunch of guys squattin' on their tails?' (201). In contrast to this immobility, the ubiquitous presence of the train reminds the reader that industry continues apace despite the apparent economic crisis. When the strikers arrive in Gath, for example, they continue to spend their days in idleness: 'A line of boys sat on the sidewalk outside the Quanta House on the fifth day of the occupation. They had been sitting there most of the afternoon, knees up, arms hanging, cigarettes drooping from their mouths, idly eyeing the passers-by. The heat made them listless' (168). The soporific diction of this description is contrasted with the energy emanating from the nearby railroad yards: 'The sound of shunting came from the railroad yards, the heavy dong-dong of the engine bell, the jar of couplings, the blasting of steam' (168). The participles 'hanging' and 'drooping' wilt against the decisive gerunds 'shunting' and 'blasting,' which bring the force of noun and verb together. The description of the transients is silent and lacking in action, save the 'eyeing,' but even this is done only 'idly.' By contrast, the machines burst with a plosive verbal and physical energy that has, it is implied, replaced the male body's energy.

Because *Waste Heritage* tames the prospect of social chaos through these patterns of immobility, it also seems to distance itself from radical art. Reportage, for example, is often theorized as a leftist literary technique, but Baird's use of it arguably manifests her anxieties about being understood as a subversive or 'red' writer. Lukács first defined reportage as a leftist literary technique that mimics journalistic objectivism to create detailed, realist accounts of contemporary social situations in both fictional and non-fictional forms ('Reportage' 45–75). Working with a much broader definition of reportage that does not insist upon its usage as a leftist technique, Hill views Baird's method as 'direct reportage' – a detached narrative style that attempts 'complete omniscience' and 'utter objectivity' ('Critical Introduction' xxxv); yet Baird's method seems more aligned with what Hill has called 'mediated reportage' – the use of an objective narrator who reports from or through a 'sustained subjective perspective' that is often metafictional in character ('The Modern' 263).

Some aspects of Baird's use of reportage clearly serve to distinguish *Waste Heritage* from its more radical literary counterparts and to establish the author's claims to objectivity. Employing mediated reportage, the novel's third-person narrator reflects on Baird's role as writer through the figure of Kenny Hughes, an unemployed teacher whose involvement in the strike inspires him to write a novel about the transient culture he has entered.[31] Though Hughes often mirrors Baird's role as author, the objectivity of his writing project is ultimately undermined in relation to *Waste Heritage*, which is consequently distinguished from 'red' propaganda or radical reportage. The novel that Hughes claims to be writing, *Bloody Sore*, is a parody of the styles that were favoured in radical periodicals like *Masses*. Accordingly, a striker wonders if a book with a deliberately provocative title like *Bloody Sore* 'ain't quite nice to have around the house' (171). By contrast, Baird's restrained but powerful title, *Waste Heritage*, speaks for the quality and tone of her novel. The publishing history of the novel begins to assert its importance with relation to the title. According to a 16 July 1973 article in *The C.C. Free Press* in which Baird reminisced on the writing of *Waste Heritage*, Macmillan rejected Baird's own somewhat sensational title – *Sidown, Brother, Sidown!* – as too 'strong' (6). Archival records show that Baird also offered the title *Wrath to Come*, but did not object when Bennett Cerf, the president of Random House in New York, declared that the title must be *Waste Heritage* (which Baird and Hugh Eayrs had initially suggested as a possibility).[32] This final title is a reflection of the publishers' desire for austerity and moderation, and Baird's acquiescence indicates her willingness to trust their conception of her audience.

Yet Kenny Hughes is not simply a foil for the novel's moderate politics; the way in which Hughes's character assumes and absorbs Baird's undercover role – the way that she cross-dresses *through* him – is significant in terms of the novel's political ambivalence. *Waste Heritage* may mock Hughes's 'propagandistic' tendencies, but his presence also reveals Baird's desire to narrow the social distance between her and the strikers and to establish solidarity with them. That Baird was often thwarted in this pursuit is made clear by the fact that she can only achieve the desired proximity to the strikers through a surrogate character. As a man, Hughes is sometimes successful at narrowing the class divide between himself and the other strikers, but Baird did not achieve this success so readily.

Recourse to Baird's unpublished letters and published articles demonstrates the difficult position she was negotiating. Her uneasy position as an outsider – a middle-class woman – is carefully documented in her comments on the research she undertook to write the novel. After *Waste*

Heritage was published, Baird claimed (with some false modesty, perhaps) that writing it was 'not a woman's job, I knew nothing about that side of life.'[33] In the second part of her retrospective article on *Waste Heritage* in *The C.C. Free Press* (23 July 1973), Baird described the research methods that she used to gain intimate access to the world of the strike. Like many contemporary women journalists, Baird transgressed gender norms during her undercover work for the novel. She convinced her family doctor, who was also Victoria's City Medical Officer, to let her accompany him on his inspections of the buildings where the striking men were housed, and she reports that he was 'scandalised' at her strategy for observing the strike first-hand (6). One would assume that many middle-class readers would have shared his opinion about the proper place for a wife and mother. Her 1976 reflection on her undercover work for the novel articulated similar issues: '(Needless to say none of my friends and family had any idea what I was up to.) My family practically gave me up; I think they feared I should be picked up with the jobless and tossed into jail' ('Sidown, Brothers' 84). This contradictory statement – her family did not know what she was doing yet they practically gave her up – suggests Baird's persistent lack of comfort with the relation between her divergent roles. That she should be equated with and indeed mistaken for one of the transients is a source of humour, but it also reveals that Baird and those in her social class thought it ludicrous that she could be so misapprehended, which further emphasizes her difference from the strikers.

Baird and her New York agent, Marion Saunders, were obviously anticipating criticism of Baird's 'unfeminine' audacity. Saunders clearly felt the need to deflect potential negative responses when she was attempting to secure a contract with Random House in 1939. In her sales pitch, she defensively argued that Baird did not need to adopt a male pseudonym for *Waste Heritage* because her cross-dressing style of writing might prove titillating for readers: 'With the exception of a few pages *Waste Heritage* has all the earmarks of masculine writing. It is a marvel to find a sensitive woman writer able to produce a strong meaty story of this type.'[34] Echoing Saunders's statement, columnist Bruce Hutchison's laudatory review of *Waste Heritage* in the *Victoria Daily Times* (30 December 1939) playfully questions how 'such a charming little lady' learned 'so many bad words.' Hutchison's review indicates that, while Saunders was right about the titillation of gender transgression, Baird was nonetheless risking great censure.[35]

The role of Kenny Hughes can therefore be thought of as a manifestation and deflection of Baird's understandable anxiety about her project:

Hughes, like Baird, may be crossing class lines, but this is diffused by the fact that he shares a gender with the strikers and can witness and evaluate the actions of the cursing, poorly educated, and physically unkempt men around him without impropriety. While the character of Hughes enables Baird to get much closer to the objects of representation – the strikers – the novel paradoxically thematizes the difficulty of this endeavour, as if reflecting on the challenges Baird faced. Hughes is described as working from a vantage point that will make him an 'insider,' but this perspective is only achieved with great physical discomfort and sacrifice:

> When the truck finally started the restaurant man fell up against Hughes with a jerk and Hughes' notes were shot onto the floor. He got quite dizzy scrambling for them and getting his head pushed around by the bumping of the truck. There were a lot of little things like that kept happening all the time, like Gabby showing his cards to Saul and then trying to collect a nickel. Things no outsider could know about or get interested in because they were not important from an outside point of view. (122)

The narrator's attention to the privations Hughes experiences authenticates his undertaking, and, by extension, Baird's.

Most importantly, Hughes functions in a role that Baird cannot assume – that of the mobile road figure. Baird could follow the strikers to Victoria, and indeed she did, but she could not become one of the mobile men whom she observes. The dichotomy of the static female and the mobile male has a narrative parallel in the relationship between Matt, who follows the strikers to Gath (Victoria), and his girlfriend Hazel, who must stay in Aschelon (Vancouver), where she lives with her aunt and works in the basement meat counter of Lincoln's department store. Hazel's brief sojourn to Gath in Part III perhaps parallels Baird's own visit to Victoria during the sit-down insofar as both experiences are temporary: both women must return to Vancouver, although for different reasons. Yet if the novel's discourse and the material processes of its writing divide mobility and immobility along a male/female binary, this division is far from neat. As the work of feminist cultural theorist Janet Wolff argues, the ways in which people move – as women, as men, as tourists, as immigrants, as racialized migrant workers – differ considerably; moreover, such differences can affect a single individual differently at different moments. For example, Baird's articles and letters about the writing of *Waste Heritage* indicate that, despite the constraints she experienced, she was a tourist insofar as she could sightsee among the strikers and then return home. Nevertheless, crossing over – the act of becoming one of the male strikers – was not available to Baird, and Hughes functions as her proxy in this regard.

Analysing Baird's negotiations with her Canadian and American publishers augments my contention that her experience of authorship was politically ambivalent. Archival evidence points to the ways in which Baird's publishers were both attracted to and wary of the novel's controversial subject – a subject that was treated almost exclusively by leftist periodicals (rather than novels by mainstream publishers) during the Depression in Canada. In a letter to Random House in New York, Macmillan of Canada's president Hugh Eayrs noted the fact that Lippincott, the house that published Baird's first novel, the pastoral romance *John* (1937), in both Canada and the United States, felt that *Waste Heritage* was 'far too strong, in its language' and, therefore, 'doesn't want to take up the Canadian end.' Eayrs offered a terse and somewhat inscrutable reason for going ahead with the 'Canadian end': 'Personally, I do.'[36] However, records indicate that Macmillan of Canada were initially cautious about the novel because editors were concerned about the possibility of anti-state sedition. In his first reader's report, Carl Eayrs – former labour editor for the *Toronto Evening Telegram* and brother of Hugh Eayrs – stated somewhat warily that Baird's manuscript was powerful enough to impact the impending federal election:

> What I'm getting at is that if this is published before the election it can become a powerful weapon in the hands of Manion and the Conservative party. I'm not exaggerating when I say that. Even if the novel only reflected on the B.C. Government, whi[c]h is Liberal, it would help the Tories, but it is also a reflection of the Federal Government. Whether you or I think they could have done anything is beside the point. That novel is dynamite, becauee [*sic*] it's so powerful and because it portrays conditions so truthfully. A good many people are going to ask, after reading it, why King allows a condition to exist where the unemployed and the youth of the country appear to have no future.[37]

Carl Eayrs avoided calling Baird's novel seditious, but his tone is clearly cautionary.

Hugh Eayrs must have heeded his brother's warning because the 1939 contract that he offered to Baird included a libel clause that the agent found unusual. Baird's agent Marion Saunders expressed concern and stated the necessity of protecting the author, whom she represented as entirely willing to accept editorial changes: 'I also hope that you will watch over any statement or reference to an existing condition in this novel of Canadian sit-down strikes, as the author is quite inexperienced in such matters and has no money for libel suits.'[38] Significantly, Kenny Hughes also frets about the potentially controversial character of the narrative he is creating: '"This is going to be a hard book to write, far harder than I figgered on," he said. "Quite apart from the actual writing and the entire absence of plot, there are a lot of technical difficulties. One is keeping clear of anything that might border on libel"' (206). Baird's willingness to accept changes indicates a desire to distinguish *Waste Heritage* from radical works of art, such as *Eight Men Speak*, that were censored during the 1930s, but it also shows how fearful she might have been of jeopardizing her emerging and fragile literary career.[39] In response to Saunders's letter, Eayrs agreed to have the novel combed 'for any possibility of libel.'[40] Carl Eayrs's second report was much less concerned about the potential political impact of the novel and was reassuring in tone. He concluded that although the novel was 'critical of the Government,' it was not aimed 'at undermining constitutional authority' and was, in fact, 'anti-Red.'[41] It could, therefore, be published without significant changes.

The novel's 'redness' was also a concern for Random House in New York, a publishing house that was both leery of a 'warmed-over Steinbeck' and convinced that strike novels did not sell well in the United States, 'especially when they are about sit-down strikes – a labor device that is now illegal in the United States.'[42] Indeed, prior to finalizing the agreement to publish *Waste Heritage*, Bennett Cerf, the president of Random House in New York, asked Baird to make a case for the originality of her character Eddy, who, as I have discussed, bears a strong resemblance to Steinbeck's Lennie.[43] Moreover, as mentioned above, Cerf firmly rejected Baird's suggested title for her novel, *Wrath to Come*; the implication is that the title was too evocative of Steinbeck's controversial *The Grapes of Wrath*, which was published in 1939 and consequently censored in cities and counties across the United States.[44] As a result of their misgivings, Random House chose to buy the printed sheets for *Waste Heritage* from Macmillan rather than producing their own edition, and indicated that the novel would not likely sell more than one thousand copies in the United States.[45] Baird nevertheless defended her novel to Cerf: 'cash or no cash I could not have resisted taking a crack at the subject as the stuff was going on all round me and I got close enough to feel it deeply.'[46]

In her correspondence with Cerf, Baird clearly distinguished her novel from works like Steinbeck's *In Dubious Battle* (1936) and *The Grapes of Wrath*. Indeed, she adamantly rejected the idea that hers was a 'strike novel': 'The strike is incidental, it is the men themselves and the irony of their status that is the substance of the story.'[47] The author repeated her defence in her description of *Waste Heritage* for the Macmillan sales catalogue, claiming that 'although the book deals with the sit-down it is not primarily a strike novel.'[48] Moreover, Baird's proposals for future novels, which she sent to Cerf throughout 1939, indicate that she took his advice about marketability to heart. Baird sent these proposals to Cerf so that he could vet her application for a Guggenheim Fellowship, which she asked him to support. Although her first proposal to Cerf was for a 'novel of heavy industry using Pittsburgh as a base,' she dismissed this idea herself and instead suggested a novel set in California that would attract war-weary readers 'by providing a brief pause for minds tense and tired by news of perpetual crisis, reminding them incidentally that there still remains one country where life can be lived in freedom, security and peace.[49] Cerf responded that this was fine, but cautioned that the 'labor angle' had been covered by Steinbeck's California novels.[50] Later, he told her that she should put some of her characteristic humour in her next novel: 'The world definitely does not want to be improved; it wants to be amused. Let's give the boys and girls what they want!'[51] Cerf is clearly urging Baird to write a less politically incendiary and more easily marketable novel, but his comments also reflect the fact that the Depression-era social protest that had garnered *The Grapes of Wrath* so much public attention in North America was, by late 1939, largely overshadowed by the war in Europe. It is therefore somewhat surprising that the description on the dust jacket of the Random House copies invited readers to compare Baird to Steinbeck.[52] Despite his obvious reservations about political 'redness,' Cerf was certainly aware of and willing to capitalize on Steinbeck's popularity, but rightly predicted that Steinbeck's style of social protest would be less marketable in a wartime climate.

The onset of war created other palpable effects for *Waste Heritage*. Baird's commitment to her novel was further tested in late 1939, when, in the early days of Canada's involvement in the Second World War, *Waste Heritage* was subjected to the state censorship of the Defence of Canada Regulations. After the pages for Random House had been printed but before the novel was released in the United States or Canada, Hugh Eayrs wrote a panicked letter to Baird, in which he informed her that he would have to excise sections of the novel that were likely to be interpreted as seditious in light of the Defence of Canada Regulations, which were made public in September of 1939.[53] He suggested three (fairly minor) changes, all of which appear in the Canadian text and which remove any reference to the hypocrisy of the government's recruitment efforts.[54] For example, on pages six and seven of the original text that was published in the United States, Matt Striker's friend Harry comments that it 'seems like the country's waitin' for Hitler to give you boys a job so you can all be heroes overnight.' Matt replies: 'Sure, an, get blown to hell an' damnation in the morning! That's one job I don't take. If we was a bunch of beef cattle at least we'd get gov'ment grading.' In the altered Canadian text, Harry avoids referring to Hitler as a potential employer: 'Seems like the country's waitin' to get a real scrap on its hands so all you guys can be heroes overnight.' Matt's response is much less militant: 'Yeah? An' where do we wake up the next mornin'? I asked guys that an' they just look at me. Maybe I didn't ask the right guys.' Baird's social critique is, therefore, significantly softened in the Canadian text.

Although the archival evidence shows that Baird was willing to make changes, she did not, in any case, have much choice. As Hugh Eayrs wrote to Bennett Cerf at Random House, changes had to occur in the Canadian text due to 'a private tip from the highest possible circles that it was either that or the book wouldn't come out.'[55] Yet Baird's communication with Bennett Cerf about the issue of state censorship reveals that she was not bothered by the intervention; indeed, she saw a potential marketing opportunity:

> Random House will be bringing out the 'unexpurgated' version. 'Unexpurgated' is a such a grand sales word. Want to make something out of it? The 'reactionaries' have reacted and my apologies to your blurb man. To my knowledge this is the first time in war or peace that a Canadian book has been censored. That makes history two ways; it is the first labor novel to come out on this side of the line and the first to get in the official hair. So what does that make us? ... As a loyal British subject I would not want to do anything to dis-help [sic] Canada win the war, but as a hard-working writer dependent on royalties I hope we raise a beautiful stink.[56]

Baird's capitulation to editorial decisions and publishers' concerns sheds light on the novel's careful negotiation of sympathy with and control of the strikers. Yet this correspondence also reveals that she was not a passive observer of the novel's fate or its meaning for political culture.

Indeed, she was an avid correspondent of Cerf's, and she used her letters to interpret *Waste Heritage* for the publisher, despite the fact that many of her suggestions for the novel were ignored or solicitously declined by Cerf.[57]

The publishing history of *Waste Heritage* offers a particularly revealing example of how the dialectic of protest and restraint that marked many Depression-era texts is embedded in the contested field of cultural production in 1930s Canada. In this way, Baird's novel anticipates the ways in which social protest and the novel form, which was itself undergoing a new kind of commodification in this period, are articulated together in the postwar years. Baird did not become a celebrated novelist, despite her success with her first novel, *John*, largely because she took a full-time job after she published *Waste Heritage*. In 1942, John Grierson hired her to work at the NFB, from whence she was eventually posted to the job of chief information officer with the Department of Indian Affairs and Northern Development until she retired in the late 1960s ('Novel of Depression' 6). Baird's work on the novels *John* and *Waste Heritage* helped her to secure the position she obtained with the NFB ('Novel of Depression' 6), and it is revealing that the novel that followed *Waste Heritage*, *He Rides the Sky* (1941), documents not unemployment but the mass *employment* provided to men and women by the state's involvement in the Second World War. Baird's cultural work, like that of so many of her contemporaries, thus becomes part of the history of Canada's 'passive revolution.'

Chapter Four

The Postwar Compact and the National Bildungsroman

This chapter forms a bridge between the 1930s and what might be called the Centennial period – the nationalist years around Canada's Centennial celebrations in 1967. The Centennial period coincided with what McKay has designated the fourth formation of Canadian socialism (1965–80), a New Left movement fuelled by its opposition to an Old Left, an 'obsolete communism,' and a bureaucratic socialism, and united by a 'new politics of resistance founded on authentic emancipation and human freedom, a "socialism" of self-management, anti-imperialism, and direct democracy' (*Rebels* 183). Using the complex textual history of Hugh Garner's largely unexamined novel *Cabbagetown* (1950; 1968) as a guide across this temporal bridge, this chapter explores how the political and cultural work of protesting unemployment in the Depression era is formally and ideologically transformed as it crosses this bridge. Published in two distinct editions in 1950 and 1968, *Cabbagetown* straddles the modern and contemporary periods. The initial part of this chapter considers how Garner's literary labour, as well as the form and content of his Depression-era dissent, were embedded in the postwar compact between state and labour. The latter half of the chapter analyses how the rise of the New Left and the growing identification between the realist novel and a national literary canon, the national Bildungsroman and narratives of Depression-era unemployment, and state-sponsored culture and conceptions of literary labour have shaped the material and symbolic production of the 1968 edition of *Cabbagetown*. If the alterations within the field of cultural production effected by state-sponsored culture are to some extent responsible for breathing new life into Depression-era narratives of dissent in the late 1960s and early 1970s, these transformed narratives are better understood as products of the contemporary, rather than the interwar, period.

Cabbagetown, Hugh Garner's well-known, semi-autobiographical Bildungsroman about Depression-era Canada, has become almost synonymous with the 1930s in Canadian literary history. Although the edition of *Cabbagetown* that Ryerson Press published in 1968 has formed the basis for all critical assessments of the novel and, indeed, is largely responsible for Garner's reputation as a realist writer, the novel has a complicated textual history that is belied by the physical appearance of its current reprint. Echoing the critical consensus that has condensed around *Cabbagetown*, the cover art of this reprint urges the consumer to read the narrative as a realist documentary that was produced in the era that it records: black-and-white photographs of Depression-era Cabbagetown from the City of Toronto archives adorn the cover and serve to divide its three sections. Reinforcing the seamless crossover from reality to representation, the cover's shoutline proclaims the book's status as the 'classic novel of the Depression in Canada.' Reading the 1968 edition of Garner's *Cabbagetown* as realist, as most critics have done, belies not only its tendency to sentimentality and melodrama, but also its complex textual history. A critical preoccupation with distinguishing Garner's work as a literary realist from the hack journalism for popular magazines and the popular fiction he wrote in order to remain financially solvent has obscured the way in which the uneven aesthetics and politics of his oeuvre are embedded in the particularly precarious cultures of authorship and publishing that existed in Canada prior to the advent of state-sponsored culture.

Documenting the Depression in the *Canadian Forum*

Garner's career-long preoccupation with representing Cabbagetown, the Toronto slum he grew up in, dates to the mid-1930s, when he published· his first documentary pieces, 'Toronto's Cabbagetown' (June 1936) and 'Christmas Eve in Cabbagetown' (January 1938), in the social-democratic periodical the *Canadian Forum*. After spending the first part of the 1930s as an unemployed transient on the roads and rails of North America, Garner returned to Toronto for a brief period and joined the CCF, which likely made him a known entity to the LSR crowd at the *Forum* (Garner, *One Damn* 29–30; Stuewe, *The Storms* 45). Like much of the fiction and poetry that appeared in the *Forum* in these years, Garner's pieces encourage social change by attempting to enlist the reader's sympathy; the observed poor possess no threatening mobility. The first of these pieces was Garner's first publication in any genre, and its concatenation of journalistic and literary conventions offers early evidence of his attempts to mimic the convention of the objective eyewitness that he found in the documentary fiction of U.S.-American magazines like *Story*, which he read avidly (according to his own account in the 9 May 1953 issue of *Saturday Night*) during a Depression-era sojourn in New York as one of the continent's innumerable unemployed (10). Yet even these early attempts at documentary indicate Garner's difficulty with the convention of dispassionate narration.

Using the technique of omniscience, the narrator of these Cabbagetown pieces palpably strains against the impulse to narrative intervention. In 'Toronto's Cabbagetown,' the narrator's roving eye objectively witnesses the social geography of Cabbagetown, describing in austere prose the appearance of the neighbourhood and the seasonal rituals of its inhabitants: 'In the summer most of the young people go swimming in Lake Ontario at the foot of Cherry Street, or for walks in Riverdale Park, north of Cabbagetown. The small boys roam the streets in gangs and play Cowboys and Indians down on the railroad tracks' (13). Like the forms of sociological analysis that emerged in the first part of the twentieth century, Garner's documentary often strives for a dispassionate account of an observed subject. Yet the narrator opens with a second-person address that is aimed at the middle-class reader and that undermines accompanying efforts at detachment: 'You strike Cabbagetown as soon as you cross Parliament street on the west, or the Don river on the east. Of course, if you cross the river by the Bloor street viaduct you won't find Cabbagetown' (13). Presumably, the *Forum* reader must be told how to find this neighbourhood, and Garner's insider-narrator acts as a knowing guide. Significantly, this convention also implies the mobility of the narrator and reader in relation to the fixity of the Cabbagetown subject, who is hemmed in by the class barriers that construct Toronto's social geography. However, the trust that is intimated by the narrative outstretched hand is eroded as the narrative develops and Garner's willingness or ability to restrain intervention recedes. The reader becomes subject to the narrator's ironic questions and didactic, often melodramatic, harangue:

> There is love in Cabbagetown … There is the love of children for parents who sit around stoves in the winter and on the steps in the summer, fading away, old before their time. People who a few years ago were the ones who sat next to you on the picnic ship to Port Dalhousie, who rented the cottage next to you at Bala, or crowded you over the record counter at Eaton's or Kresges. (14)

The reader's prejudices must be corrected, and Garner's narrator assumes the task by oscillating between detached description and heavy-handed moralizing. As William Stott's classic study of the documentary in the Depression-era United States contends, such a tension is typical of the leftist documentary in the interwar period and reveals contradictory desires – to see accurately the social crisis that various media had obscured, and to 'sharpen' facts with 'feeling' in order to encourage social reform (72, 18–21). Indeed, the adaptation of Soviet-style reportage in the 1930s often led, in the United States, to 'sentimental' representations of the deserving poor, such as Dorothea Lange's now iconic photographs (Stott 57–9).

'Christmas Eve in Cabbagetown,' published two years after Garner's initial appearance in the *Forum* and shortly after his return from fighting facism in Spain with the International Brigades, is much more successful at restraining the narrator's judgment. This piece also provides evidence that Garner was beginning to develop his literary sense of Cabbagetown, meaning that it draws more fully on the plot and character conventions of the short story. Garner diminishes his third-person narrator in order to document the simultaneous experiences of misery and joy during one Christmas eve in the neighbourhood, but the narrator's presence asserts itself in one conspicuous way – through the trope of dramatic irony. We are told, for example, that 'down near Queen street a family stood around the bed of Betty McGuire five years old who was dying of the flu' (354). The pathos of little Betty's illness is extended through the narrator's knowledge that sickness will lead to death: 'Nobody in the family thought that Betty was dying, they were all trying to cheer her up with stories about what Santa Claus was going to bring her' (354). The unwitting poor of Garner's story thus become sentimentalized victims of a system they can neither comprehend nor change, but which Garner and the *Forum* reader are savvy enough to understand and potentially reform.

Narrating the Depression as Mass-Market Paperback

As is the case for the transient strikers in Baird's *Waste Heritage* and the marching men of *Bonheur d'occasion*, Garner's chronic unemployment was absorbed by the Second World War and his duty in the navy. Upon his return to Toronto in 1945, Garner, like many other veterans of the war, was the beneficiary of numerous programs that were aimed at reintegrating men into the Canadian labour force. For example, Garner profited from a veterans' housing project in the suburb of Etobicoke,

one of the many programs that emanated from the National Housing
Act (1944, replaced in 1950 by the federal Central Mortgage and Housing Corporation). The act, and the subsequent federal body, aimed
to employ state funding to encourage private home ownership (Guest
127–8), and, in the case of the public housing project of Regent Park
that replaced Cabbagetown in 1957, to settle low-income families in de-
cent housing.[1] Funded by a Department of Veterans Affairs course in
Co-operative Management and later by his work for the War Assets Corporation – a demobilization project of the federal government – Garner
began his quixotic attempt to earn enough by writing that he might become what he later called a 'professional writer' (*One Damn* 76). Quixotic is the appropriate adjective here: in the late 1940s, there were few if
any Canadian authors who supported themselves solely by writing fiction
(Davey, 'Economics and the Writer' 103), and Garner had little formal
education and no contacts in the literary world. Indeed, Davey points
out that 'professional authorship' did not appear as a separate category
in Statistics Canada studies of the Canadian labour force until 1978, and
even then, median earnings were less than half of the median income for
the Canadian workforce as a whole ('Economics and the Writer' 104).
Garner's somewhat unreliable testimony bears out these facts: despite
the initial euphoria he experienced in 1949 when he finally sold his first
manuscript (the novel *Storm Below*), the remarkable sales of this novel
earned him only $461 in 1949, much less than he had earned as a ship-
ping clerk or punch-press inspector – two of the many other jobs he held
in the late 1940s (*One Damn* 102–3).[2] Despite the lack of direct state support for authors prior to the 1960s, however, one small building block of
the postwar welfare state – unemployment insurance – was in place when
Garner began his writing career. Indeed, Garner later quipped that the
unemployment insurance he received in the early 1950s was the 'Canada
Council grant in those days' ('An Interview' 23). After 1952, however,
Garner eschewed sporadic work and periods of unemployment for the
'easier' and more 'lucrative' work he found in magazine writing (*One
Damn* 108). Like Garner, many Canadian writers in the period 1940–
60 turned to journalism as a means of earning their primary income:
some, such as Pierre Berton, Morley Callaghan, and Gwethalyn Graham,
benefited from indirect state support as employees of the CBC (Davey,
'Economics and the Writer' 105), and others, such as Garner and Callaghan (when he was not working for the CBC), earned their bread by
writing for private magazines and newspapers. Attention to the material
conditions of authorship in late 1940s Canada is particularly important

for thinking through Garner's particular relation as writer to the post-war compact between state and labour. If, after demobilization, Garner the worker benefited from housing schemes, improved labour market opportunities, and the advent of unemployment insurance, Garner the writer had few resources to draw upon.

As Garner's archival records indicate, the novel manuscript that he wrote in the late 1940s from his Depression-era stories is a Bildungsro-man that features the political radicalization of Ken Tilling, a semi-au-tobiographical protagonist who hails from Cabbagetown and who, like Garner, eventually travels to Spain to join the international forces fight-ing against fascism. This manuscript clearly resuscitates the ideologies of the Popular Front period, and its conclusion, which places Ken in the hopeful light of dawn, draws on a leftist trope that appeared on the covers of many Depression-era periodicals. In 1946, Garner submitted a typewritten manuscript to Peggy Blackstock at Macmillan of Canada that numbered more than six hundred pages.[3] At least twice in early 1947, Ellen Elliott contacted Garner to let him know that the novel was 'too verbose and often repetitive,' which created a realist aesthetic the firm did not find pleasing: 'There is still too much detail in every incident and every character which, while realistic is so in a photographic rather than in an artistically impressionistic way.'[4] Although there is no extant manuscript of *Cabbagetown* from this period, it is clear from Garner's cor-respondence that he took the advice from Macmillan seriously, pruning the novel by almost two hundred pages and presumably attempting to create the 'impressionistic' quality that Macmillan sought. In any case, the firm ultimately rejected the book.

While still in negotiations with Macmillan in the late 1940s, Garner, who was impatient to see his novel in print, submitted it to J.M. Dent. The firm recommended many changes, some of which Garner carried out, but C.J. Eustace at Dent declined the book and subsequently di-rected Garner to Charles Sweeny at William Collins Sons, a British sub-sidiary in Toronto that introduced its line of White Circle paperbacks in the early 1940s in an attempt to capitalize on the emerging mass mar-ket in Canada (Parker, 'Trade and Regional' 172).[5] White Circle Pocket Editions featured reprints and original titles from popular British and American writers, such as Agatha Christie, romance novelist Maysie Greig, and crime fiction writer Peter Cheyney, as well as reprints and new titles from lesser-known Canadian writers who were learning to write romances and mysteries for the popular market. Featuring vivid picto-rial covers and a standard design that identified the genre of each title on the back cover, these paperbacks encouraged spontaneous purchase and light reading. The growing normalization of the paperback in the postwar period is apparent in Irene Baird's attempts in the early 1950s to get *Waste Heritage* reprinted in Harlequin or White Circle paper covers; however, the disconnect between postwar and Depression-era political ideologies – the gap that Earle Birney evokes in the title of his 1955 novel *Down the Long Table*, that Hugh MacLennan probes in *The Watch That Ends the Night* (1959), or that the fallout from the 1945 Gouzenko affair demonstrated – is apparent in Hugh Eayrs's reluctant agreement to look into the possibility of reprinting Baird's novel: 'The interest in books on the subject of depression and labour troubles is not of course nearly as great as it was.'[6] If Lorne Pierce at Ryerson Press published Vera Lysenko's novels of the Depression in the 1950s – *Yellow Boots* (1954) and *Westerly Wild* (1956) – certainly the fact that the former makes almost no reference to the economic crisis of the Depression and that the latter is a romance that employs the dreary Saskatchewan dustbowl only as a contrast for the narrative's passion speaks to the zeitgeist of the postwar era. 'Labour troubles' were no longer politically tasteful in the context of the Cold War; moreover, it must be remembered that the unemployment crisis of the 1930s had retreated and the urgency of unresolved questions about the state's relation to the unemployed had retreated with it. Unemployment spiked in the winter of 1950, but for the next three years, the Korean War stimulated employment and thus removed any government incentive to act on the lingering question of federal responsibility for the millions of Canadian workers who were not eligible for or who had exhausted employment insurance benefits (Struthers, 'Shadows' 10–18). Joblessness and the radicalism engendered by dire economic conditions were simply not timely topics while unemployment rates were well under 3 per cent.

It is crucial to add that in his appraisal of the possibility of reprinting Baird's strike novel, Eayrs acknowledged the question of popular appeal. One implication of his comments is that the mass-market paperback was not a likely home for unpopular political ideologies. It is therefore unsurprising that, despite Garner's enthusiasm for his novel, Charles Sweeny and Robin Ross-Taylor of Collins initially refused to publish *Cabbagetown*, citing its 'complete absence of humour,' its bewildering proliferation of characters, its bombastic dialogue, and, most significantly, its 'weak' ending. Garner's original manuscript took Ken to the Spanish Civil War, and Robin Ross-Taylor at Collins questioned this ending in frank prose: 'Why take Ken to Spain when nothing whatsoever happens there? To be in keeping with the rather "hopeless" character of the boy, surely the ending should have some ironical twist.'[7]

In an undated reply to Ross-Taylor that appears to have been written in the early autumn of 1948, Garner indicated that he had attempted to deal with all of the firm's criticisms; to this end, he had rewritten the 'last third of the book' and had given the ending, as Ross-Taylor had urged, an 'ironical twist' that enabled him to 'cut out all of the political allusion regarding my main character, realizing, as you doubtless did, that the politics of the 1930s no longer deserve sympathy today.'[8] In this letter, Garner claimed to have long believed that the 'chase' scene originally involving two childhood friends of Ken Tilling's who turn to crime as a way out of their poverty is the 'best chapter' in the novel, and argued that putting Ken at the centre of this scene vastly improved the pace and excitement of the narrative:

> Instead of him [Ken] becoming a Communist fellow traveler and going to Spain, he becomes desperate after a winter spent sleeping in a box-car along Toronto's waterfront, and when through a fortuitous meeting with Bob McIsaacs he begs the other to take him along with him and give him an opportunity to take part in one big hold-up [sic]. However before they have a chance to plan this they are surprised while breaking into a grocery store, and McIsaacs shoots a policeman. Their car is wrecked and McIsaacs is blinded in the crash. Ken Tilling, suffering from a broken arm, is pursued by the police and shot while trying to escape.[9]

Garner's peripatetic life of unemployed transience was accommodated within the postwar compact between the state and the veteran; Ken Tilling's mobility would be curtailed within the context of mass culture. This is not to suggest that a 'text's political effects can be read-off from, or calculated solely on the basis of, an analysis of its formal properties' (Bennett, 'Marxism' 253) as popular fiction, but it is clear that the historical coincidence of the mass-market paperback and what I have been calling the postwar compact combined to produce a crime novel whose primary goal was sensation rather than social interrogation.

If conditions in the market economy and within the political field dramatically shifted between the 1930s and the '50s, it nonetheless remains tempting to assert that Garner's lack of both symbolic and economic capital made him unlikely to offer, as Bourdieu puts it, 'resistance' to the 'external demands' of his publishers (41). Yet the question of what the mass-market paperback meant in postwar Canada is complicated.

The appearance of the mass-market paperback in this country in the late 1930s (Parker, 'Trade and Regional' 171) roughly coincided with the postwar formation of a newly defined canon of Canadian literature; these two phenomena are examples of how what Bourdieu calls the sub-fields of large-scale production and restricted production deepened existing striations in the field of cultural production in postwar Canada (39). With the rise of state-sponsored culture beginning in the 1950s, the internal differentiation of the literary field accelerated – one might think of the insistence of the Massey Commission that popularity was no measure of a national literature, for example. Not coincidentally, the 'worker' specific to the field of restricted production – the professional literary author – emerged in a new way in this period. As I have already suggested, professional literary authorship was not a viable career option in Canada prior to the Second World War; this meant that writers such as Ted Allan, Morley Callaghan, Hugh Garner, Charles G.D. Roberts, and Robert J.C. Stead, among others, wrote for hire as a matter of course. Entering this contested literary field with little cultural or symbolic capital in the late 1940s, Garner perhaps had only a vague apprehension of the distinction between 'popular' and 'literary' authorship.

Despite Garner's obvious willingness to accommodate any changes that Collins demanded in the *Cabbagetown* manuscript, it was not until 1950, after Collins had achieved some success with two other novels that Garner had hastily composed, that they finally agreed to put his novel of the Depression in print. On the advice of the firm in 1949, Garner quickly finished a manuscript about a North Atlantic convoy during the Second World War, which Collins published in hardcovers as *Storm Below* later that same year. Refusing to abandon *Cabbagetown*, however, Garner turned his new chase-scene conclusion into a short story called 'The Go-Boys,' which was published in the popular magazine *National Home Monthly* in April 1950.[10] As 'The Go-Boys' hit newsstands, and after the publication of both *Storm Below* and *Present Reckoning* (a potboiler that Garner quickly cooked up over the summer of 1949 for publication as a White Circle paperback), *Cabbagetown* appeared in drug and department stores across Canada as a White Circle paperback.

As a result of the changes that Collins demanded, the tension between observation and didacticism that characterized Garner's *Canadian Forum* stories was pushed in the direction of sensationalism. While the 1950 *Cabbagetown* appeared in the standard White Circle design, its back cover declared its status as 'A Novel,' which distinguished it from the standard generic categories Collins used to identify its paperbacks to potential readers. Yet as the letters cited above indicate, Collins encouraged the author to transform his manuscript into a more recognizable form of genre fiction – the crime novel. As Tony Bennett has shown, popular forms of fiction can be 'profoundly, if anarchically, subversive of the dominant ideological discourses of class, nation, sexism and so on' (250), but the first edition of Garner's *Cabbagetown* mostly confirms the ideologies that prevailed in 1950s Canada. For example, rather than opening out onto the possibility of a transformed world, the paperback edition of *Cabbagetown* closes in on Ken's bullet-ridden body hanging from a fence, 'looking like a one-armed Christ against the darkness' (160). Interestingly, the conclusion of Garner's story 'The Go-Boys' retained some of the wording from his original Spanish Civil War narrative, but the revolutionary discourse seems out of place in the context of the chase scene and disappears from the conclusion of the 1950 edition of *Cabbagetown*. In 'The Go-Boys,' Ken hangs from the fence as the third-person narrator closes the story with what appears to be a comment on the social transformations that must occur in order for young men like Ken to live meaningful lives:

> The dawn can be seen to the east, but really it comes from the west. It comes across the watcher's shoulders and envelops him in its light while he watches for it. It starts as a narrow ribbon of light darkness, then squeezes together before it fans high into the sky. As the watcher looks for its birth, it begins at his feet, and lights him so that he becomes a part of it. The dawn is in the crease of his trousers and the new-appeared eyelets of his shoes. The dawn is in the new shapes around him, and the lightened fields. The dawn is a widened earth – a populated earth. The dawn is not only the beginning of the day, but the ending of the night. (37)

With some very minor emendations, this is the paragraph that concludes the 1968 edition of the novel, which restores the chapters that send a radicalized Ken off to the Spanish Civil War. Garner was clearly reluctant to sacrifice this passage when he altered the ending of the novel for Collins, and 'The Go-Boys' testifies to the conflicting aesthetic and political ideologies that Garner the fledgling writer was negotiating in the immediate postwar period. More generally, 'The Go-Boys' might be read as a transitional text that signals the tensions between the residual leftism of the interwar period and the dominant ideologies of the Cold War and the incorporation of the former by the latter within mainstream journalism.[11]

With regard to the treatment of gender, however, the 1950 paperback accords much more agency and sexual power to the character of Myrla Patson than is apparent in the later 1968 edition, which is based on Garner's original manuscript. In both editions of *Cabbagetown*, Myrla is Ken's childhood sweetheart, and she eventually turns to prostitution as a result of Depression-induced poverty. The cover of the 1950 edition, which bears the subtitle 'The Song of the City,' complements the narrative's fashioning of the reader as voyeur: in dimly lurid colours, one sees the racy interior of a tavern and the titillations it offers – the possibility of sex and the guarantee of a whiskey (see figure 4.1). In a review for the *Globe and Mail* (17 February 1951), William Arthur Deacon worried that this packaging would misinform readers of the 'seriousness and dignity' of the author's intent (10), but what he called the novel's 'sexual incidents' were undoubtedly shaped to titillate. For example, when Myrla is seduced by her employer, Claude Leroy, the reader is invited behind the closed door:

> As she walked along the hall to the stairs she heard the sound of breaking glass, and Claude Leroy's footsteps coming across the floor. Before she reached the bottom step, he caught her and she allowed him to kiss her, pressing herself against him, trembling with an urgency not altogether new. He took her in his arms and carried her up the stairs, his face against her neck. He pushed open the door of her room with his foot, and shut it behind him. After he had undressed her, she lay on top of the bed watching him take his clothes off in the light from the window. A half-drunken smile played around her mouth as she felt his weight beside her on the bed. (61)

The cover of this edition strongly suggests that it was marketed to readers of popular fiction, and Claude Leroy's conquest is clearly shaped for such readers. Yet Myrla's active participation in this sexual encounter – her frank gaze over Claude Leroy as he undresses, for example – also challenges conventional standards of female sexuality. By contrast, the 1968 edition emphasizes neither the illicit thrill of gazing through an erotically closed door nor Myrla's sexual anticipation, but her impression that everything seems 'confused and unreal' and her growing cynicism about love (123–4). In the 1950s, when Garner was earning his bread by writing popular fiction for magazines, including women's magazines such as *Chatelaine*, he relied again and again on the reader-as-voyeur convention and the type of the desiring woman in stories such as 'Desire' (*Liberty*, November 1954), which features a middle-aged female

4.1 Murray Smith's dust jacket for the 1950 edition of Hugh Garner's novel *Cabbagetown*. Library and Archives Canada e010858642. Every effort has been made to secure permission for this reprinting.

protagonist who, against her better judgment, attempts to seduce her much younger, 'brown, muscular' farmhand (55). Given its obvious attractions, it is not surprising that the 1950 *Cabbagetown* was a bestseller: according to Garner's autobiography, it sold more than forty-five thousand copies (*One Damn* 103). To put this figure in context, one can refer to George Parker's observation that McClelland and Stewart achieved 'extraordinary sales' of forty thousand copies with Ralph Connor's 1919 novel *The Sky Pilot in No Man's Land,* a success that Parker claims was not duplicated by a Canadian-authored book published in Canada until the 1960s ('Trade and Regional' 169).

Despite its sensationalism, the back-cover copy of the 1950 edition attempts to place the novel in the tradition of realism, citing the book's 'realism and power and emotional appeal.' Some reviewers in the mainstream press (such as Deacon) took this copy at its word, praising Garner as 'rigidly and apparently coldly objective' and applauding the 'stern realism' of Garner's 'social document' (10). For postwar leftists, however, the novel's politics were far from appealing: in its 2 April 1951 issue, the Labour-Progressive Party's *The Canadian Tribune* pans Garner for his 'political capitulation' and the novel for its acquiescence to the pressures exerted by 'red-baiters' and capitalist publishers (13). In particular, the reviewer condemns Garner's decision to pander to fear mongering about 'foreign' communists, which was as prevalent in 1950 as it had been in the middle of the Depression. The *Tribune* reviewer cites the scene in which Ken, after being persuaded to attend a communist rally, retreats from socialism because it threatens his sense of home and cohesive ethnic identity:

> He had allowed Jimmy to persuade him to join a protest march to the Provincial Parliament Buildings. He had been amazed and disconcerted, however, to find that the marchers were not the people of Cabbagetown, but strangers, foreigners mostly, who had been recruited by their Communist leaders. He had helped to carry a large sign in the parade, striding straight ahead, his eyes defiant, resolved to set an example to his own people who stood on the sidewalks and looked on apathetically. At the meeting which followed the march he had listened to a re-hash of all the Party slogans, 'Free Tom Mooney, Solidarity Behind the Spanish Workers, Aid to the anti-fascist German proletariat,' until, sick and disgusted with the whole rotten farce he had walked quickly from the crowd. (144)

The *Tribune* reviewer vehemently rejects the idea that interwar working-class solidarity was or should have been undercut by racism, insisting that 'Canadians of all racial origins played courageous roles in the Cabbagetown relief fights' (13). For the Labour-Progressive Party (formerly the CPC), the issue of unemployment did not retreat in the 1950s because so many Canadian workers remained outside the state insurance scheme. Contributors to the *Tribune* therefore repeated and extended the demands for universal, non-contributory unemployment insurance that their Depression-era counterparts had articulated.

Significantly, Garner's experience of more or less writing for hire shaped the decade that followed: during the 1950s, he published almost no literary short stories or novels and instead focused on the lucrative market in popular magazine articles. As Garner candidly admitted in his later years, the income he earned from writing novels for Collins in the late 1940s and early '50s was not sufficient to maintain his family (he had a wife, Alice, and two small children) *and* his drinking habit, so he turned to writing for magazines because it was easier and more lucrative work (*One Damn* 108). Garner therefore spent the 1950s working as both a full-time and freelance writer and editor for various magazines and newspapers based in Toronto, including *New Liberty* (the Canadian edition of the popular U.S.-American magazine), *Saturday Night*, the *Globe and Mail*, and the *Financial Post* (*One Damn* 111–28). While his occasional use of pseudonyms such as 'Jarvis Warwick' in this period suggests that he wanted to maintain some distance from his popular writing, the fact that he did not use a pseudonym consistently offers more evidence of the fact that Garner was negotiating the differences among high and low forms of print culture.[12] The *Canadian Index to Periodicals* lists no fewer than eighty-seven articles and stories for the decade between 1948 and 1959, including popular pieces such as 'Father's Day: Manufactured Tradition' (*Saturday Night*, 5 June 1954) and 'My Recipe for Eating Out and Staying Alive' (*Maclean's*, 4 January 1958), as well as the nostalgic pieces about Cabbagetown, such as 'Some Ghosts of Christmas Past' (*Saturday Night*, 26 December 1953), that Garner would continue to produce throughout his career. As several critics have noted, Garner was skilled at recycling material: he recast his experiences as a transient and as a soldier in the Spanish Civil War for countless popular periodical publications in the 1950s and '60s. Moreover, he used the story of Myrla Patson as the basis for 'All the Gay Days,' a titillating, sentimental story about a fallen woman that was published in the women's magazine *Canadian Home Journal* in March 1957, and created a hard-edged, confessional version of the 'Go-Boys' narrative that formed the conclusion of the 1950 edition of *Cabbagetown* for a short crime story – '... The Fall Guy' – that was published in *New Liberty* in July 1951. These forays into crime fiction indicate Garner's early attraction to the genre, which he later developed in his detective novels *The Sin Sniper* (1970), *A Nice Place to Visit* (1971), *Death in Don Mills* (1975), and *Murder Has Your Number: An Inspector Dumont Mystery* (1978).

As Garner took up his heteronomous position as a popular magazine personality, he recast his Depression-era radicalism in a manner that was in keeping with the general political cringe of the 1950s. In the immediate wake of the 1950 paperback publication of *Cabbagetown*, Garner began to write non-fictional pieces for popular periodicals about his memories of the Depression, and what emerges is a figure who can find a place in postwar North America – a deliberately anti-authoritarian, individualistic, iconoclastic man. On 24 October 1953, for example, Garner wrote an article suggestively titled 'The Tired Radical' for his *Saturday Night* column 'If Memory Serves.' In it, Garner recalls the 'anti-authoritarian' Reid, a former 'Wobblie' and 'one of the last native American radicals,' whom he met during his time in Spain (10). Reid, who later formed the basis for the character of Noah Masterson in the 1968 edition of *Cabbagetown*, challenged Garner's unthinking acceptance of communist doctrine and taught him 'two things which I still believe: to think things out for myself, and to stand up for my convictions' (10). In 'My Memories of the Great Depression,' an unpublished and undated article that Garner likely wrote in the 1950s or early '60s, he distances himself from every political response to the Depression. The article sneers at 'the odor of sanctity and old church pews' enveloping the 'Fabian socialists' of the prairie provinces, and calls Tim Buck the 'Communist knee-dummy of the ventriloquist dictator Joseph Stalin' (10).[13]

Yet when leftist politics could be aligned with the literary, Garner was less hesitant to evoke them. Despite all his popular work in the 1950s and '60s, Garner's career as a journalist paradoxically also gave him the opportunity to shape his own legend as a literary author – a position that was slowly being institutionalized by emerging bodies such as the Canada Council in these decades. His three-part series on the Spanish Civil War, for example, which appeared in *The Star Weekly* in April 1960, provided him with the opportunity of suggesting his political and aesthetic proximity to the British and American writers who had also joined the cause: 'It was a great war for the literati, and the Loyalist forces probably had more distinguished novelists and poets per capita than any fighting forces since Caesar's. Elliot Paul was in the Balearics and Ernest Hemingway,

John Dos Passos and Josephine Herbst were in Madrid' ('A Loyalist Soldier Returns to Spain, Part 2' 33). As a fellow writer/journalist, Garner implies, he cut his creative teeth on the same material as the 'distinguished novelists and poets' of this 'literati.' Despite his considerable popular success and despite the fact that he 'actively fulminated' against literary pretension (Stuewe, *Hugh Garner* 7), by 1960 Garner clearly hankered after the symbolic capital that the interwar realists were acquiring.

The Revival of *Cabbagetown*

After many unsuccessful attempts throughout the 1950s and early '60s to bring the Collins edition of *Cabbagetown* back into print (Reimer 26–7), Garner decided in 1967 to revive the one full-length manuscript he had preserved from the 1940s. This appears to have been a choice shaped by the fact that, throughout his career, Garner attempted to keep all his work – no matter what its quality – in print in order to maintain some income from it, and the fact that he wished to see his original, and, in his opinion, artistically superior, version of *Cabbagetown* in print. Many additional factors likely combined to create the right moment for the revival of the original manuscript: Garner had accumulated more symbolic capital as a literary writer (he appeared at the now-famous Canadian Writers' Conference at Queen's University in 1955, and his selected stories won the Governor General's Award for fiction in 1963); Cold War politics had become decidedly more temperate; the rise of the New Left was invigorating literary and political cultures in Canada; and unemployment was gaining renewed political attention in Canada as rates of joblessness rose throughout the late 1960s and the state committed itself to new solutions through the creation of the Department of Manpower and Immigration in 1966 (Pal 46–7). Indeed, nostalgia for the Depression era in the late 1960s and early '70s gave Garner many opportunities. A piece called 'On the Road through the Thirties,' for example, appeared in both *Weekend Magazine* (27 February 1971) and in Michiel Horn's edited collection of Depression-era documents, *The Dirty Thirties*. In 1969, the CBC adapted the revised *Cabbagetown* as a two-part radio drama series.[14] Moreover, as Filewod and Irvine have observed, the New Left had a decided preference for Popular Front narratives of the 1930s ('Performance and Memory' 70; 'Among *Masses*' 206), and, in particular, the story of the Spanish Civil War. This narrative enabled former communists to defend their youthful radicalism. 'I Was a Young Communist,' the retrospective memoir of Peter Hunter, the secretary of the Young Communist League (YCL) in Toronto during the 1930s, clearly functions in this way. Selected by Dorothy Livesay for inclusion in 'the Thirties' issue of *CV/II* (May 1976), Hunter's apologia defends the YCL (and communists more generally) against charges of extremism by emphasizing the idealism, humanism, and internationalism of those who fought against 'the extension of Italian fascism and German Nazism to yet another country' (18). There is other evidence of a New Left revival of the Spanish Civil War: in 1969, Victor Hoar's history of Canadian participation in the conflict, *The Mackenzie-Papineau Battalion*, was published, and the author drew on Garner's account of the 'tedium, routine, and more tedium' of life on the front (Hoar 79); in the early 1970s, Mac Reynolds was collecting Spanish Civil War narratives on tape for the CBC archives and asked Garner to participate (*One Damn* 249); and in 1975, *Weekend Magazine* commissioned Garner to write an article about his experiences in Spain, which he titled 'Spain, 38 Years Later.'[15] Garner's first *Cabbagetown* manuscript, which takes Ken to Spain and aligns him with the internationalist ideologies of the Popular Front, must have appeared ripe for the picking in the late 1960s. The revised edition of Hugh Garner's *Cabbagetown*, published as a hardcover trade edition by Ryerson Press in 1968, restores the political radicalization of Ken Tilling and the Bildungsroman structure and amends racist statements in order to make the novel more consistent with the cultural politics of the New Left. While the original manuscript from which Garner created the 1968 edition is no longer extant, he claimed in letters to Robin Farr at Ryerson Press that the 're-writing was in syntax, grammar, and composition rather than in content,' and blamed the sensationalism of the 1950 paperback on 'editorial legerdemaine' that was 'perpetrated' – without his approval, he implied – by Ross-Taylor and Sweeny of Collins.[16] If the editors at Collins had circumscribed Ken Tilling's mobility and his politics in order to increase the novel's circulation, Garner's editors at Ryerson Press saw no reason to do this and, indeed, celebrated their 'uncut and unexpurgated' edition in a 1968 press release.[17]

By the late 1960s, the divisions between the fields of large-scale and restricted production were eminently apparent to Garner and his publishers. Garner's claim that the 1968 edition of *Cabbagetown* was the 'unexpurgated' text of a novel that had been corrupted by Collins can be understood in the context of his desire to consolidate his perpetually precarious share of the symbolic capital that was increasingly available to Canadian writers after 1960. As John Moss points out in a 1972 interview with Garner, 'there seems to be a continuously widening split between the popular writer and the serious writer, the literary figure' ('A Conversation' 50). Garner replies that he began writing with the desire to 'be a literary figure,' but that his carelessness about aesthetics had likely prevented that from happening ('A Conversation' 50). Although Garner's autobiography *One Damn Thing after Another* is bursting with vitriol against the 'literati,' it is also full of evidence that he sought many of the forms of recognition available to professional literary authors in Canada after 1960, such as Canada Council grants, various forms of support from the CBC, and, in the early 1970s, the sale of his papers to Queen's University, a form of indirect state support for Canadian writers that emerged as a result of the establishment of Canadian literature as a doctoral program field (*One Damn* 153, 244–5; Davey, 'Economics and the Writer' 107). For all his apparent disregard of the 'continuously widening split' between 'popular' and 'serious' writers, Garner worked very hard in the period of *Cabbagetown*'s 1968 publication to fashion himself as a 'serious' literary realist. Not long after the 1968 edition appeared, for example, Garner claimed that, like Morley Callaghan, he had been one of the modern writers 'who were attempting to change the Canadian literary scene by writing realistic urban-setting fiction' (*One Damn* 44). Moreover, in his introduction to the first edition of Alice Munro's first short-story collection, *Dance of the Happy Shades* (1968), Garner compliments Munro's use of 'familiar' situations and 'ordinary' characters, noting that, like Callaghan, he believes the 'literary artist' can render the banal interesting, whereas the 'second-rate writers, the writers manqués, the professional-commercial writers, find it impossible to write about ordinary people in ordinary situations' (Foreword vii). Garner thus retrospectively attempted to fashion himself as a writer of the realist fiction that was privileged by those critics and scholars who shaped Canada's literary canon in the postwar period.[18] As Denning observes, the continental recuperation of the Depression era in the late 1960s and early 1970s similarly favoured realist aesthetics, and, in particular, the 'documentary and folk authenticity' that the 1930s seemed to embody (119).

In staging the seamless encounter with truth that is often touted as the hallmark of documentary realism, Ryerson Press insisted on the purity of its 'uncut' 1968 edition and suggested its restored proximity to the Depression era. The publisher's 1968 fall catalogue, for example, presents the new edition of *Cabbagetown* as an improvement on the 'cheap paperback' that had been published in the 1950s. Ryerson thus chose to forfeit the economic capital attached to this bestselling edition and instead sought the symbolic capital that a 'powerfully realistic' 'sociological study' marked by 'Hugh Garner's rather special sincerity' might accrue.[19] In an interview in the early 1970s, Garner supports this representation of the novel, calling it 'a sort of textbook' of the Depression ('A Conversation' 53). The 1950 edition of *Cabbagetown* was likely to help neither author nor publisher in making their claims on literary realism. Accordingly, the dust jacket for the 1968 edition bears a sombre colour illustration that features Ken Tilling in the foreground; unlike the racy cover of the 1950 paperback, this cover places Ken in the middle of a dismal Cabbagetown street, and instead of smiling and pouring a whiskey, Ken averts his sad gaze from the reader and wears the classic body language of the Depression-era unemployed – thumbs hooked in pockets. Behind Ken's back, Myrla, dressed in pink, looks directly at the reader with a coy expression. Black ink outlines augment the clarity of the illustration and further distinguish it from the hazy bar atmosphere suggested by the 1950 cover. Even the Ken Tilling of the 1968 text, who is so clearly based on Garner's own experiences, distances himself from the sentimental idealization of popular journalism. In a scene from 'Transition,' the middle section of the novel that Garner either restored or created in the late 1960s, Ken is about to leave Cabbagetown for a period of tramping in the United States, and, as he is making his preparations, he finds a 'copy of a national magazine' in his mother's house that he then flips through. Soon, however, he discards the magazine in disgust, calling its narration of 'the beauteous Clarissa ... languid on a pink beach chair' 'Crap!' (275)[20]

As in the 1950s, some reviewers in the late 1960s took the book for what it claimed to be – a novel of 'graphic realism.'[21] According to Ross Hayball, 'as sociology, history and art, the new *Cabbagetown* is a great improvement on the original.'[22] Taking his friend Hugh Garner at his word, the venerable Bob Weaver notes (in the 2 November 1968 issue of *Saturday Night*) that '*Cabbagetown* was previously published in 1950, but only in a pocket book edition, and it was edited (not by the author) in such a way that the narrative became badly disjointed and the ending melodramatic and patly symbolic' (36). In Weaver's opinion, the newly released edition allows the reader to 'judge what a solid piece of realistic fiction that book was always intended to be, with an ending far less melodramatic and much more in tune with its protagonist than the climax of the pocket book' (36). Echoing Garner's own self-fashioning, Weaver concludes that the author 'is a social realist in the manner of James T. Farrell and John Dos Passos, a man of the 1930s with a wide personal experience of the hard side of Canadian life' (42). In the second edition of the *Literary History of Canada*, which appeared in 1976, Hugo McPherson observes that *Cabbagetown* 'records with naturalistic energy the case histories of residents in Toronto's worst slum'; given that McPherson incorrectly states 1951 as the first date of publication, it seems likely that he is commenting on the 1968 Ryerson Press edition of the novel (218).[23]

The 1968 edition forms the basis for all recent critical evaluations of *Cabbagetown*, and these tend to agree with earlier critics regarding the novel's aesthetics. Chen, for instance, reads *Cabbagetown* as an example of the social realism that reigned in Canadian fiction from 1920 to 1955, and which featured conventions of verisimilitude, authenticity of language, resistance to figurative language, and a separation of author and text in order to maintain the appearance of objectivity (84–92). Roxanne Rimstead considers *Cabbagetown* in the context of her study of Canadian 'poverty narratives' and contends that it is an example of 'hard-boiled social realism' or 'documentary realism' (13, 191). Similarly, Hill asserts that 'the narrative almost cinematographically moves in and out of the minds of numerous characters, striving for psychological realism on the level of the individual mind, but always subtly emphasizing the connection between the individual life and the spirit of the times' ('The Modern' 230–1). In Hill's view, but not in Chen's or Rimstead's, these characteristics of the novel are in no way aligned with 'social commentary,' and the narrator 'avoids drawing moral conclusions about the events that take place in the novel' ('The Modern' 231–2). Yet discussions of the social-protest element of Garner's realism feature in most contemporary critical treatments of Garner, most of which do not even mention the existence of the 1950 edition. Such critical responses to Garner, and the fact that such characterizations of his aesthetics and politics form the basis for all arguments that attempt to claim his place in the modern literary canon, have perhaps encouraged McGraw-Hill Ryerson to market the most recent reprint of the novel as documentary realism.[24]

There are indeed many basic documentary conventions in the 1968 edition of *Cabbagetown*, but, significantly, they are also evident in the 1950 paperback. Garner's desire for realist representation is demonstrated most obviously in the particularity of the novel's setting – its street names, hotels, and restaurants – and in his attention to the portrayal of a Cabbagetown idiom. However, the 1968 edition of *Cabbagetown* is not as realist as its initial reviewers, its contemporary critics, and its current packaging suggest: while it exhibits some of the documentary conventions that Garner first experimented with in the 1930s and more or less maintained in the 1950 edition, it retains the didactic and often sentimental third-person narrator that characterized his early use of the documentary form and later became an entrenched feature of the various writing personas he cultivated in his career as a writer of popular fiction and magazine journalism. In his author's preface to the 1968 edition, which explains to the reader that the Cabbagetown of the novel was 'bull-dozed to the ground' after the Second World War to make way for the public housing project of Regent Park, Garner seems aware of his own narrative indulgences: following his description of the 'umbilical ties with the Cabbagetown that had gone,' Garner adds, 'but perhaps Ken Tilling would have said, "Talking like that borders on the sentimental, and nobody should get eulogistic over a slum"' (vi). Due to this maudlin habit, and also because he continued to produce popular detective fiction until the end of his life, Garner's literary reputation has remained contentious among some critics and scholars. Although Doug Fetherling, a New Left critic who advocated Garner's work in the 1970s, blames the anti-realist preferences of his contemporaries for Garner's failing reputation in this period, it is more likely that the feminization and degradation of the sentimental that postmodernism inherited from modernism is to blame. Indeed, some young critics in the late 1960s were willing to judge Garner by the standards of interwar realism, but nevertheless found his work lacking.[25] Despite these critiques of Garner's style, and, later, critic Paul Stuewe's characterization of the 'sentimental and reactionary strains' in Garner's writing (*Hugh Garner* 5), the dominant critical assessment of *Cabbagetown* as realist has shaped the positioning of the novel in the contemporary field of cultural production.

The narrative that Garner refined when revising his manuscript in the late 1960s transforms the conventions of popular genre fiction that define the 1950 edition. The crime novel plotline remains, but Ken plays no role in the robbery that leads to Bob McIsaacs's death. Early on in the 1968 edition, McIsaacs's criminal character is contrasted to the adolescent mistakes of Ken and his friends, whose mischief is more generally aligned with the 'clean-fun, knockabout type of story' that Garner would have encountered in the public-school story papers that he loved so much as a young man (Orwell 82). But the narrative voice of the revised *Cabbagetown* is often more intrusive than in the 1950 edition: after decades of writing for hire and instructing his readers what to think, Garner had likely lost whatever ability or inclination he once had to cultivate the convention of the detached narrative voice. In the 1950 edition, when Myrla Patson's young lover Herb attempts to rape her after she refuses his marriage proposal, the narrator tells us simply that Myrla flees, while

Herb 'sat watching her from the car, knowing it was all over between them' (34). In the 1968 edition, the passage is much more elaborate:

> Herb watched her go, surprised at the suddenness of their breakup, unable to comprehend what had happened in such a short space of time, wondering what had changed him from a young man plighting his troth one minute to a rough slavering rapist the next. His thoughts were unable to line the events in proper sequence, and he still could not grasp what had happened between them. As the streetcar pulled away he felt a sinking inside, feeling he had lost something both ephemeral and lasting, something he would never find again. (51–2)

This kind of direct intervention, which instructs the reader how to respond to each character, is typical of the revised *Cabbagetown*.

Such narrative didacticism also serves to distance Garner the author from some of the aspects of Cabbagetown in the 1930s that readers in the late 1960s might have found offensive. When Ken's mother and a neighbour visit the home of a young eastern European couple that has recently settled in Cabbagetown, the 1950 edition lets the reader judge Mrs Tilling's incredulity at the fact that there's not 'a cleaner house on the street' (128). While the first edition makes it clear that Mrs Tilling's racist prejudice is challenged by her visit with the immigrant family, the narrator in the 1968 edition risks no misunderstanding:

> The 'foreigners' were just beginning to spread in the city's East End, but it would be years before they ousted the Anglo-Saxon majority from the district immediately west of the Don River. When this happened some of the Cabbagetown women, who still could not be convinced that foreigners and Jews were not dirty, used to watch the European immigrant women washing down their front porches and steps every day, and put it down to showing off or being clean publicly to hide their houses' inside dirt. The sight of an immigrant woman placing her mattresses outside her windows to air them was looked upon as being a filthy and unhealthy habit. Most Cabbagetown housewives lived their whole lives and went to their deaths believing these things. The truth was, of course, that the dirtiest families in the city of Toronto, and probably everywhere else, were the poverty stricken welfare recipients of English, Scots and Irish birth or descent. (307)

Such irony is familiar: the dramatic irony of Garner's 1938 'Christmas Eve in Cabbagetown,' for example, attempts to motivate the sympathy of the middle-class *Forum* reader. Yet here the ironic gap between the narrator and the unwitting characters of Cabbagetown permits a heavy-handed critique of the way that racism inhibits class solidarity.

The 1968 edition depends on Ken's adoption of this narrative perspective, and this forms part of the Bildungsroman structure through which the protagonist comes to political consciousness. In opposition to his friend and foil, Theodore East, who becomes involved in the pro-fascist, xenophobic 'National Canadian Youth' organization, Ken takes to the rails and learns that racism can fracture class solidarity. (Because the 1950 edition does not emphasize Ken's political education, there is no need for a fascist character foil and the Theodore East chapters do not appear.) If Ken's experiences of transience in the 1950 edition only confirm his belief that 'foreigners' are political agitators rather than unemployed victims of an unjust system, in the 1968 edition, Ken's time on the road teaches him to deplore the racism that divides the working class.[26] These lessons culminate in his decision to travel to Spain to fight with the loyalist International Brigades, which are to Ken's delight 're-ally international,' comprising men from places as diverse as the U.S., Austria, Cuba, Canada, Germany, Ireland, and Romania (412). The lack of an extant manuscript from the late 1940s makes it impossible to know if such progressive identity politics were present in the original manu-script, but it is nonetheless clear that the revised novel departs from the 1950 edition in its efforts to represent the politics of the Old Left in a way that would be appealing to what McKay describes as the anti-racist, anti-imperialist ideologies of the New Left (*Rebels* 183–8), which located in the Popular Front an appealing example of internationalism.

Given the rise of second-wave feminism in the late 1960s, the period during which Garner was revising his manuscript, it is also interesting to examine the character of Myrla Patson and the more general relation between gender and mobility in the 1968 edition. Indeed, in this lat-ter edition Ken's transient mobility is central to the development of his political radicalization and personal maturity. Like the first edition, the second initially pays great attention to the fact that differential access to mobility is the consequence of a society that carves out rigid public and private spheres for men and women, but to emphasize Ken's growing difference from those around him, and particularly from the women around him, the 1968 edition makes the inability to move an essential flaw of character rather than a symptom of structural inequalities.

In both editions, Ken's transient adventures are continually juxta-posed with scenes from the domestic world of Cabbagetown, and the fate of Myrla Patson, Ken's former girlfriend, is central to these sections. Before the narratives split in two, the reader is clearly shown the social context in which men have access to mobility and women do not. The first part of both texts, 'Genesis,' contains a scene in which Ken berates Theodore East for giving his name to the young woman with whom he has just made love in Riverdale Park and whom he might have gotten in 'trouble' (56; 113). Ken and Theodore are agents; they do not have to accept the consequences of behaviours that would otherwise tie them to homes and families. By contrast, the chapter that follows in both editions narrates Myrla's troubled situation: she has just lost her job, can no longer help her family pay the bills, and daydreams about how she and her friends had hoped to 'marry tall handsome' men who could afford a 'nice apartment and a maid' (57; 118). Such ideal visions are not to be realized in Cabbagetown, and Myrla ends up as a servant in the middle-class home of a Forest Hill family where she finds herself exchanging sex for money and favours from Claude Leroy, the family patriarch. Myrla eventually becomes pregnant, and her slow descent into the nadir of prostitution is chronicled alongside Ken's gradual growth outward into the world.

In the 1968 text, Ken's mother compares Ken's transience to his father's and wishes that she were a man and 'could run away too' (273), yet this same text privileges Ken's ultimate dismissal of Myrla's situation and his belief that she is to blame for her fate. In their last meeting in the 1950 edition, Ken accepts and even empathizes with Myrla's fate; by contrast, in the 1968 text Ken tells Myrla that, like a 'real criminal,' she has a 'psychological quirk' in her makeup. It is not her 'environment or poverty' that have made her, but an innate psychological imbalance (389). Like the squirmy homosexual Clarence Gurney, whose fusty, bourgeois apartment stands in contrast to the mobility that allows Ken to become a confident and politically effective male, Myrla's body is innately aberrant. Ken's damning judgment thus seems to explain Myrla's (and other women's) absence from the final chapters of the 1968 edition, which take Ken to Spain and place him in the midst of an open-ended dawn – 'not only the beginning of the day, but the ending of the night' (415). Women cannot enter the public sphere because their particular, individual, private identities cannot be articulated there. As contemporary feminist critiques of liberalism and liberal citizenship observe, many problems issue from this public/private dichotomy. Chantal Mouffe, for example, challenges the liberal reliance on discrete public and private realms, wherein the public is abstract and universal (and so must exclude the particularity of women's experiences) and the private is the location of particularity and difference ('Democratic Citizenship' 237). Mary Dietz, among others, posits that this liberal dichotomy nourishes a conception of citizenship that does little for women, who have historically been excluded from the public realm and allied with a private realm 'where the state cannot legitimately interfere' (66–7). Although it seems that Garner attempted to account for the shifting politics of the left in the 1968 edition, the gender politics of the novel repeat the masculinist discourses of the Old Left and reinforce the private/public binary that informs liberal conceptions of citizenship and programs of the postwar welfare state, such as unemployment insurance.[27]

The National Bildungsroman and Unemployment

As the foregoing arguments illustrate, the 1968 *Cabbagetown*, which has effaced the earlier edition in Canadian literary history, must be read as a text of the Centennial period rather than of the 1930s. This has ramifications for readings of the 1968 edition as a Bildungsroman, particularly because the coming of age that the novel narrates has important parallels with other recuperations of the Depression in the Centennial period. Indeed, by the late 1960s the crisis of the Depression was frequently cast as a sort of national crucible – one in which the nation had been tested but from which had emerged the benevolent welfare state. Not all writers were convinced that the Depression had left the legacy of a wiser nation: F.R. Scott's poem 'Regina 1967' queries the forgetting that paradoxically accompanied the nation's Centennial celebrations and implies that the supplanting of 'hunger-marchers' by 'oil-men' and 'miners' is not necessarily a sign of the social progress celebrated by the Centennial (16), and Juan Butler's novel *Cabbagetown Diary: A Documentary* (1970) both alludes to Garner's *Cabbagetown* and critiques the spirit of nationalist optimism of the Centennial period. Others read the legacy of the Depression more sanguinely in this period. Indeed, the Depression years proved to be a powerful foundational narrative for many artists, writers, and critics in the late 1960s and 1970s, many of whom had come of age in the 1930s and viewed rising unemployment rates with trepidation. As H. Blair Neatby notes in her introduction to her 1971 history of the Depression, *The Politics of Chaos*,

The fascination for the 1930s is relatively recent. For those who lived through the depression the first reaction was relief that it was behind them.

Only later could they remember with nostalgia the personal bonds forged by common hardships and economic disaster. For the younger generation, the 1930s is now part of history, a remote prewar decade, tinged with the romance of a period when life seems to have been simpler and less confusing. But this contemporary vogue for the 1930s is also linked to the concern for Canadian identity. In many ways the decade marks the beginning of modern Canada. The Canadians of that era were grappling almost for the first time with many of the problems which are still with us. (1)

Around the 1967 Centennial, when many writers were searching for myths of nation, the Depression – what Neatby calls 'the beginning of modern Canada' – served as one site of national origin.

For example, Al Purdy drew on and extended the earlier transient identities that he had developed in the 'vagabondia' poems of his first collection, *The Enchanted Echo* (1944), in his 1965 collection *The Cariboo Horses,* which contains several poems that interpret the Depression as a foundational moment for the nation and the national citizen.[28] If 'Bums and Brakies (1937)' emphasizes stasis – the 'plodding' movements of its transient subjects and their accompanying lack of identity and humanity (82) – 'Transient' celebrates the poet's experiences riding the rails during the Depression. In 'Transient,' the national folk-hero poet and the transient speaker of the poem are clearly collapsed; the assumption of a national identity is inevitable for the speaker ('you are where you were always going'), represented as a physical trait ('the shape of home is under your fingernails') that emerges as the white, male speaker rides through the space of the nation on a freight train (108). Many writers and activists in the 1930s posited the rights of the transient unemployed to a program of what was later called social citizenship; by the mid-1960s, an Anglo male poet like Purdy could assume transience – and by extension, the experience of Depression-era if not contemporary unemployment – as the very foundation of national citizenship. According to Brodie, the 'Social Canadian' – the national subject conjured in the citizenship discourse of the 1960s – was the bearer of the social rights of citizenship that had been imagined in the interwar period as rights that would vitiate the instabilities of capitalism (384–6). Such a 'state-orchestrated vision' of 'an inclusive pan-Canadian nationalism' strove, in the 1960s, to adhere the 'citizen to the state' (Brodie 382, 380).

As D.M.R. Bentley points out, Purdy's cultivation in the late 1960s of a 'hinterland transient' identity appealed to the popular media of the period (110): on 28 May 1965, for example, the Canadian edition of *Time* magazine featured 'The Purdy Pigment,' an article that revels in Purdy's 'hobo' credentials, linking his experiences riding the rails and working odd jobs to his anti-authoritarian streak (Purdy is quoted as saying that he quit the RCAF during the war because 'I didn't like other people telling me what to do') (11). The article, however, documents the fact that Purdy's success with *The Cariboo Horses* garnered him a Canada Council travel grant in 1965, which he used to go to the Arctic (and to write the poems that appeared in the 1967 collection *North of Summer: Poems from Baffin Island*). Despite this state-sponsored mobility, the *Time* article remains committed to the Depression-era image of Purdy riding the rails, 'scribbling poetry on scraps of paper' (11). A poetics of transience may form an element of *The Cariboo Horses*, but it is a vestigial trace that is clearly overwhelmed by a poetics of place, nurtured, one might argue, by a new relation to the state. Indeed, the place-based poetry for which Purdy is known – the poetry of Roblin Lake, Ameliasburg, and the 'country north of Belleville' – emerged from a now somewhat famous cottage on the shore of Roblin Lake that he built in the 1950s, as a zeugmatic line from 'One Rural Winter' tells us, 'with Unemployment Insurance / and pounded thumbnails' (Purdy, *The Cariboo Horses* 68).

Slightly before Purdy's and Garner's excavation of the Depression-era transient, John Marlyn published his novel of the Depression, *Under the Ribs of Death* (1959).[29] Like Garner, Marlyn employs the form of the Bildungsroman to narrate his protagonist's coming of age just prior to and during the Depression years, and like Ken Tilling, Sandor Hunyadi hails from a working-class slum – in Sandor's case, North Winnipeg. Unlike Garner, Marlyn depicts a protagonist whose Hungarian ethnicity marks his experience of adolescence, and whose ambition and disavowal of his ethnicity (he renames himself 'Alex Hunter' in the second part of the novel) creates disastrous consequences, ultimately resulting in unemployment, destitution, and estrangement from his family and community. Daniel Coleman reads the novel as an ironic critique of the 'allegory of manly maturation' that constitutes an 'oft-repeated story of national legitimation,' and which more often than not employs the Bildungsroman form to map out a male immigrant's assimilation to Anglo-Canadian norms ('Immigration, Nation' 85). Joseph R. Slaughter's work on the 'sociohistorical and formal correspondences' between international human rights law and the idealist Bildungsroman is instructive here, particularly insofar as he observes the limits of universalist and internationalist discourses: 'Historically, what the Rights of Man and the *Bildung* cultivated were not primarily universalist sensibilities about the inherent and inalienable equality of man but patriotic senses of national particularity, of what it means to be, and how to become, a French or German citizen' (1407, 1416). According to Coleman, it is Ralph Connor's best-selling 'allegory of manly maturation' and immigrant assimilation, *The Foreigner: A Tale of Saskatchewan* (1909), that Marlyn resists; however, as Coleman notes, the conclusion of *Under the Ribs of Death* contains 'renewed elements of the old allegory of maturation' insofar as Sandor's/Alex's redemption depends on his connection to a patriarchal 'genealogical continuity' embodied in his infant son, who bears his ethnicity ('Immigration, Nation' 103).[30] So, although it is an 'allegory of manly maturation' with a difference realized through irony, it retains the patriarchal assumptions of its avatar.

Coleman construes Marlyn's irony in light of a more general scepticism of the 'national-maturity allegory' that arose in the wake of the First World War and the Depression ('Immigration, Nation' 103), but reading *Under the Ribs of Death* and the 1968 edition of *Cabbagetown* together suggests that the Depression eventually generated a 'national-maturity allegory' of its own. In *Under the Ribs of Death*, the Depression is cast as the necessary if painful stage that precedes the multicultural nation allegorized by Sandor's son. In *Cabbagetown* it is the period that shapes the consciousness of the forthcoming welfare state and its citizens, allegorized by Ken Tilling, whose mobility suggests that Canada's postwar future is a 'widened' one appropriately figured as 'the beginning of the day' (415). The restored conclusion of the 1968 *Cabbagetown* is embedded in the internationalism of the Popular Front, but its Centennial-era citation also functions as a celebration of the nation's triumph over the Depression.

Indeed, it is revealing that in his 1964 introduction to the New Canadian Library reprint of *Under the Ribs of Death*, Eli Mandel reads the novel as a foundational narrative of nationhood:

His setting is Winnipeg in the late 'twenties, and one of his main concerns is the economic collapse which led to the great depression. Yet, oddly enough, it is this very concern with the past which accounts for the contemporary feeling of his work, for the great cracks which then opened in our social structure allowed us to peer at least momentarily into its very foundations and thus into our own selves. Those, like Marlyn, who dared to look, saw not ancient history but the face of contemporary man. (7)

While Purdy's transient figures are explicitly Anglo-Canadian, Mandel's reading of *Under the Ribs of Death* suggests that, in the Centennial period, it was the *male* subject who had experienced the ravages of Depression-era unemployment who could be recuperated as a figure for the national citizen or the nation-in-process. The Bildungsroman form of Garner's 1968 *Cabbagetown*, which might easily be read as an allegory of a nation-in-the-making, makes a similar assumption. Brodie points out that such gendered exclusivity characterized the postwar discourse of social citizenship, as well, despite the ostensible universality of the 'Social Canadian': 'social security programs tended to be constructed for the male breadwinner while social welfare, usually less generous and means-tested, was reserved for women and others on the fringes of the paid labour force' (384).

This Centennial-era version of the Bildungsroman may seem from the perspective of the early twenty-first century to be surprisingly optimistic. A much more recent immigrant Bildungsroman that traverses the same geography as Garner's *Cabbagetown* (although it is now called Regent Park), Rabindranath Maharaj's *The Amazing Absorbing Boy* (2010), indirectly critiques the sanguinity of Garner's and Marlyn's allegories of national development and the way they link national citizenship to unemployment and immigrant status. Narrated from the historical perspective of the destruction of Regent Park – a postwar experiment in public housing – Maharaj's novel has little reason to celebrate the national citizen who is nurtured by welfare-state benevolence. Yet *Cabbagetown*, situated at the crossroads of twentieth-century political and aesthetic debates, takes its meaning from the relation between the literary leftism of the 1930s and the New Left ideologies of the late 1960s. Informing this relation is the terrain across which Old Left thought must pass before it can arrive in the contemporary period – the Cold War ideologies and the postwar welfare state of the political field, and the rise of mass culture and a national literary canon in the field of cultural production. Attention to this terrain is a necessary part of reading *Cabbagetown*, which mobilizes the Depression under shifting political, economic, and social conditions. It is to this phenomenon of mobilizing the Depression era in the contemporary period that I turn in the next chapter.

Chapter Five

New Left Culture and the New Unemployment

Unemployment was, in a certain sense, 'new' in the 1970s. If joblessness was rising in ways that by the early 1970s were looking worryingly old to many media commentators, the phenomenon of joblessness was being interpreted in policy discourse in new ways: it was a 'problem' exacerbated by the increased participation of women and youths in the labour market that could be tackled with a new spin on demand management. In the early Trudeau years, job-creation strategies were designed to ease labour-market problems while simultaneously engaging a youthful population that demanded autonomy and meaningful (rather than make-) work experiences. An influential segment of this youthful demographic resided in Quebec, and the particular militance of the New Left in Quebec played no small part in shaping the discourse of job creation in the first half of the 1970s. Women, too, were making demands on the state in unprecedented ways. Their activism resulted in the Royal Commission on the Status of Women (1967–70), and their increased labour-force participation – and unemployment – contributed to the urgency motivating federal job-creation schemes (Keck 39, 35).[1]

Unsurprisingly, in the context of rising unemployment in this period, the legacies of the welfare state were being evaluated: competing interpretations included celebrations of its accomplishments, denouncements of its incompleteness, and critiques of its inability to ever eradicate structural inequality in society. Linked to this debate about the role of the welfare state in late twentieth-century Canadian society were conflicting conceptions of citizenship, which was increasingly imagined as a collective practice rather than an individual right, a shift that challenged entrenched liberal ideas of national citizenship. Nevertheless, state conceptions of citizenship in this period endeavoured to manage the radical implications of such thinking through programs that initially emphasized but subsequently limited the meaning of citizenship participation.

Rather than the direct address of the state that one finds in many of the cultural texts of the 1930s, representations of unemployment in this period often indirectly address the state via the narratives, images, and tropes of the Depression, which reflects the fact that, by the 1970s, such devices had become staples in the pantry of the nation's self-image, thanks in part to the work of writers such as Hugh Garner, John Marlyn, and Al Purdy, and to popular historians such as James Gray. This chapter investigates how a variety of New Left and socialist-feminist literary, intellectual, and artistic cultures engaged worklessness as a feature of contemporary life in Canada in the 1960s and '70s and, in particular, how the Depression was mobilized in these engagements.

The Political Economy of the Arts in 1970s Canada

In keeping with the kinds of questions that I have been posing throughout this book regarding the material conditions of work that produce narratives of unemployment, this chapter first examines the relation between labour market policy – especially job creation – and the arts in 1970s Canada. The reiteration of the figures of the 1930s left in the cultural texts of the New Left connects the political economy of the 1930s to a global economic order that began to assume new characteristics in the 1970s. The welfare-state reforms that came about in Canada in the postwar period and that have been described in previous chapters coincided with a period of prosperity in the capitalist world economy that endured from 1950 to the early 1970s.[2] The lesson of the Depression for governments in the West was that the autonomous market could not guarantee the precious combination of low unemployment and economic growth, and the Keynesian solution, hammered out at the 1944 Bretton Woods conference, proposed state intervention in the market as a means of securing 'full employment capitalism' and thus defending liberal democracies from socialism (Muszynski 254–5). Fuelled by the development of markets in western Europe and the recycling of world liquidity provided by Cold War military conflicts, the United States led the postwar period of expansion in world trade and production, yet this phase of material expansion led directly to a crisis between 1968 and 1973 (Arrighi 296–8). In the early 1970s, the United States abandoned the fixed gold-(U.S.) dollar exchange standard that had prevailed since Bretton Woods in fa-

vour of flexible or floating exchange rates, and this, in turn, was a key
factor in the global financial 'revolution' of the late twentieth century – a
'revolution' powered by trade and speculation in foreign currencies, as
well as by the removal of controls on the movement of capital (Arrighi
299–300). These last two transformations encouraged the 'geopolitical
diversification' of corporations wishing to escape the new challenges of
fluctuating exchange rates, the diminishment of state power over the
production and regulation of world money, excessive borrowing, and
accelerating inflation; meanwhile, real wages in western Europe and
North America and prices, particularly the price of oil, rose at staggering
rates in the first half of the 1970s. This rise, coupled with the 'intensified
transnationalization' of U.S. and non-U.S. capital seeking new foreign
markets, created the crisis that straddled the late 1960s and the early
1970s (Arrighi 310–13, 304–5).

In most industrial nations, stagflation followed: in Canada, for example, inflation exceeded 10 per cent by 1974 and 1975, and unemployment
increased from an average rate of just under 4 per cent between 1965 and
1969 to just under 7 per cent by 1975 (Keck 356, 358). Although Canada's
postwar federal government was never fully committed to the Keynesian
notion of state intervention as a means of securing full employment, the
state did periodically use Keynesian 'demand management' to stabilize
the economy (Campbell, *Grand Illusions* 43–4; Muszynski 253). In the
postwar period, unemployment insurance played this role. As unemployment rose in the late 1960s and early 1970s, unemployment insurance
was extended to more workers and unconventional community-based
job-creation programs, such as Opportunities for Youth (OFY; 1971–6)
and the Local Initiatives Program (LIP; 1971–6), were introduced.[3] However, on the heels of the 1968–73 economic crisis, federal policy makers
increasingly felt that Keynesian economic theories could not adequately
explain the stagflation that industrialized nations like Canada were ex-
periencing, and in the mid-1970s the Canadian government turned to
conservative monetarist policies (such as the wage and price controls
of 1975), which affected labour market policy in the form of reductions
in unemployment insurance benefits and direct job-creation spending
(Muszynski 253, 270–3; McBride 152–3).[4] In this context, social programs
were portrayed as a 'drain on the economy rather than as a right of
citizenship,' and thus the 'Social Canadian' ceased to be an object of
state policy discourse (Brodie 387). The mid-1970s, therefore, is a pivotal
period that witnessed the transformation of the global economy and the
alteration of the relation between workers and the state that had been

developing since at least the interwar period and the crises of the Depression years.

Describing the effects of this emergent economic globalization and the rise of neoliberalism on the cultural field, Barbara Godard notes that 'literature no longer "expresses" and so binds territory, nor does it retain its utopian dimensions as an ideal human realm of value. Instead, culture is caught up in struggles for economic domination through cultural exchange in a different economy of value that turns not on the mediating power of labour but on speculation on the market itself' ('Notes' 222). Just as the 'mediating power of labour' and Keynesian liberal doctrine were becoming less relevant to state actors in the globalizing economy, one finds in Canada (as elsewhere in the industrialized world), the rise of a state 'cultural industries' strategy that indicates a shift from the postwar conception of culture as *compensation* for economic dependency to a new conception of culture as a means of 'economic independence' (Dowler 342). Kevin Dowler makes it clear that this shift in the late 1970s did not entail supplanting a 'cultural mandate' with an 'industrial strategy' but rather a 'blending of these two areas into a combined strategy' (341). This convergence since the mid-1970s of industrial, economic, and cultural policy has a precedent in the job-creation programs that were introduced in the early 1970s to stimulate the economy and employment but that also had mandated roles in cultural initiatives such as the national unity program (Dowler 341). For example, one of the explicit goals of the OFY program, which was initially under the direction of the Secretary of State, was to nurture 'national unity through creating a general awareness and affection for the country' ('Opportunities for Youth'). What becomes apparent is that in the early 1970s job-creation programs bore a conflicted if not contradictory relation to the quasi-Keynesian postwar and emerging neoliberal orders. On the one hand, such programs offer evidence of the federal government's retreat to the Keynesian demand-management strategies that had characterized the postwar era; on the other hand, job-creation programs tied federal labour-market policy to cultural initiatives, arguably for the first time in Canadian history, and presaged a new conception of the arts as industry.

The spectre of contemporary unemployment clearly motivated New Left interpretations of the Depression and its legacies; simultaneously, unemployment altered the conditions of artistic labour in this period because the state was involved in the labour market in ways that had been almost unthinkable during the 1930s. In 1971, the Department of Manpower added job-creation programs to its roster of policy mechanisms as a means of responding to rising unemployment, but this unemployment was conceptualized as 'new' insofar as it was largely attributed to rising rates of unemployment among women and youths.[5] Such programs were not without precedent – the 'public works' projects launched during the Depression (and earlier), and the Municipal Winter Works Incentive Program (1958–68), which was a seasonal fixture throughout the Pearson years, are earlier variations on a theme – but the OFY and the LIP did reflect a new emphasis on 'citizen participation' that was a hallmark of the early Trudeau government (Keck 98–103; Pal 42–9).

A summer employment program aimed specifically at students, the OFY was initially administered by the Department of the Secretary of State, the ministry in Trudeau's government that assumed responsibility for citizenship participation programs. This department had already administered the Company of Young Canadians (1965–9), which provided youth volunteers and resources for community development projects (Keck 101–31). The yoking of the OFY to citizen participation was particularly pressing in the context of a road-tripping youth culture that flourished in the early 1970s, when thousands of high school and post-secondary students in search of seasonal work or meaningful experiences during the summer months opted to hitchhike across the country. According to a 1972 federal study of the OFY program, 'significant numbers of so-called "alienated youth"' first became apparent to the federal government in the summer of 1967, and over the next year, media attention to the number of transient youth in summer months, illegal drug use, and 'youth culture' in general increased (Cohen 11–12). In August 1969, the Department of the Secretary of State appointed a Committee on Youth to investigate 'the aspirations, attitudes and needs of youth' and the 'government's present role in this area' (Cohen 12). This led to a strategy that unfolded in the summer of 1970, when the Department of the Secretary of State oversaw the temporary conversion of armouries into hostels across the country (Canadian Council on Social Development 3, i–ii). This plan ominously recalled the carceral strategies of Depression-era relief camps for the single unemployed, which were administered by the Department of National Defence and which also used existing military infrastructure. The Department of the Secretary of State soon shed this association with the Depression-era strategy of government and announced that it would provide funding during the summer of 1971 for hostel and auxiliary services to be generated from the local level; that same summer, the OFY appeared as an employment strategy that had as one of its aims the reduction of youth mobility and alienation (Canadian Council on Social Development ii, 13, 16). While unemployment rates for youth were certainly high in this period, federal studies of the 'problem' of road tripping did not conclude that the majority of the youths on the road were actually in search of work. In 1971, for example, the Canadian Council on Social Development interviewed 237 transient youths in twenty-one different Canadian cities and found that just over 60 per cent of the respondents would have travelled anyway if 'full-time work had been available,' and only 5 per cent claimed to be seeking work actively (43–4). It was in the context of information like this that the federal government developed its job-creation strategy for youth with a specific emphasis on 'meaningful' experience.[6]

The LIP program was also influenced by the concept of governing through citizenship participation. Under the LIP program, the state solicited proposals from individuals and community groups rather than, as in the case of traditional public works projects, prescribing the nature of the work that would be done, and grants tended to go to projects that promoted civic participation and betterment. For example, in the winter of 1973 a $32,000 grant went to the North West River Indian Band in Newfoundland to construct an outdoor skating rink, produce and promote Native handicrafts, cut firewood for the elderly, and convert a school into a community centre.[7] Jennifer Keck situates this emphasis on citizen participation in the political and social nexus of the late 1960s and early '70s: the emergence of the New Left, the rapid increase in the number of students enrolled in post-secondary institutions, the simmering politics of separatism in Quebec, and the agitation among youth and activist groups for 'alternative' services all informed the Trudeau government's discourse of democratization (103).

The radical, Depression-era stage of the Worker's Experimental Theatre used unemployed workers and thus functioned as an alternative form of employment in the absence of state intervention (Ryan, 'Canadian Theatre' 110). By contrast, the artistic initiatives of the 1970s that benefited from job-creation programs were clearly much closer to the state, and yet the emphasis on citizenship participation and the values of a 'public economy,' at least in the early years of these programs, created an interesting kind of autonomy for the arts projects that benefited from them, not least of which was autonomy from the standards of artistic merit established by the Canada Council and the provincial granting councils (McKinnie 432–3). These values of the 'public economy' created something that looked, for a brief period, like the Depression-era WPA Arts Projects in the United States, which depended on and encouraged a discourse of art as 'necessary' and as 'emblematic of how the welfare state might transform the relation between markets and the national community altogether' (Szalay 6).

Given the policy emphasis on citizenship participation, it is perhaps not surprising that job-creation programs like the LIP inadvertently benefited the arts. Nourished by state subventions generally, small presses abounded in the 1970s – thirteen appeared in 1976 alone. Many of these, such as Toronto's Coach House Press, benefited directly from LIP and OFY funding (McKnight 315). As Murray has shown, the 'innovative' reader surveys and nationalist promotion of Canadian literature undertaken by the Toronto-based CANLIT action-research team similarly drew on LIP and OFY dollars ('The CANLIT Project'). Like many emerging small presses and other nascent cultural initiatives, small theatre companies found themselves in the early 1970s more or less ignored by large cultural granting agencies such as the Canada Council; programs like the LIP therefore offered seductive sources of funding that emerging theatres were 'able to find and creatively use' in service of the belief that 'a professional career was not just a dream but an ideal that could be a reality' (Rubin, 'The Toronto Movement' 396–7). Michael McKinnie, the only scholar to analyse systematically the effects of the LIP on theatre in Canada, explains the significance of the program:

> Of the LIP grants awarded to artistic projects in 1971, theatre accounted for 75 percent. In 1971–72, LIP allocated nearly $2.3 million to theatre projects; since the national, provincial, and municipal arts councils combined awarded just over $6 million to theatre in 1970–71, this injection of subsidy represented a 37 percent increase in overall funding for the sector in a single year. Furthermore, only 2 percent of LIP funding was for existing professional companies, so the vast majority of this increase went to new, and newly expanding, ventures. LIP was the most significant single form of industrial investment that Canadian theatre had received for a long time, and perhaps ever. (431–2)

As McKinnie notes, however, of the theatres most commonly associated with what is now known as Toronto's alternative theatre movement, it was the Toronto Free Theatre, in particular, that benefited from LIP funds, particularly in 1972, its founding year (432). Unlike the large regional companies that received the lion's share of Canada Council funding and that staged what playwright Carol Bolt later mocked as colonial 'museum theatre' ('An Interview' 146) – reproductions of well-known British, European, and American plays – small, alternative theatres based in Toronto, such as the Toronto Free Theatre, the Factory Theatre Lab, and Theatre Passe Muraille, while different in many ways, were influenced by the international traditions of revolutionary agitprop and documentary theatre, the anti-authoritarian sensibilities of 1960s countercultures, and the anti-colonial impulses of leftist nationalism (Filewod, *Collective Encounters* 3–23; Johnston 5–6).

Despite the effect of the LIP on struggling arts communities in Toronto and beyond, it is important to recall that the majority of LIP funds were directed elsewhere. Of the almost six thousand approved LIP projects in 1972–3, nearly half were construction initiatives, and about one-fifth of the projects were related to social and health services. Artistic and cultural projects received less than 6 per cent of the total funding (Canada, *Local Initiatives Program, 1972–73* 1–2). McKinnie observes the 'disproportionate' amount of negative press that arts initiatives attracted, given how little relative funding they received, and suggests that the LIP 'unwittingly exposed state employment policy to social anxieties about the status of artistic labour and suspicions about the economic utility of the arts in general' (435–6). Indeed, the link between labour-market policy – traditionally considered an economic tool – and culture initiated by the OFY and the LIP adumbrated the cultural-industries strategies that became a regular part of policy discourse by the late 1970s.

Moreover, as Keck astutely demonstrates, the governance of citizen participation quickly became a matter of harnessing radical politics, and as the OFY and the LIP were reviewed each year, the mechanisms for preventing subversive political groups from securing funding became more complex and rigorous (139–47, 177–8, 283). Indeed, even with early federal initiatives such as the Company of Young Canadians, the state was confronted almost immediately with the contradiction posed by, on the one hand, its earnest incorporation of the concerns of youth who claimed disenchantment with the welfare state and, on the other hand, its definition of citizen participation within the framework of liberalism and its imposition of strict limits on political dissent, particularly in Quebec (Keck 112–14).[8] Such a contradiction points to the complexity of governmentality: job-creation programs, like other policy mechanisms, were not 'top-down impositions by political authorities,' but rather signalled the mobility and flexibility of government, whose policies 'frequently incorporate forms of ethical identity and self-government which already existed in other spaces' (Walters 6).[9] After the first year of the OFY and the

LIP, specific mechanisms were put in place to curtail political dissent and encourage 'real' work. Political newspapers and groups were excluded from the 1972 OFY program, for example, and applicants were required to obtain a letter of support from an 'established' community group (Keck 146). Similar moves were afoot in the context of the LIP. In 1972, the Department of Manpower and Immigration prepared a pamphlet entitled *Projects by People* that described the LIP as a success but cautioned that the federal government had decided to renew the program 'on a more selective basis': 'Priority will be given to those projects that best combine the dual objectives of job creation and a realistic and identifiable contribution to the quality of life' (i). Offering thirty-four examples of such 'realistic' and 'identifiable' contributions, the brightly coloured *Projects by People* suggests only four projects that might be classified as cultural initiatives: local television programming to encourage cross-cultural understanding; full-time jobs in theatre; recording pioneer legends; and puppets for children. Significantly, all of these arts projects emphasize educational and/or historical value, particularly as these relate to children. Under the 'Full-Time Jobs in Theatre' description, one finds:

> Canada's Centennial Year showed that people are fascinated by local history and amateur theatre ... In a large western community this interest has developed into a full-time occupation for a small corps of writers, producers, and actors who used a L.I.P. grant to bring live theatre to people. Using authentic historical records, they write plays about the incidents that were important to the founding and growth of the local community ... Student audiences especially have shown appreciation for local history that is 'taught live.' And for the general public the dramas have awakened a new pride and awareness of the events that have made our country. (6)

Above this description is an illustration of two white actors: a redcoat soldier is wielding a bayonet and talking to a blonde woman in colonial dress. *Projects by People* models a form of theatre that privileges mimesis, settler myths of origin, and, in keeping with the message of national unity promoted by the Trudeau government in the context of political unrest in Quebec, national 'pride.' The 'labourist and civic values' promoted by the LIP and by the arts organizations that were receiving LIP funds were thus actively supported by the state for only a very brief period of time in the early 1970s (McKinnie 435). Job-creation programs, with their residual commitment to the quasi-Keynesian ideals of the postwar period, put the concept of what Brodie calls the 'Social Canadian' under stress (382–6): the notion of citizenship participation, in particular, challenged the unifying vision of Canadian society that the social rights of citizenship were meant to encourage.

Citing and Circulating Depression-Era Unemployment: Drama

The left nationalism of the 1970s, which in anglophone Canada 'integrated conventional nationalist themes' of the previous formation with 'contemporary discourses of anti-imperialism, participatory democracy, and feminism' (McKay, 'For a New' 111), asserted its presence in countless cultural milieux. As McKay observes, the fourth socialist formation – the New Left – embraced 'self-management, anti-imperialism, and direct democracy,' while reacting against the socialisms of the second and third formations, and, in particular, the accommodation of these formations within the postwar liberal order (*Rebels* 183–6); however, as Rifkind demonstrates, many New Leftists also celebrated the accomplishments of the previous formations (*Comrades* 210). For example, some of those who had been active in the 1930s English-Canadian cultural left, such as Toby Gordon Ryan and Dorothy Livesay, published memoirs of their experiences during the Depression in the 1970s and early 1980s. Clearly, such texts must be read as New Left interpretations of the 1930s, and, as I argue in chapter 4, the New Left exhibited a marked preference for the non-sectarian Popular Front narratives of the Depression. A good example of this is Livesay's own interpretation in the 1970s of her work with the CPC in the early 1930s – what she called in the April/May 1970 issue of the *Canadian Forum* her 'past sins' (35).

Due in part to LIP funds, the 1970s was a crucial decade for the growth of indigenous theatre in Canada, and citations of Depression-era unemployment abounded in this context. Although it would make for fascinating cultural history to link the two plays that recuperated the unemployment crisis of the 1930s – *Buffalo Jump* (1972) and *Ten Lost Years* (1974) – to job-creation funds, neither of these plays originated in theatres that benefited from LIP or OFY dollars. *Buffalo Jump* was an early form of the collective documentary that became the signature of Toronto's Theatre Passe Muraille, which was not joining 'the rush for LIP funds' in the early 1970s because director Paul Thompson 'felt that the program was upsetting a fragile ecology in Toronto's small theatre scene, and he suspected (rightly, in many cases) that it would create problems of bureaucracy and dependency beyond its value to a company' (Johnston 122). Indeed, the administrative records for Passe Muraille for the early 1970s offer no evidence that the company applied for or received job-creation funds, even if Bolt (and some scholars) have assumed that the 'institutionalized employment' of LIP funds encouraged 'great, sprawling epics with huge casts,' such as *Buffalo Jump*, 'because then you could employ more people' ('Carol Bolt' 273).[10] *Ten Lost Years* was the product of a more established theatre – George Luscombe's Toronto Workshop Productions. Founded in 1959 and professionalized in 1963, Luscombe's theatre was receiving almost $70,000 from the Canada Council by the 1972–3 season (McKinnie 432). Filewod posits that, although an older theatre, Toronto Workshop Productions was the 'first of the alternative theatres in Canada' because it stems from the same theatrical traditions as those more commonly associated with the movement (*Collective Encounters* 51).[11]

First produced in 1971 as *Next Year Country* at Regina's Globe Theatre, *Buffalo Jump*, a much different play, came out of the collective playmaking processes favoured by Theatre Passe Muraille director Paul Thompson.[12] Committed since its founding at Rochdale College in 1968 to the concept of theatre as 'event' and theatre 'without borders,' Passe Muraille produced collective, documentary creations such as *Doukhobors* (1971), *Free Ride* (1971) – a play about the phenomenon of cross-country hitchhiking that Thompson researched by going on the road during the summer of 1971 – *Bethune* (1971), *Buffalo Jump* (1972), and *The Farm Show* (1972). *Buffalo Jump* interprets the events of the 1935 On-to-Ottawa trek through the analogy of the 'buffalo jump' (the traditional method that Plains Aboriginals developed for killing buffalo en masse by urging them over a cliff). The play thus engages the political economy of the 1930s in a thematic sense, but it also performs this engagement in a methodological sense. Filewod's work on documentary theatre in Canada shows that the collective documentaries of Passe Muraille owe a debt to both the 'tradition of didactic historical drama in Canada' and 'the international tradition of documentary theatre that originated in Europe in the 1920s,' but that appeared in Canada via the Workers' Theatre Movement of the 1930s (*Collective Encounters* 5–8). Indeed, techniques such as direct address and exhortation, imagistic montage, circularity, and polyphony – what Filewod calls the 'mise-en-scène of cultural resistance' – were established in Third Period agitprops and later incorporated into the toolkits of theatres such as Passe Muraille ('The Comintern' 29; *Collective Encounters* 7); however, in Filewod's view, Passe Muraille documentaries also transformed these Old Left traditions of 'political documentary' by challenging the 'very idea of the dramatic text' with performances of 'findings' based on the field research of actors (*Collective Encounters* 52, 78).

The backward glance performed by *Buffalo Jump* is thus inflected by New Left preoccupations. Of crucial importance in this regard is the fact that Bolt's source material derived not just from primary historical documents, such as the papers of R.B. Bennett (Bolt, 'Carol Bolt' 267), but also from histories of the Depression published in the late 1960s and early 1970s. The 1972 house program indicates, for example, that Bolt used material from Michiel Horn's *The Dirty Thirties* (1972); 'original interview material and massive documentation' provided by Victor Hoar, who edited Ronald Liversedge's *Recollections of the On to Ottawa Trek* (1973); as well as the essays that appeared in the 1969 collection *The Great Depression: Essays and Memoirs from Canada and the United States.*[13] Bolt recalled in the late 1970s that she wanted to make the 'theme' of *Buffalo Jump* – the argument that the trekkers and their families were 'being manipulated by both sides, the politicians of the Left and of the Establishment' – 'entertaining' ('An Interview' 147). This analogy of the 'Left' and the 'Establishment' is certainly present in the play's typically New Left critique of organized politics. Such New Left positions frequently criticized the '"passive party" allegiance' and the bureaucratization of the labour movement that was understood to represent the absorption of the Old Left within the liberal welfare state (McKay, 'For a New Kind' 109). The parody of the union meeting at the end of act 1, for example, in which a motion (against smoking in bed) is carried despite the fact that most of the strikers vote against it, satirizes complex rules of order and bureaucratic socialism. Significantly, by the 1970s, New Left critique also frequently incorporated feminist ideologies and discourses of decolonization (McKay, *Rebels* 183–4), and these concerns are evident in the self-conscious way *Buffalo Jump* explores the gendering of political and cultural/caregiving work in the 1930s,[14] as well as in the play's skewering of R.B. Bennett, whose fondness for a Kiplingesque, Anglo-Saxon, Christian masculinity is represented as an anachronism in the scene that interprets Bennett's bombastic performance at the 1932 Imperial Economic Conference in Ottawa (1.15–17). This is indeed a play indebted to what Filewod identifies as the 'disruptive' techniques of agitprop – imagistic montage, circularity, and polyphony – ('The Comintern' 29), but in the final scene, when uniformed police instruct audience members to 'clear this area,' *Buffalo Jump* queries the extent to which Old Left strategies of resistance continue to be relevant or compelling.[15]

With regard to Bolt's desire to make the play's critique 'entertaining,' it is clear that, *despite* the lack of LIP funds at Passe Muraille, the large cast and a collective playmaking methodology encouraged an aesthetic of abundance in the 1972 production:

> Paul Thompson turned it into a circus. We had a huge cast and wonderful cartoon sets by John Boyle. There were songs and dances and funny stories and we didn't really go deeply into the politics of the event. It was more of a comic strip, perhaps not so much as my later play about Duplessis, *Maurice*, but it was very episodic and highly coloured. Paul wanted to turn it into something picaresque, a journey across the country. He wanted to experiment with as many different theatrical forms as he could; there was a scene based on a Marx Brothers film, another scene was a highly structured improvisation, then there was one derived from Noh theatre, but we cut it because it didn't fit into the play. There was also a very operatic scene. ('An Interview' 147)

In contrast to the aesthetics of abundance Bolt is describing here, the 1930s are often cast as a time of lack. For example, the 1935 On-to-Ottawa trek that *Buffalo Jump* imagines is an event deeply marked by the 'epithets' of 'scarcity,' such as 'hungry,' 'lean,' 'dirty,' and 'angry,' that have come to dominate cultural memories of the Depression (Rifkind, *Comrades* 12).

Indeed, Rota Lister, the interviewer who prompted Bolt's response above, offers evidence of the persistence of such epithets in the dominant cultural memory of the Depression. After Bolt states the politicized theme of *Buffalo Jump*, Lister asks, 'What made you think that that would be entertaining theatre?' ('An Interview' 147). In other words, how can a play about the 'dirty' thirties be 'entertaining'? Reviewers of the 1972 Passe Muraille production of *Buffalo Jump* concurred with Lister. Urjo Kareda, the extremely influential theatre critic who wrote for the *Toronto Star*, utterly rejects the production (in his 19 May 1972 review) as a ludic 'romp' that is 'nostalgic,' disrespectful, and depoliticizing: 'One knows that the actors adore playing poverty and despair. But there is something patronizing in these performers' radiant glee in enacting economic misery' (30).

Such sentiments have been echoed in more recent assessments of Bolt's oeuvre. Cynthia Zimmerman, for example, reads the 'epic-romance' engendered by the collective playmaking process as an apolitical form that transforms the trekkers' journey 'into a mythic quest undertaken by larger-than-life characters.' For Zimmerman, this means that Bolt's 'wish to entertain was obviously more important than fully engaging the socio-political complexities of the tragedy' (36). One implication of Zimmerman's critique is that anti-realist aesthetics have no purchase on the political. In a 1982 interview with Zimmerman, Bolt describes her anti-realist conception of the documentary:

> I don't think they are documentaries. A documentary implies that the value of the piece rests in its faithfulness to history and its factual base. I would like to think that the value of my plays lies in their theatricality and their entertaining qualities. I think they're 'true,' but history is really only their starting point. What I'm trying for in all of the things I'm doing now is an epic kind of adventure or romance form. ('Carol Bolt' 268)

Bolt's resistance to the mimetic denotation of the term 'documentary' anticipates the work of many critics and theorists in Canada and elsewhere who, a decade or so after this interview, insisted on theorizing the term 'documentary' not as the frumpy realist alternative to modernist and postmodernist experimentation, but rather as a form that estranges the document's claim to truth through the use of juxtaposition, for example.[16]

Contrary to many readings of *Buffalo Jump*, I contend that the sometimes surreal aesthetics of abundance in the play effect at least four important moves, all of which are politically charged. First, the mobile bodies of the actors in the Passe Muraille production of *Buffalo Jump* resist the carceral strategies of government aimed at the unemployed of the 1930s (and, to a lesser extent, the 1970s), while offering a playful rebuttal of an image that circulated frequently in right-wing newspapers in the 1970s – the image of the lazy, inert, self-indulgent, unemployed but grant-dependent youth.[17] To be sure, the Passe Muraille collective had avoided job-creation grants but was actively seeking funds from the provincial arts council and the Canada Council in these years, and this stereotype was likely one that resonated deeply with the members of the collective. Indeed, their 1971 collective creation *Free Ride* attests to an awareness of the stereotype of the 'deliberately' unemployed youth, staging, according to Urjo Kareda's review for the *Toronto Star* (1 October 1971), a 'comic evocation' of road tripping that is full of 'irony' and 'self-criticism' (60). Kareda exemplifies this interpretation with a description of a clearly satirical sequence in which each member of the cast sits in a 'little spot of isolation,' chanting adjectives about his or her situation.

The dissonant sounds of 'alone,' 'desperate,' 'rejected,' and so on eventually merge into a collective 'whimper of baby sounds' (60).

Second, the aesthetics of abundance in *Buffalo Jump* reminds the audience of a contradiction: if the 1930s was a decade of scarcity, it was simultaneously a decade of plenitude. As Rifkind argues, this was a 'period of remarkable activity and innovation,' marked by 'counter-images and oppositional narratives of impassioned speeches, secret meetings, clandestine presses and radical pamphlets, workplace organizing, agricultural cooperatives and agrarian radicalism, the On-to-Ottawa trek, parades, rallies, banners, and celebrations of a culture of resistance and defiance' (*Comrades* 12). *Buffalo Jump* explicitly plays on the 'dialectic of scarcity and abundance' that Rifkind identifies. In act 2, for example, the strikers are riding the rails 'on to Ottawa' in order to demand 'work and wages' from the Bennett government. In Kamloops, their first stop after departing from Vancouver, they fail to find the hot meal promised by the local Orange Lodge, and the strikers construe this as a betrayal of both their bodies and their spirits. However, Red Evans – Bolt's amalgamation of trek leaders Red Walsh and Arthur 'Slim' Evans – insists that the lack must be converted into plenitude: 'But when we get to Ottawa, who is it going to be able to talk from the gut? R.B Bennett. Iron Heel Bennett with an apple in his mouth? Or guys who've been hungry. I thought you were hungry to get to Ottawa' (2.5). The scene that follows is set in Golden, and it is a riotous bricolage of opera, barbershop harmonics, and union barn burners. Complementing this aural celebration is a feast laid out by the community in the 'sylvan glade':

> Mayor: Welcomed be! Welcomed be! Welcomed be!
> As mayor of the village of Golden
> I greet you with open arms
> With infinite love and compassion
> And virtues old fashion … ed.
> We have prepared food for you. (2.9)

The strikers are invited by the dryadic members of the Ladies Aid to fill their growling bellies with 'beef stew with cabbage, beets, and celery too,' 'macaroni salad, Russian salad, Jelly salad and toss-ed salad,' 'cauliflower, radishes and rhubarb,' 'chocolate cake and strawberry shortcake, home made ice cream, apple pie' (2.9–10). Clearly embodied in this demonstrative, even excessive, welcome is a strong civic spirit and desire to make conditions better for those in the community and passing through it.

The third aspect of the play's commentary on the abundance of the 1930s is less celebratory. Indeed, *Buffalo Jump* is sensitive to the problems that attend a recuperation of the decade's plenitude. In Zimmerman's 1982 interview, Bolt insists that what distinguishes her plays from the mimetic conception of documentary is her use of 'heroic,' 'larger than ordinary' characters ('Carol Bolt' 268). Crucially, Bolt claims that such treatments of historical figures depend on documentary evidence – in this case key 'images' and turns of phrase that Bennett infamously deployed in his speeches – but she insists that the final, inflated character is 'a cartoon of himself, really' ('Carol Bolt' 267–8), a parody which is clearly reflected in set designer John Boyle's large cartoon cut-outs of Bennett. This strategy of inflation for satirical effect obviously critiques Bennett's bombast, but it also comments on the problem of inflating individuals in the process of historical recuperation. More interestingly, it is not just Bennett but also Red Evans who is the inflated object of parody, a fact most obviously indicated in the way the play collapses two historical figures into the portmanteau of Red Evans. Towards the end of act 1, Evans identifies his role as leader of the trek by gesturing to his own cut-out and saying, 'That's Red Evans there. 1914 Hero. 1935 Bum' (2.34). By acknowledging the processes by which individuals become messianic, larger-than-life leaders, the play critiques a nostalgic recuperation of the Depression. Indeed, even the trekkers in *Buffalo Jump* are the objects of a distorting idealization and inflation, a fact that is particularly clear during the march through Calgary when the 'Lady Poet' who swoons over the men quotes line after line of verse and prose that commemorates or romanticizes masculine bravery in war (2.63–5).[18] Moreover, while other histories of the Depression from this period, such as Barry Broadfoot's *Ten Lost Years* (1973) and Liversedge's *Recollections of the On to Ottawa Trek*, claim to offer the reader pure, documentary encounters with the Depression (and to this end silence editorial intervention), *Buffalo Jump* ironizes these encounters through, for example, transparent scene changes.

Finally, the aesthetics of abundance staged in *Buffalo Jump* provokes the audience to consider what full employment would *actually* look like. Full employment was both R.B. Bennett's quixotic 1930 election promise – as the first scene of *Buffalo Jump* reminds us – and, later, a stated goal of Keynesianism. As discussed above, federal policy makers in Canada were never strongly committed to the goal of full employment in the decades that followed the Second World War, preferring instead to emphasize the role of the private sector in the labour market (Muszynski 253); indeed,

Keck's analysis of the OFY and the LIP indicates that even intervention-ist strategies like job-creation programs were considered 'residual' tools and, unsurprisingly, did not have a significant effect on lowering rates of unemployment in the early 1970s, a contention that contemporary government reviews of OFY, for example, corroborate (212).[19] It is re-vealing in this context to consider that the Economic Council of Canada had pegged full employment at 3 per cent unemployment in the 1960s. By the 1970s the rate was 5 per cent, and at the end of that decade, when unemployment averaged 7.5 per cent, the council had discarded the Keynesian concept altogether (Muszynski 278).

The Passe Muraille production of *Buffalo Jump* had a cast of eleven actors who played a total of more than twenty-nine different parts. In addition to this large cast, Bolt and Thompson exploited the potential of the audience and the props to create a 'mass' effect. Recalling the tech-niques of agitprop, the stage directions frequently instruct the actors to move through the audience and to treat them as fellow strikers, commu-nity members, and so on. Moreover, the massive 'cut-out workers' creat-ed by Boyle are used to suggest a 'sense of mass,' when, for example, the strikers march through the streets of Calgary in act 2 (2.14). The fullness of the cast and these 'mass' effects, coupled with the plenitude evoked in the play's aesthetics and its activation of Depression-era protest against unemployment, urge the audience to recall the unfulfilled promise of Keynesian demand management – the promise that formed a central component of the postwar compact between state and labour.

Job-creation grants like the LIP encouraged a new dependence on the state for many fledgling cultural organizations – a dependence that Passe Muraille director Paul Thompson claimed to be resisting in the name of creative flexibility and autonomy. The Passe Muraille produc-tion of *Buffalo Jump* staged its commentary on the legacies of Canadian labour-market policy just as the post-Fordist global economy and the shift to monetarist economic policy were transforming the relation be-tween the state and workers, shifting labour-market policy toward 'real work' on infrastructure and private-sector initiatives; transforming the social rights of citizenship into what would become, by the 1990s, a con-cept of 'entrepreneurial citizenship' (Brodie 390); and turning artistic labour to more narrowly economic ends via an emerging cultural-indus-tries strategy.[20] The emerging emphasis on 'real work' in labour-market policy after the mid-1970s had much to do with the changing conception of unemployment. As Keck shows, the shift to monetarism in federal policy in this period reflects, among other things, a growing belief in government that those who constituted the highest proportion of the unemployed – women and youths – were often secondary wage earners who were 'choosy' about work and thus artificially inflated unemployment rates (220–1). This was called, in the words of Harvard economist Martin Feldstein, the 'new unemployment,' and it 'raised considerable scepticism' about the state's responsibility for ensuring high levels of employment (Keck 221, 223).

In her 1982 interview with Zimmerman, Bolt recalls that she began revising the script of what became *Buffalo Jump* with George Luscombe at Toronto Workshop Productions before she began her work with Paul Thompson at Passe Muraille. Prompted to describe the differences between the styles of these two directors, Bolt muses:

> I was very influenced by George and I still use a lot of his terminology, 'objectives' for example, and the way that he breaks down a script into units. A 'unit' for Luscombe is the French scene. There's a real technique to working with George. You sit down and analyze the script, and every actor decides what is his object in each unit. You have to go through this process endlessly which I don't really find valuable now. It's too rigid. It's meant to codify the script and I don't think that's useful for a writer. ('Carol Bolt' 267)[21]

Filewod's reading of documentary theatre traditions similarly articulates this gap between Luscombe's method and the collective documentary work of the alternative theatres. While Toronto Workshop Productions, like Passe Muraille, 'represents an extension of a theatrical tradition that can be traced back to the Workers' Theatre Movement of the 1930s and ultimately to [German playwright Erwin] Piscator,' documentaries such as Luscombe's *Ten Lost Years* did not influence the alternatives because it does not 'embody the process of radical redefinition of theatrical form' – i.e., the rejection of the theatrical text and the roles of director and playwright in favour of a 'performance of findings' based on local materials (*Collective Encounters* 78). Consequently, *Ten Lost Years* is a play of the Old Left – 'retrospective rather than active,' 'didactic' rather than interventionist (*Collective Encounters* 78).

The play *Ten Lost Years* is a full-length musical adaptation of Broadfoot's bestselling oral history of the Depression (although it also includes material from James Gray's 1966 memoir *The Winter Years* and Horn's *The Dirty Thirties*), and it opened at Toronto Workshop Productions just three months after the publication of Broadfoot's book by Doubleday

Canada. Although actors chose the material from the book that compelled them, the material was then arranged by Toronto Workshop Productions veteran Jack Winter and scored by Cedric Smith (Filewod, *Collective Encounters* 62). The play was 'highly successful': it played for seventeen weeks to a sold-out house in Toronto and subsequently toured western and then Atlantic Canada. With sponsorship from the Department of External Affairs, it was produced at the Holland Festival and in theatres in the United Kingdom. A finalist for the Chalmers Award in 1974, *Ten Lost Years* was remounted by Toronto Workshop Productions in 1975 and 1976, and was adapted for a sixty-minute television play for the CBC in 1975 ('Jack Winter' 185–6).

Key factors in Filewod's reading of *Ten Lost Years* as a 'retrospective' rather than 'active' documentary are the source material on which the play draws and the method by which this material was interpreted for performance. Intensified because distilled and condensed several times, the anecdotes of the 'people' that form the 'presentational montage' of the play present the Depression as 'romantic nostalgia' – 'as a time of greater extremes than our own, a time in which moral issues were less ambiguous and shared adversity gave birth to a social unity since lost' (Filewod, *Collective Encounters* 63). Broadfoot was clearly aware of the nostalgic power of a past figured in terms of its social and moral cohesiveness; in an interview in the *Toronto Star* (2 February 1974), he described the project that followed *Ten Lost Years* (an oral history of the Second World War) as a 'natural sequel,' but noted that he planned to follow this project with a history of the settlement of the west because 'from 1945 Canada becomes fragmented' (H1). Crucial to the 'retrospective' quality of the dramatic adaptation of *Ten Lost Years* is the maintenance of the past-tense narration that is a feature of Broadfoot's book. This is not a play about contemporary economic or social problems, despite the fact that many reviewers of the play and its television adaptation make connections to 'the oil crisis, ever-mounting inflation and mass layoffs in the auto plants.'[22] Cast in the terms familiar to Canadian audiences by the mid-1970s, the Depression as presented in the play is a unifying experience for the nation. Each region is represented, and often anecdotes from different regions share the space of the stage simultaneously. While there are some conflicting points of view in the play, the emphasis is clearly placed on unity: for example, the frequent use of mimed freight-car hopping underscores, as in scene 19, the way in which each man helps out the one behind him. Recalling the character types employed in agitprop, the characters in *Ten Lost Years* are abstractions only – a 'Quiet

Man,' a 'Farm Wife,' a 'Salesman' – and their typicality is emphasized in comments such as 'really there was nothing unusual about us' (Smith and Winter 142). The frequent use of the second person also actuates the effect of typicality, drawing the audience into a shared past.

The 1974 western Canadian tour of *Ten Lost Years* drew actively on this concept of a lost social unity embodied in the Depression. Funded by a new body within the Canada Council – the Touring Office – the mobility of the tour speaks to the changed conditions in which unemployment was articulated by artists in the 1970s. Unlike the mobile agitprop troupes of the early 1930s that relied on private donations and borrowed vehicles, the *Ten Lost Years* troupe enjoyed state-sponsored mobility of a new kind, and with them they took a message that was more about the unity of the Popular Front than the polarizing politics of the Third Period. In jarring contrast to the transient mobility of the play, in which freight trains are 'covered with men, going absolutely nowhere' (Smith and Winter 143), the vividly red promotional brochure for the national tour boasts 'an exciting touring concept!':

> Though *Ten Lost Years* will open its 78 day tour with a week-long run in the magnificent Hamilton Place, in that city [*sic*], play the National Arts Centre in Ottawa for a week and enjoy extended runs in major centres such as Vancouver, Calgary and Winnipeg, it will also visit communities like the copper mining town of Manitowadge, the paper making towns of Marathon, Terrace Bay, Dryden and Fort Frances, all in Ontario, the atomic research center of Deep River, Ontario, the Okanagan Valley communities of Kelowna and Penticton and small and medium size places across Saskatchewan and Alberta.[23]

The 'concept' of going into small working-class communities alludes (perhaps unintentionally) to the mobility of the agitprop troupes of the 1930s and authenticates the play's connection to the 'people.' Ironically, then, it was in the smaller centres of southern Saskatchewan that *Ten Lost Years* brought the touring office of the Canada Council under fire for 'being insensitive to regional interests and foisting bad-language plays' that are 'overly concerned with sex' on audiences.[24] Although such controversies suggest that Toronto Workshop Productions' interpretation of a national past was not uniformly shared by all Canadians, the promotional poster brims with assurances that this is 'theatre that tells us about ourselves and our past ... To this day, there are none among us not in some way touched by the Great Canadian Depression.' The poster goes on to emphasize the documentary appeal of the play, which permits transparent access to a common past: 'In *Ten Lost Years* the actors become real live human beings, who speak to us directly of an important stage in our past.'[25]

Documentary authenticity was clearly central to the success of the play, which opens with a casual reminder to the audience: 'Something else you oughta know is that the songs and stories you're about to hear are the real stories of the real people all across Canada who survived the Depression. And they're all true' (Smith and Winter 138). Staging a transparent encounter with the past in the same manner that the current cover of Hugh Garner's *Cabbagetown* does, the play and the promotional discourse it generated largely silence the slippage between event and memory, oral anecdote and edited text. Yet the play is not entirely absent of self-consciousness about the act of representation: in scene 9, for example, a typically unreliable radio garbles the voice of the Prince of Wales as he announces his abdication, and a 'decision that will affect us all very deeply' is nothing more than incomprehensible static (Smith and Winter 146). However, such irony is entirely absent from the promotional material.

There is irony of another sort in the house program for the 1974 show at Hamilton Place (which inaugurated the first national tour): in addition to a photograph of a family of Saskatchewan 'drouth refugees' (taken from Gray's *The Winter Years*) who look surprisingly like John Steinbeck's Joad family, the program features a reproduction of Dorothea Lange's 1936 photograph 'Migrant Mother,' a central image in the artistic canon of the Resettlement Administration and one of the most famous images of the U.S.-American Popular Front (Denning 80, 137). If the national tour of *Ten Lost Years* was telling 'us about ourselves and our past,' these iconic U.S.-American images of the Depression suggest that such a narrative of homogeneous experience and recovery overlaid complex political, economic, and social histories. Importantly, they also link the popular recuperation of the 1930s in Canada to what Denning calls the U.S.-American 'grapes of wrath' narrative of the Popular Front. This narrative, popularized in the 1940 film adaptation of Steinbeck's novel, gained much of its discursive and visual power from the fact that it figures the crisis of the Depression as a natural disaster, situates a 'New Deal utopia' as its 'happy ending,' and is 'told as a story of white Protestant "plain people"' (Denning 265–7). While *Buffalo Jump* uses Depression-era unemployment to critique the incompleteness of the contemporary welfare state, *Ten Lost Years* offers a good example of a popular recuperation of the Depression that casts that decade as a time of folksy simplicity and lost national unity – a time of crisis, to be sure, but one that was created less by the contradictions of capitalism than by unavoidable calamities of weather.

Citing and Circulating Depression-Era Unemployment: History, Memoir, Popular Culture, Fiction

Like the playwrights of the period, historians such as Victor Hoar, Michiel Horn, and James Struthers turned to the 1930s in order to document a national history of radicalism, citizen participation, and the struggles of the Depression-era unemployed, and to urge Canadians to remember the importance of these histories in a period of rising unemployment. As Todd McCallum observes, the popular and academic histories of the 1960s and '70s played crucial roles in shaping contemporary conceptions of the 'images and stories' of the Depression (89); however, McCallum finds much more consistency in these historical narratives than I do. Like Garner's 1968 edition of *Cabbagetown*, some tend to fashion the Depression as a foundational moment for a nation that has now come of age. Gray's popular history of the Depression as it played out in the prairie provinces, *The Winter Years*, certainly falls into this category. Gray's thesis is that 'so much was learned from the depression that it will never happen again' (7). Armed with the land-management techniques developed at the Dominion Experimental Farms and the Keynesian vision of the welfare state, the mature nation may confront natural and economic disasters in the future, but such problems 'can now be managed and lived with, an impossibility during the depression' (215).

By contrast, however, the academic histories of Horn and Struthers are critical of an incomplete welfare state and wary of narratives that cast the Depression-era unemployed as victims saved by the courageous, interventionist state. Historians such as Horn were uneasy with popular readings of the Depression for other reasons, as well. For instance, in a 1976 analysis of the legacies of the Depression, Horn suggestively argues that 'the current interest in the Depression' has less to do with the fears of the poor than with middle-class paranoia: the very poor, Horn reminds us, live in much the same fashion that they did during the 1930s ('The Great Depression' 47–9).

The efforts of academic historians were complemented by the memoirs of Steve Brodie, Ronald Liversedge, and Sydney Hutcheson. Those memoirs penned by Communist Party members, such as Brodie's and Liversedge's, insist on the radicalization of the working class in the 1930s. Liversedge's memoir of the 1935 On-to-Ottawa trek, *Recollections of the On to Ottawa Trek*, idealizes communist solidarity for young Canadians of the 1970s, and Brodie's account of his leadership of the 1938 Vancouver Sit-Down Strike, *Bloody Sunday* (1974), eviscerates the claim that the CCF resolved the strike with a politics of conciliation and insists on the collective power of the strikers' passive resistance. Given the documentary appeal of so many of the historical and artistic representations of the Depression in the 1970s, it is crucial to note that historian Victor Hoar edited Liversedge's text and silenced his interventions, creating a set of 'recollections' that must be read not as transparent representations of Liversedge's experiences, but as an academic's rendering of a retrospective worker's account. Sean Griffin, who introduces and concludes Brodie's memoir, notes that 'renewed public interest in the depression years' led Brodie to worry that precisely this kind of editorial intervention would destroy his text: according to Griffin, Brodie did not want his account to be distorted or 'recast' in the image of an editor who would not respect the straightforwardness of a 'working-class story' (qtd in Livesay, *Right Hand* 271). Griffin (who was also a former organizer for the CPC in British Columbia) thus casts Brodie's history as the true account in a struggle for the past that was being waged in the 1970s. The principal opponent motivating Brodie's and Griffin's sectarian history was Harold Winch, the leader of the British Columbia CCF during the Sit-Down, who published what Griffin calls a 'self-glorifying account' of the strike in the *Vancouver Province* and who was being hailed in the 1970s as the politician who engineered the peaceful departure of the strikers from the Vancouver Art Gallery (qtd in Livesay, *Right Hand* 271).[26]

Other memoirs are less convinced about the widespread radicalization of the unemployed in the 1930s but do find in the decade a lesson about the nation's failure to mobilize real political and economic change. For example, Tom McGauley reads worker-writer Sydney Hutcheson's *Depression Stories* (1976) as proof that the social-democratic 'solution' to the 'pain' of the 1930s was and is able 'to do no more than humanize the face of capitalism,' and urges contemporary readers in the midst of 'another major economic rupture' to 'more progressive political action' (ix–x). McGauley casts Hutcheson as a 'Classic old CCF'er,' and faults this commitment with limiting Hutcheson's ability to call for radical social change (vii). Yet Hutcheson, who spent his life working in the east and west Kootenays, narrates stories of the Depression that similarly insist on a failed reformism. For example, he offers a critique of the present by lamenting the 'freedom' that was lost with the advent of the bureaucratic socialism of the postwar welfare state, epitomized by the Unemployment Insurance Act:

> From the time I left school in 1929 until 1941 I was as free as a bird. I could go where I wanted to, live as I wanted to, work if I wanted to, play around if I wanted to – because I was an individual with a name and I had a thousand personal friends who were all as free as I was. But with this freedom was also responsibility. As an individual I could do all the things stated, but it was up to me to fend for myself and maintain a standard of living. Therefore if I did not work I did not eat, and after going hungry for a few days, the responsibility to myself came in a real hurry. The young people of today have a kind of freedom that I hate because there is no responsibility with it. In 1940–41 the Unemployment Act was brought into being, and after every citizen in Canada had been stamped with a permanent number for the first time, that was the beginning of the end. (115)

In many ways, Hutcheson's political commentary is paradoxical. On the one hand, his argument provides evidence of his internalization of interwar state discourses of work and worklessness. The greatest source of concern for relief administrators in 1930s Canada was that aid from the state (whether in the form of relief or contributory unemployment insurance) would create a disincentive to work, and so relief measures were modelled on the nineteenth-century conception of 'less eligibility' (in which any and all relief is rendered 'less eligible' than the worst-paid work) (Struthers, *No Fault* 7–9). By suggesting that he would be able to find work and feed himself in the direst of economic crises, Hutcheson presents himself as the model citizen for interwar policy discourse. Despite this very suggestive example of the principle of self-governance – in which state discourse is instrumentalized through an individual – Hutcheson actively resists the notion that the state should govern the work ethic of individual citizens and instead engages a concept of 'freedom.'[27] According to Hutcheson, the coddled youth of the 1970s had no understanding of his notion of freedom; nonetheless, many New Leftists of the period championed the power of grassroots and community-level action over the bureaucratic administration of a top-heavy state, and, in this sense, Hutcheson's memoir shares some ground with New Left thought. Indeed, *Depression Stories* brims with anecdotes of men and women helping one another out in ways that deliberately ignore, circumvent, or render unnecessary the possibility of state intervention: 'whist drives' at the local Union Hall, picnics and sport days at the city park in Fernie, a reading room maintained by the unemployed that featured a radio 'donated by someone,' a borrowed truck that enables him to hunt deer and caribou for food (and which he barters for dressed and roasted meat), a meeting hall in Naksup donated by the local mill owner that is converted into a gymnasium by the men in the community, and a snow-slide that is cleared by volunteer workers who 'felt they were contributing something to the town and society as a whole' (52). Furthermore, it is the period before relief was available from the provincial and federal governments that Hutcheson remembers most fondly – and in the most detail.

Notwithstanding his reservations about Hutcheson's political 'vision,' McGauley is enthusiastic about Hutcheson's unrefined narrative style, which he represents as the epitome of documentary transparency: 'There is rather a vogue of "oral history" at the moment – and the tape-recorded interview has its own valuable brand of authenticity. But Sydney Hutcheson's achievement is more remarkable in that he did not have an interviewer to egg him on and tell him that what he was doing was valuable' (McGauley viii–ix). McGauley disdainfully refers to but does not name journalist Barry Broadfoot's tremendously popular oral history of the 'everyday' experiences of the Depression, *Ten Lost Years*, which was published three years before *Depression Stories*. The most popular recuperation of the Depression in 1970s Canada, Broadfoot's oral history was inspired by U.S.-American Studs Terkel's *Hard Times: An Oral History of the Depression* (1970) and might also be situated in relation to 'the 1960s obsession with documentary and folk authenticity,' a continental phenomenon evident in the reprinting in this decade of James Agee's and Walker Evans's *Let Us Now Praise Famous Men* (1941) (Denning 119). Like Liversedge's account, the stories of 'ordinary,' unnamed Canadians in *Ten Lost Years* were edited, and Broadfoot does not indicate his presence in the text. Insisting that this is nevertheless a book of and for the people, Broadfoot admits in his preface that 'I had to do some editing of most interviews because people just do not talk simply and economically. Listen to anyone tell a story and you will understand; they ramble. So I did compress the story where necessary, although I always tried to keep the individual flavour of the storytellers' tale' (vi).

The tremendous popularity of Broadfoot's history – in 1982 it was in its seventh printing, and in the mid-1970s it was adapted for the stage (by Toronto Workshop Productions) and screen (by CBC Television) – offers evidence of how the Depression functioned as a site of popular nostalgia in 1970s Canada, particularly for those who had lived through the decade. In Sid Adilman's article for the *Toronto Star* about the success of *Ten Lost Years* (2 February 1974), Broadfoot gloats that he had predicted his book's 'roaring success': 'As far as I was concerned, it was always a winner. It was riding a wave; the 1930s are nostalgia now – the music, the Waltons. I picked up that wave and rode the crest like a good surfer' (H1). In his preface to the catalogue for the 1975 exhibition Canadian Painting in the Thirties at the National Gallery of Canada, John Sutherland Boggs (then director of the National Gallery) similarly observes the 'fashion' for the 1930s in 'films, revivals in dress, music and literature' but is careful to distinguish the high-cultural 'seriousness' of the exhibition from popular recuperations (Hill, *Canadian Painting* 7).[28]

As McCallum points out, a central feature of liberal-nationalist histories of the Depression, such as Broadfoot's but also L.M. Grayson and Michael Bliss's *The Wretched of Canada*, is an emphasis on the helplessness of the Depression-era poor, who passively waited while 'reform-minded politicians led them to the promised land of the welfare state' (93). Bliss pursues a similar argument in his preface to the 1975 reprint of Leonard Marsh's 1943 *Report on Social Security for Canada*, in which he contends that the growth of the 'modern welfare state since the end of the 1930s' is a 'major event in the society's history': 'No one can minimize the importance of our transition from a society in which provision for destitution was largely an individual responsibility to one in which a variety of programs guarantees a level of social and economic security to all citizens' (ix). According to Bliss, the 'social minimum' that postwar reformers such as Marsh were calling for was actually realized; according to other histories of social security in Canada, such as Guest's *The Emergence of Social Security in Canada* or Alan Moscovitch and Jim Albert's *The 'Benevolent' State*, this is far from true.

Like some historians and memoirists, left-nationalist literary historians and critics in English Canada found much to celebrate in the cultural history of the 1930s. Several anthologies and collections corralled texts from the 1930s as proof of a storied socialist tradition and as a means of asserting an independent national culture. For example, the socialist publishing collective New Hogtown Press of Toronto contributed explicitly leftist collections to the New Left revival of the 1930s. Richard Wright and Robin Endres edited a collection of plays from the Canadian Workers' Theatre in 1976, and the publishers' preface to the collection insists on the continued relevance in 'post-industrial society' of both the condition of joblessness and the Third Period tactics for representing this condition: 'Similarly, at a time when unemployment has again become a familiar aspect of our common everyday life, the agitprop version of the experience of joblessness is still closer to the mark than that of our best journalists and most of our politicians' (New Hogtown vii). If the publishers' preface interprets the Workers' Theatre movement as one that was 'cut off' by the movement of the CPC toward Popular Front tactics (New Hogtown x), Endres's introduction explicitly contradicts this argument, following what had become by the 1970s 'party orthodoxy' insofar as it posits the 'evolutionary continuity' of the theatre movement and avoids linking the Workers' Theatre to the CPC (Filewod, 'Performance and Memory' 71). According to Filewod, such a contradiction speaks to the conflicted conditions in which New Leftists recalled the 1930s in the 1970s, and to the effects of the 'culture of secrecy' nourished within an underground party and 'fossilized by the real persecutions of the 1950s (and beyond)' ('Performance and Memory' 70). In 1979, New Hogtown Press also published Donna Phillips's *Voices of Discord*, an anthology of English-Canadian short fiction from the 1930s, all of which originally appeared in *Masses, New Frontier*, the *Canadian Forum*, and *Queen's Quarterly*. In his lengthy introduction, Kenneth J. Hughes identifies two tasks for cultural critics in 1970s Canada, both of which are equally pressing: he calls for a reappropriation of 'Canadian literature' from the 'liberal' 'ruling establishment' and a non-sectarian definition of a 'left literary and critical tradition' (11–12).[29]

More liberal than leftist in its reading of the legacies of the Depression, the 1976 anthology *The Depression in Canadian Literature* (1976) emphasizes the thematic importance of this period in the nation's literature. Unlike *Voices of Discord*, the collection omits material originally published in *Masses* and favours the voices of those writers who congregated around the social-democratic *Canadian Forum*. Edited by Sheila A. Brooks and Alice K. Hale, the collection forms part of Macmillan's 'Themes in Canadian Literature' series, which also features thematic studies of 'Canadian Humour and Satire,' 'Isolation in Canadian Literature,' and 'Canadian Myths and Legends.' In their terse introduction, Brooks and Hale note the 'renewed interest in the Depression era' in 1970s Canada (of the eighteen fictional and non-fictional texts reprinted in the book, six are contemporary representations of the 1930s), but do not speculate at any length about the causes of this interest, aside from noting that the Depression years 'permanently changed the political nature of Canada,' while paradoxically scarring and enriching 'our literature and our very identity' (2). *The Depression in Canadian Literature* thus suggests that its interest in the 1930s hinges on an imagining of the decade's scarcity that serves as a contrast to the more affluent present. The editors' choice of a story like Alice Munro's 'Walker Brothers Cowboy,' which first appeared in her debut collection *Dance of the Happy Shades*, seems an ironic one in light of this contrast. Much of Munro's short fiction from the 1960s and '70s explores Depression-era southwestern Ontario from the perspective of the narrator's present, and some have critiqued the way that the 'retrospective glance' that characterizes this fiction implies that 'the narrator and character have both been transported from the lived situation and are commenting from some safely remote place' that 'does not resemble poverty' (Rimstead 109–10). Yet if 'Walker Brothers Cowboy' boasts a retrospective narrative point of view, it is nevertheless a particularly evocative treatment of the richness – the 'weathers, and distances you cannot imagine' – that lies beneath the apparently colourless, noiseless, and threadbare 'nineteen-thirties' (Munro 18, 8).

New Left ideas assumed a different form in Quebec, where an anti-colonial movement critiqued foreign economic and political domination within the province and resisted the homogeneity implied by ostensibly progressive English-Canadian appeals to the 'people.' After 1960 and until about 1980, francophone Quebec was the 'storm-centre' of New Left politics in Canada, a politics that was 'constructed, in part, as a formation that rejected the active centralizing federal state' imagined in social-democratic texts like David Lewis and F.R. Scott's *Make This Your Canada* (1943) (McKay, 'For a New Kind' 112). As McKay observes, the Quiet Revolution, which merged socialist and nationalist ideologies to powerful effect, posed a tremendously thorny problem for anglophone socialists of the third and fourth formations because it 'inherently called into question the "Canadian subject position" with which Canadian socialists, both Communist and CCF, had identified since the late 1930s' ('For a New Kind' 112). The mostly English-Canadian 'Waffle' movement similarly troubled the nationalism of the New Democratic Party (NDP). For its 'Manifesto for an Independent Socialist Canada,' which called, among other things, for a recognition of the existence of two nations within Canada, the Waffle was expelled from the NDP in 1972 (Penner, *From Protest* 101–2).

If ownership of the means of cultural production was a key issue for the English-Canadian left-nationalists who congregated around presses such as New Hogtown, New Canada, and Steel Rail, this issue also played a crucial role in left-nationalist movements in Quebec: 'Books and printed matter were at the centre of a huge undertaking: a rereading of the past, a rewriting of history, and a reform of political and cultural institutions' (Gerson and Michon, 'Editors' Introduction' 8). McKay similarly notes the importance of 'extra-parliamentary' phenomena to the activities of the gauchistes, including a 'thriving left-wing press' that produced periodicals such as *La Revue socialiste, Parti pris, Québec Libre, Résistance, Révolution québécoise,* and *Socialisme québécois* ('For a New Kind' 113). According to McKay, this radical press was complemented by a 'mass media alive to marxisant and independentist ideas,' which is proof of a 'socialist cultural ferment whose only close parallel in Canadian history was the radical labour upsurge of 1917–1922' ('For a New Kind' 113–14).

As in English Canada, some of the texts that emerged from the left-wing press of this period explicitly recall Depression-era unemployment: a very early example is Jean-Jules Richard's *Journal d'un hobo: l'air est bon à manger,* which was written between 1958 and 1965 and published by Parti pris as a livre de poche in 1965. *Journal* is a retrospective, semi-autobiographical account of the author's experiences as a transient and as a participant in the Hunger March on Ottawa in the 1930s. Although Richard was not well known even within Quebec during the 1960s, his leftist themes and his exploration of working-class settings and conflicts (in novels such as *Le feu dans l'amiante* [1956]) profoundly influenced the writers associated with the political and cultural periodical *Parti pris* (1963–8) (Solie 965). As Victor-Laurent Tremblay observes in one of the only critical studies of *Journal d'un hobo,* the fact that *Parti pris* operated as the representative of the sexual countercultures of the U.S.-American beat generation in Quebec makes it unsurprising that the publishing enterprise associated with the periodical published *Journal d'un hobo,* 'livre qui, selon la publicité du temps, avait été refusé auparavant par tous les autres éditeurs à cause de son pouvoir d'étonnant' (63).[30]

Uniquely, Richard's novel employs as its protagonist an androgynous transient ('une bardache') who struggles to come of age in a repressive, prejudicial, and bourgeois environment. Given the characteristics of New Left politics in Quebec during the latter half of the 1960s, such a figure seems an obvious trope for the marginalization of the Québécois within predominantly anglophone Canada; however, this is not Richard's primary theme. Neither is unemployment a central concern of this text, which is perhaps unsurprising given that it, like Gray's *The Winter Years,* was written in the early 1960s rather than the early 1970s, when rising unemployment rates were beginning to attract considerable media and state attention. If writers and activists in the 1930s and the 1970s tended to employ the transient figure as a comment on a problem of

political economy, the cross-country itinerary of Richard's jobless youth
creates a form for a Bildungsroman of sexual, sensual, and emotional
awakening that celebrates the mobility of the transient. The opening
lines of the novel, for example, declare this thesis:

> Des années que ça dure, cette vie d'appétits! Tel un courrier des Incas, ma
> fonction consiste à dévaler d'une ville à l'autre pour l'embrasement, le soir
> venu, des étoiles filantes. Mangeur d'air; hobo: crève-faim professionnel.
> Au moral comme nature, de corps et d'idéal, ès lettres et sciences. (11)

The novel's critique targets the sexual parochialism of Roman Catholic
Quebec and Protestant English Canada alike, while skewering the ostensible solidarity of the Depression-era unemployed by making the train
that transports the jobless the site of repeated sexual violations perpetrated against the protagonist by his 'comrades.' Unlike the nationalist
myth-making work undertaken by Al Purdy's transient, which finds in
the moving train an analogue for both the speaker's and the nation's
coming of age, the Bildungsroman form of Richard's *Journal d'un hobo*
ultimately insists on the continued marginalization of the sexually different within the space of the nation, going so far as to suggest that the legendary treks of the jobless in the 1930s sought to cure the wrong malady
– state lassitude rather than human rigidity and insensibility.[31] Richard's
reinterpretation of the utopian impulses of socialist realism or socialist romanticism insists not on revolution, but rather on the necessity of
an alternative space for the physical and psychic survival of its ravaged
protagonist. In line with the novel's representation of indigenous and
eastern conceptions of hermaphrodism as the perfection of humanity;[32]
Richard situates this alternative, utopian space in the Chilliwacks of British Columbia, where a legendary tribe of 'géants' embraces the pregnant
hermaphrodite and where 'l'ère de l'amour et celle de repeuplement de
la terre' offers a counterpart to the destruction signalled by the date of
the protagonist's escape into the mountains – 4 September 1939 (288).
Richard was not as fortunate as his fictional counterpart: he enlisted
when Canada joined the Second World War, his regiment was 'decimé,'
and he was wounded, all of which he represents in his searing first novel,
Neuf jours de haïne (1948) ('Jean-Jules' 46).

Just as Richard was at the vanguard of writers in Quebec who were,
in the 1950s and '60s, beginning to prise apart a rigid sexual morality
(Tremblay 63), *Journal d'un hobo* anticipates an element of leftist politics
that continues to this day to struggle for recognition in Quebec and in

the rest of Canada. McKay suggests that it would be 'wishful thinking' to designate 'queer leftism' as one of the leftist formations that have 'attracted or influenced thousands of people, generated hundreds of publications, and created long-lasting and large institutions, libraries, archives, and literatures' (*Rebels* 133). Despite his own commitment to 'queer leftism' and his belief that there is clearly a 'language of leftism oriented to the ideal of liberating sexual minorities,' McKay concedes that '"queer leftism" is a hopeful projection into the future, not a historically significant counter-hegemonic formation that can be documented in Canadian left history' (*Rebels* 133).

In English Canada, Helen Potrebenko's novel *Taxi!* (1975), like Richard's *Journal d'un hobo*, avoids explicit parallels between Depression-era experiences of unemployment and the rising spectre of joblessness that haunted the fragile welfare state of 1970s Canada. *Taxi!* documents the lives of working-class Vancouverites in the early 1970s, when 'recession and inflation and unemployment and war and devaluation' were features of quotidian life (11). The resolutely present-tense perspective of the narrative resists the popular and often nostalgic citations of the Depression in this period – what Rimstead calls the 'tendency in Canadian culture to locate "true" and "deserving" poverty in the distant and discontinuous past while stigmatizing and blaming people who are currently poor' (291). In this sense, Potrebenko's novel might be located in a broad New Leftist interrogation of work and worklessness that includes writers such as Milton Acorn (his 1972 poetry collection *More Poems for People* is a good example), David Fennario, and Patrick Lane, and which anticipated the later work of the writers affiliated with the Kootenay School of Writing in the 1980s. Yet Potrebenko's engagement with contemporary labour-market conditions nevertheless bears intriguing traces of Depression-era Canada.

The child of working-class Ukrainian immigrants, Potrebenko is best known for her leftist interpretation of Ukrainian-Canadian history, *No Streets of Gold: A Social History of Ukranians in Alberta* (1977). Her little-known novel *Taxi!* along with the stories collected in *Hey Waitress and Other Stories* (1989), offers a rarity in English-Canadian writing – fiction about work narrated from the point of view of a working-class woman. What makes *Taxi!* particularly unusual is the type of work its young protagonist does: Shannon drives a cab, and this never fails to solicit a predictable response from her customers, who wonder if she is 'allowed to work nights' and complain that her 'husband shouldn't let [her] do this' (140). If Shannon's work obliges her to navigate the bowels of east-side

Vancouver and thus to practise a mobility that her motley crew of clients finds unsettling, the narrator nevertheless makes it clear that women's mobility is restricted by the collusion of patriarchy and capitalism: 'It was, after all, only men who had enough money to buy airplane tickets in any significant numbers. Women rode buses, or stayed at home' (75). Yet for Shannon, the taxi is a paradoxical physical space that is both precarious – it is owned by someone else and working conditions in the industry are terrible – and relatively safe: 'The car is safe on cold winter mornings. She hates to leave the car even to get a coffee because a woman walking is subject to danger and ridicule whereas in the car she is safe' (14–15). Almost certainly influenced by its Vancouver avatar, *Waste Heritage* (which was reprinted by Macmillan in 1973), *Taxi!* examines the dialectic of threatening mobility and containment, but with a crucial difference embodied in its female protagonist.[33]

A documentary novel like Baird's, *Taxi!* seeks to describe the everyday life of its beleaguered protagonist against the facts and figures of her era. The novel is set in the two years following the October Crisis of 1970, a period of considerable political and economic upheaval, and in sporadic, didactic narrative interventions, the age is described:

> Until the 1960s there had been growth in the manufacturing industries in Canada. This growth ceased and in both primary and secondary industries, technology increased productivity. Thus a large proportion of men were no longer required as workers. There was no war to send them to and historical developments precluded the bourgeois from gassing them, so any number of other strategies were devised. One was to increase the age of youth. Instead of being adults at 16, men were still considered children at 30. Universities increased and expanded to accommodate more students, and trades which had been learned by apprenticeship were now taught in technical schools. All this meant that men were kept off the labour market longer. The service industries continued to expand so that most women did not suffer, or benefit, from an equal extended training period. (10)

Embedded in this economic and demographic abstraction – which surely functions as a satire of the 'bureaucratese' of the day – is Shannon and her friends Bradley and Evelyn, all of whom have painful experiences coming of age, negotiating changing gender roles, and finding autonomy in the unstable labour market of the early 1970s. Driving a cab, the back cover of the first paperback edition tells us, was Potrebenko's solution to her own violent encounter with underemployment in the early 1970s: 'Although all the characters in this novel are fictional, Helen Potrebenko drove a cab in Vancouver for a number of years. At first she was a spare driver while putting herself through University ... upon graduation in 1971, she discovered she was overqualified for a better job and continued driving a cab for several years.' In a reportage piece cheekily entitled 'Woman Driver' (which appeared in *The Pedestal* in October 1970), Potrebenko confirms this history and makes it clear that her fictional character Shannon is modelled very closely on her own experiences 'pushing hack' (7). If the narrator's voice in *Taxi!* is quite clearly an experienced Potrebenko persona, Shannon is treated as the narrator's younger, inexperienced self.

Insofar as the novel critiques the mythology of the welfare state from a perspective that is cognizant of structural racism as well as sexism in the labour market, it participates in a discourse of the period that might also be found in the work of Austin Clarke – the novels of his Toronto Trilogy are notable here – and in George Ryga's play *Indian* (1971), for example. Shannon is a university dropout who turns to cab driving because she has lost her job, she has student loans to pay, and she might as well drive a taxi because 'all women's jobs are bad, so for a woman, it's a job like any other job' (15). Women, 'Indians,' and non-white immigrants are all mostly subject to the same fate; as the narrator tells us in one of the extended reportage sections of the novel, these groups are more or less excluded from the edifice of the welfare state:

> Labour laws are never enforced except against workers so there is no protection for cab drivers. This leads owners into excesses of abuse and all the working conditions taken for granted by all other workers (except for farm workers and domestic labourers) are not available to cab-drivers. These are: the 40 hour week, eight hour day, holidays, lunch breaks, income tax deductions, unemployment insurance, vacation pay, severance pay, minimum wage laws, safety regulations. (17–18)

There is little in the history of the welfare state to celebrate, at least for working-class women like Shannon. Alan Moscovitch and Glenn Drover's dissection of the history of the Canadian welfare state makes a similar point insofar as the authors underscore the basic 'contradiction of the welfare state': 'When social expenditures rise, there is no evidence they fundamentally change the structural basis of Canadian society' (37).

This thesis regarding the limitations of the postwar compact between state and labour touches on a significant bifurcation in 1970s Canada:

if liberal discourses often celebrated the mythology of the welfare state, New Leftists positioned themselves against such liberal myth making, taking issue with the incompleteness of the welfare state or critiquing its role in the maintenance of a capitalist society. Simultaneously, many New Leftists were sceptical of 'an "obsolete communism" and a "sold-out social democracy"' (McKay, *Rebels* 183). Shannon is critical of both of these ideologies: her 'revolution,' for example, is distinctly New Leftist in its challenge to Russia's legacy of 'dictators' (162). Moreover, the 1972 provincial election, in which the NDP took power for the first time in British Columbia, functions as a 'document' in the novel's exploration of the problem of an emptied-out social democracy. Shannon, who regularly lectures her clients about socialism and women's liberation, believes that 'Social Democrats who were seriously out to reform capitalism without changing the economics of it, could indeed cause a few problems' (152). Along with a suspicion of social democracy comes the charge that a middle-class creep endangers the politics of the New Left. The 'hippie philosophy,' embodied in Shannon's bourgeois, yogurt-imbibing friend Gerald (who abandons his parents' middle-class home in favour of the streets), allows capitalism to conduct business as usual and provides an easy target for the narrator's polemical arrows (10). So too does the OFY job-creation program, which is construed as evidence of a 'prying' middle-class encroachment on working-class women's collective undertakings (48). The novel's critique of the discourse of 'citizenship participation' that was articulated in the era's job-creation programs thus rejects the way in which more radical, feminist, and collective notions of citizenship were put to use by the liberal state.

Indeed, working-class women form the crux of this novel's political discourse. In this sense, *Taxi!* is less about New Left politics than it is about feminist challenges to the left. What McKay calls the fifth socialist formation, socialist feminism, endured from the mid-1960s to the mid-1990s and took the shape of a movement in Vancouver in the late 1960s through such organizations as the Vancouver Women's Caucus and events like the 1969 Western Women's Liberation Conference (*Rebels* 198–9; Eichler and Lavigne). Between 1969 and 1973, the Vancouver Women's Caucus published the periodical *The Pedestal*, to which Potrebenko was a 'well-known' contributor (Schofield), authoring pieces like the aforementioned 'Woman Driver'; 'Wendy' (February 1971), a meditation on the problem of befriending other women's children in a capitalist society; 'Zelda' (April 1972), an essay about Nancy Milford's feminist biography of Zelda Fitzgerald; and 'Hospitals Are Sick!' (August

1972), a critique of the 'top-heavy' structure of the B.C. Hospital Employees' Union and its failure to represent its lowest-paid members – women.
Socialist feminism (or, in its early days, 'women's liberation')

> engaged in a two-front struggle: against (and alongside) socialists, who had
> so often spoken a language of universal interests when what they really
> meant were male heterosexual interests, and against (and alongside) lib-
> eral feminists, who had so often spoken of women's advancement without
> probing the material preconditions and class interests of a revived women's
> movement. (McKay, *Rebels* 197)

In 'Marx Never Said,' a February 1972 article for *The Pedestal,* Potrebenko
expresses this ambivalence toward socialism, simultaneously defending
Marx and critiquing the socialist vanguard in Canada that claimed to be
'pointing the way to the Only True Revolution' (14). As both Shannon
and the narrator of *Taxi!* remind us, any second-wave feminism that only
accounts for women who want to be managers will ignore the largest
population of women – the poor, the non-white, and the working class.
    While revising crucial theoretical and practical assumptions of the
Old Left, socialist feminists channelled their male, Depression-era predecessors in events like the 'abortion caravan' to Ottawa undertaken by
seventeen members of the Vancouver Women's Caucus in May 1970.[34]
Protesting the abortion law passed by Parliament in 1969, which fell far
short of legalizing the practice, these women 'decided on a caravan because it was linked a bit to the On to Ottawa Trek of unemployed people
in 1935,' and imagined that they were realizing a 'national scale' of protest that no 'social movement since the thirties' had matched (qtd in
Rebick 37, 39). Although the women's mode of mobility – two cars and
a van – differed from the freight trains of the iconic 1935 trek, many of
the tactics and organizing strategies of the 'abortion caravan' were borrowed from the trek or from the Depression-era cultural left: the Caucus
had a 'guerilla theatre portraying a backstreet abortion'; they relied on
chili served in United Church basements for sustenance en route; they
orchestrated flamboyant entries into cities along the Vancouver-Ottawa
route and solicited media attention wherever it could be had; and they
submitted a list of demands to the prime minister (which were published
in *The Pedestal* in April 1970, well before their arrival in Ottawa) (Rebick
39–40). Yet unlike the trekkers, the members of the caravan all made it
to Ottawa, and were joined by three hundred women and men on Parliament Hill on Mother's Day, although an actual meeting with Prime

Minister Trudeau did not occur until after the Caucus members had returned to Vancouver (Rebick 45–6). It is important to note that the 'abortion caravan' drew on a history of women's protest, as well. In the June 1970 issue of *The Pedestal,* Barbara Hicks reminds readers that, in addition to illegal tag days, marches, and mass meetings, Vancouver women had occupied the offices of Mayor Gerry McGeer on Mother's Day, 1935, in order to support the cause of the Relief Camp strike that eventuated in the On-to-Ottawa trek. However, Hicks notes that the cause of relief-camp workers displaced a women's 'campaign for maternity insurance and birth control clinics': 'This is just another example of women's struggles which throughout history have been adjusted to the struggles of others around them. But the time has now come that women must realize the importance of organizing around the issues which directly affect their own lives' (2).

Taxi! launches a sharp socialist-feminist critique, but it is nonetheless self-consciously aware of its inability to muster a formal equivalent to its politics. If the Vancouver Women's Caucus alluded to the mobility of the 1935 On-to-Ottawa trekkers in its 1970 caravan, *Taxi!* seems more indebted to the immobility of *Waste Heritage.* To quote the strike leader Hep who appears in *Waste Heritage,* this is a novel that has 'no plot, nothing' (247). We know nothing about Shannon's past: she lacks a last name and a family, and, even when the narrator teasingly suggests that she will explain Shannon's 'early life' and how she 'ended up as a driver,' we encounter the obstacle of her passengers' assumption that 'she was given birth to by a taxi,' and an extended reportage on the taxi-driving business follows (14). Rather than following a plotline, the narrative comprises a series of dated 'reports' from Shannon's work shifts, each of which narrates a similar chain of events and conversations. Variety is provided by the fragmented style of the 'reports': the point of view is limited to Shannon, and we see and hear the world as she does, through her rear-view mirror or above the din of a traffic snarl. Yet this novel, quite deliberately and ironically (given its title), goes nowhere. If the comparable immobility of Baird's novel is embedded in the interwar field of cultural production, the stasis of *Taxi!* is produced within a labour market that offered few opportunities for working-class women.

If *Taxi!* is hardly a forward-looking novel, it is one that holds tenaciously yet pessimistically to the trope of the 'new day.' A well-worn figure of radical discourse, the 'new day' is subject to feminist revision here: 'But every morning is a new day, and the next morning Shannon was driving down Granville singing and the city was sparkling like jewels beneath a cold blue sky' (168). This 'new day,' as both a literal passage of time and a metaphor, is caught up in Shannon's method of survival, articulated in the feminist manifesto that appears toward the end of the novel. Exhausted by the role of ministering 'Mama' assigned to her by drunks, Shannon articulates her own power:

> But I like driving a cab. Receptionists, sales clerks, waitresses – they all have to look pleasant all the time. I can snarl if I want. There ain't too many wom-en who can do that. Maybe garment workers are allowed to snarl at their sewing machine. But women mostly have to look pleasant when they're fucking miserable and smile when they're angry. It's a big deal. The city is mine, too. The city belongs to those who know it. There's an arrogance that goes with being a taxi driver. You don't give a fuck about anything and it's been years since I was surprised by anything. We don't, none of us, have very many choices. We can rebel. Organize, when there's a chance. Talk. But it's all this madness. In the end, all we can choose is our kind of mad-ness. If we're strong. I'm strong. (138)

Shannon's clients continually ask her if she is a 'boy' or a 'girl,' and, although the answer is more than apparent to them, the question is prompted by Shannon's refusal to perform the gender codes of femi-nized clerical, sales, and service work, which included, in the 1970s, wear-ing 'panti-hose' (136).[35] McKay contends that this gender troubling was 'in some respects the most radical' aspect of the socialist-feminist forma-tion, calling into question as it did 'the very categories of "men" and "women" through which so much conventional experience and prac-tice were – and are – organized' (*Rebels* 193). Indeed, unlike Baird who metaphorically cross-dresses through the character of Kenny Hughes, Potrebenko insists on literal cross-dressing as a regular practice of every-day life.

To conclude an analysis of such a diverse body of material is difficult. As this history of contemporary socialist formations and their politically interested recuperations of Depression-era unemployment suggests, ci-tations of the 1930s in the 1970s were not uniformly motivated. While nostalgia for the 1930s certainly formed part of the popular recuperation of the Depression, the artistic, intellectual, and political cultures of the 1970s engaged this period diversely, on the one hand celebrating the liberal narrative of the welfare state and on the other hand revealing the fissures evident in this narrative from its inception in the 1940s. What is clear is that the 1970s, a time of rising rates of unemployment, was also a pivotal decade in terms of the discursive reframing of both artistic labour and the phenomenon of joblessness. If writers across the leftist spectrum in the 1930s conceived of the state's role vis-à-vis the jobless as a *responsibility*, many writers by the 1970s were far more skeptical of the possibility that a welfare-state edifice should or could ameliorate the lives of the working poor.

Conclusion: Unemployment in Neoliberal Canada

As I have argued throughout this book, unemployment has been subject to variable discursive framing throughout the twentieth century in Canada. Despite the fact that seasonal, mobile labour – and accompanying seasonal cycles of joblessness – were common in the first decades of the twentieth century, literary histories in Canada have privileged another story: that of the settler-pioneer. The Depression, however, rendered the phenomenon of worklessness more visible in literary culture, particularly the leftist periodical culture that emerged during the 1930s. During the interwar period, activists and writers on the cultural left increasingly construed unemployment insurance as a social right, but the federal state refused responsibility for the jobless. Nonetheless, by the postwar period, the state had affirmed this social right and tentatively committed itself to high levels of employment. Depression-era unemployment, in this context, became the basis of a national Bildungsroman that figures the postwar nation as the mature counterpart of a crisis-plagued youth. In the early 1970s, joblessness came to be seen as a problem particular to women and youth, but the demands of these workers were recognized for only a brief period before the concept of unemployment insurance as a social right of citizenship was eroded in the context of fiscal restraint. Writers affiliated with New Left cultures were often critical of the insufficiency of the welfare state and its supposed protection of the jobless and underemployed, and many of these writers also found their artistic labour framed in new ways by the state they were critiquing.

As the previous chapter argues, the intensification of economic globalization, the shift to monetarist economic policy, and the concomitant rise of neoliberalism from the mid-1970s all signalled a new relation between the state and workers and between the state and citizens. For this reason, I conclude the book in the 1970s, recognizing that the study of cultural producers and their relation to neoliberalism requires tools other than the ones I have employed in this study. In particular, the temporal limits of this book are meant to recognize that recent scholarship on the relations between globalization and the Canadian nation-state and cultural production in Canada are better equipped to analyse the neoliberal present than this project is.[1] This is meant neither to construe the present as closed and inevitable nor to deny Neil Smith's contention that the rise of neoliberalism is connected to a larger historical moment, namely, the 'social and intellectual revolutions of the seventeenth and eighteenth centuries that ushered in a new political economy of bourgeois property rights, market power, and the rule of nation states' (29); however, I do mean to acknowledge a palpable (and ongoing) *intensification* in the present of longer social, economic, and political processes. Nonetheless, in this brief conclusion I would like to offer some tentative thoughts about the current discursive framing of unemployment in relation to the now vigorously examined question of neoliberalism.

Admittedly, the 2008 financial crisis tempered some of the triumphalism of neoliberal discourse. Media references to the Depression were ubiquitous in the weeks and months that followed the collapse of major U.S. banks in the fall of 2008, and John Maynard Keynes and Franklin Delano Roosevelt had not looked so good since the 1940s.[2] Yet now that some of the direst predictions have not been realized (even if the unemployment rate in Canada has budged little), another reading of the Depression is emerging. According to Richard Florida – the director of the Martin Prosperity Institute and Professor of Business and Creativity at the Rotman School of Management in the University of Toronto and author of the bestselling books *The Rise of the Creative Class* (2002) and *Who's Your City* (2008) – the Depression of the 1930s, and all other periods of economic crisis, are 'reset' periods during which capitalism has a chance to innovate and right itself. This Florida argues in his latest publication, appropriately named *The Great Reset: How New Ways of Living and Working Drive Post-Crash Prosperity* (2010). Unsurprisingly in an era when Florida's influential analyses offer up individual innovation as the solution to economic crises, the Depression and the always-precarious welfare state that it anticipated once again look quaint, curious, and unthinkable.

Despite the mid-twentieth-century recognition of a national labour force and the advent of actuarial tools used to predict and manage unemployment, joblessness remains a common experience for many living in Canada. In the mid-1970s, an economic policy paradigm 'tolerant' of 'rising unemployment' began to assert influence (McBride 153). This period also witnessed what legal scholar Georges Campeau identifies as the shift that culminated in the 1990s in a series of 'counterreforms' that 'heralded a major policy shift' with regard to the unemployed:

> Thereafter the government reduced its direct involvement with the job-
> less to refocus on managing unemployment, primarily to serve the market-
> place. The rights that the system recognized to the jobless were radically
> challenged: qualifying conditions were tightened up, the length and rate
> of benefits were revised downward, and the penalties for voluntary leaving
> and misconduct were toughened. The numbers of unemployed with access
> to benefits would drop by half during the 1990s. (viii)

The postwar Unemployment Insurance Act enshrined 'one of the more enduring myths of the welfare state' – that 'benefits as of right are insep-arably linked to [employee] contributions' (Guest 107): what Campeau contends is that even this conception of the state-worker compact is in tatters, and he queries with scepticism the notion that the contributory system continues to 'recognize genuine rights to the jobless' (viii).

In his Foucauldian study of unemployment as a 'historically specific site of regulation' in twentieth-century Britain, Walters points sugges-tively to the ways in which the concept of unemployment has altered in recent years. He observes, for example, that current forms of govern-ment 'presuppose a form of individuality not apparent in welfare gov-ernment,' insofar as they address the unemployed person as an active 'choice-maker' who may pursue self-employment or skills training or up-grading (154). Campeau finds a similar situation in Canada during the last decade of the twentieth century, when a series of 'counterreforms' led to the end of federal contributions to unemployment insurance and to the passage of the 1996 Employment Insurance Act: following the lead of the Organization for Economic Co-operation and Development, the federal government adopted an 'active' rather than 'passive' ap-proach to labour-market management (hence 'employment insurance' rather than 'unemployment insurance'), which meant that unemploy-ment came to be viewed as 'primarily an individual responsibility' that could be assuaged with training and re-employment initiatives (128–9). As I suggest in chapter 5, state conceptions of citizenship have altered in analogous ways as neoliberal ideals have gained ascendance. Brodie observes, for example, that the social rights of citizenship – including unemployment insurance – so crucial to the imagining of the national subject in the 1960s, have been supplanted in federal Speeches from the Throne by the idea of the 'entrepreneurial citizen,' which Brodie reads as a fundamental alteration of the state's conception of its role as guarantor of social security and national unity: 'In contrast to the postwar transcripts that assigned to the federal government the primary responsibility for realizing both social security and national unity, these critical outcomes are now entrusted to the market and to the individual' (390).

The Economic Action Plan implemented by the Conservative government of Stephen Harper in the wake of the 2008 financial crisis is suggestive of the ways in which such neoliberal thinking has persisted. Admittedly, the Economic Action Plan, which was rolled out over a two-year period beginning in January 2009, addresses some of the problems inherent in the Employment Insurance Act, but it leaves others utterly untouched: for example, the Canadian Labour Congress contends that if the plan minimally extends the benefit period for some workers in some regions of high unemployment and for some 'long-tenured' workers who have not habitually drawn benefits, it leaves the stringent entrance requirements (from 420 to 700 hours) and the duration of benefits unaltered for most workers in Canada. Indeed, the plan's labour-market strategy clearly favours 'active' employment 'benefits,' such as skills training, which are funded through employment insurance and are currently administered by provinces and territories through Labour Market Development Agreements. With relation to such programs, emphasis falls on key words like 'transition' and 'adjustment,' both of which signal the need for the individual worker (especially the 'long-tenured' but now jobless worker and the 'older' worker) or the community (in the case of the 'Community Adjustment Fund,' which fosters 'economic developments, science and technology initiatives, and other measures that promote economic diversification') to innovate in order to find a place in Canada's changing economy (Canada, *Canada's Economic Action Plan*). Following David Harvey's argument in *A Brief History of Neoliberalism* (2005), Jeff Derksen points out that the individual 'choice-maker' conjured by such policy discourse embodies a contradiction: 'Neoliberalism then has accelerated individual liberty so that only that which is individual can be libratory [*sic*] (to choose otherwise is to take away choice from the individual)' (6). Choosing, for example, the collective social insurance of the 1940 Unemployment Insurance Act, which recognized the 'right to benefit' (Campeau 161), is no longer an authentic choice.

Reading Alan Mettrick's reportage-style account of his two-year stint among the unemployed and homeless of Canada, *Last in Line: On the Road and Out of Work ... A Desperate Journey with Canada's Unemployed*

(1985), Rimstead contends that middle-class conceptions of unemployment and homelessness have changed little since the early twentieth century. Early twentieth-century resistance to the concept of market-induced unemployment (a concept I discuss in chapter 1) is paralleled, Rimstead insists, in neoliberal policies of the sort that gained popularity in Ontario in the late 1990s: the imposition of workfare or the fingerprinting of welfare recipients, for example, offer evidence of the persistence of ideologies that blame the unemployed for their joblessness (96). Clearly there is not an exact similitude between conceptions of the unemployed in these periods, but Rimstead's analysis is suggestive insofar as it reminds us that neoliberal emphasis on the *individual* who is out of work is not entirely new – indeed this emphasis characterized much early twentieth-century liberal thought in Canada, which stressed the 'personal-ethical issues' that could be reformed through broad legislative changes (Allen 17). As Rimstead points out, contemporary non-fictional reportage narratives of unemployment and homelessness such as Mettrick's and Evelyn Lau's *Runaway: Diary of a Street Kid* (1989) tend to achieve more commercial success than 'collective testimonies' because they 'construct poverty, street life, and prostitution uncritically as personal choice rather than necessity' (242). Contemporary novels that represent joblessness and homelessness often reveal this tendency, as well; one might think of Richard Scrimger's *Crosstown* (1996), which represents homelessness as the result of an individual's moral misstep, or Carol Shields's *Unless* (2002), which figures a young woman's voluntary homelessness as the alternative to her mother's middle-class angst.

Like Walters, Jennifer Henderson and Pauline Wakeham read 'neoliberal norms of the functional self' in terms of how they emphasize 'the individual flexibility and adaptability required in order to survive harsh labour markets and the disappearance of the social safety net' (17). Writers in Canada have explored this particular aspect of the labour market under neoliberalism in countless ways, but I would like to offer two suggestive examples here – one from the end of the twentieth century and one from the first decade of the present century. Austin Clarke's oeuvre is rich with explorations of the relations among masculinity, ethnicity, and work. Several of the stories collected in Clarke's *Nine Men Who Laughed* (1986) suggest that male West Indian immigrants in Toronto perform tremendously clever versions of themselves in order to fit into the Canadian labour market. In the stories that follow the fabricated life of Joshua Miller-Corbaine, 'A Man' and 'How He Does It,' these performances generate a parody of 'urban Canadian norms for masculinity' (Coleman, *Masculine Migrations* 30); yet when read with 'Canadian Experience,' which follows the protagonist's degrading attempt to secure a job for which he lacks the proper qualifications and skin colour, the Joshua Miller-Corbaine stories can be understood as satirical renderings of the malleability demanded by a labour market that reserves few well-paying jobs for black immigrant men. When the illusion of masculine performance fails, as it does so palpably in the failed reflections thematized in 'Canadian Experience,' the result is suicide. Significantly, the Joshua Miller-Corbaine stories recall the plot of Katherine Bligh's (Dorothy Livesay's) 1936 story from *New Frontier*, 'Six Years,' insofar as they narrate the life of a man who is 'only playing' the role of the gainfully employed male (Clarke, *Nine Men* 208). Miller-Corbaine constructs an elaborate façade as a successful corporation lawyer but, in fact, is supported by his wife and his various lovers. Unlike Livesay's Depression-era story, in which the resolution hinges on Mrs Dakin's realization that she and her husband should not shield their situation with middle-class pride but rather should join the community unemployed movement, 'A Man' and 'How He Does It' locate no such collective solution. For example, it is clear at the conclusion of 'How He Does It' that Miller-Corbaine's individual survival depends on maintaining the complex convolutions of his daily charade.

Rawi Hage's 2008 novel *Cockroach* offers another potential site for thinking through 'neoliberal norms of the functional self.' *Cockroach* narrates the confrontation of an unnamed, underemployed Lebanese immigrant in Montreal with a bureaucratized and inadequate social-welfare system, while satirizing individual adaptability via the narrator's strategy for coping with poverty, racism, and a personal history of trauma, namely, his habit of attributing his own transgressive acts to a cockroach. The cockroach signifies a space of abjection – the underground world of the city where 'the refuse of stained faces, infamous hands, dirty feet, and deep purple gums gathered in a large pool for slum kids to swim, splash, play in' (22). Yet it is only through learning to 'pass through the underground' that the narrator survives (24). In Franz Kafka's 1915 novella *The Metamorphosis*, the transformation of the protagonist into a giant insect is an unwilled act that suggests his estrangement from his petit-bourgeois life; in *Cockroach*, the transformation is willed and is indicative of the protagonist's rejection of his well-meaning but detached psychiatrist, who would rehabilitate him and render him marriageable, employable, and taxable.

If, for a brief period around the Centennial, the Bildungsroman links national citizenship to the figure of the Depression-era unemployed male, under neoliberalism, this coupling seems once again imponderable. Arguably, joblessness has become most visible in contemporary fiction in Canada via representations of the homeless unemployed, and contemporary novels of homelessness, such as Robert Majzels's *City of Forgetting* (1998) (set in Montreal) and Timothy Taylor's *Stanley Park* (2001) (set in Vancouver), suggest that it is the very lack of a fixed address – and hence gainful employment – that obviates the possibility of meaningful citizenship. Such a configuration is hardly new; if early liberal thought insisted that 'socially meaningful labor' rather than birthright should determine access to political equality, the 'rise of a capitalist ethos' in the eighteenth century 'profoundly reinforced' the value of work, such that 'economic criteria such as property holding have involved both an inclusive and an exclusive character, presumably based on notions of merit and a moral valuation of industriousness' (Arnold 22–3). As Kathleen Arnold contends in her study of citizenship and homelessness, contemporary citizenship continues to be configured under the rubric of economic independence, and there are 'varying degrees of citizenship' based on this unexpressed norm (5). In her reading of *City of Forgetting*, Lianne Moyes suggests that recent scholarship on the subject of homelessness – she cites Arnold and Leonard Feldman – tends to treat it not as a social problem but rather as a 'problem of politics and, especially, of citizenship' (129).

This book argues that unemployment has accrued variable meanings in twentieth-century Canada. Cresswell points to an analogous discursive instability around the category of the tramp in U.S.-American history: 'The word tramp was formulated as a noun in the 1870s in America to describe homeless and mobile people. By 1940 their successors were known as migrants or migrant labourers' (10). Similarly, Sharma observes that as 'ideologies of highly racialized nations as natural homelands became more fixed' (from the mid-nineteenth century in Europe and from the late-nineteenth century in Canada), migrants became equated with vagrants: 'Moreover the imposition of the idea that homelessess is akin to godlessness allowed vagrancy to be understood as a moral (and often a criminal) offence to the community of "honest residents." Migrants were thus strongly associated not only with losing their homes but also their moral standing' (11). In other words, there is a strong association between tramps and vagrants – both names for the jobless – and migrants in twentieth-century North America: if the placelessness of the tramp and the vagrant, coupled with his dubious moral standing, excluded him from the incipient conception of national citizenship prior to the Second World War, this exclusion did not persist in the context of the postwar compact, which was shaped by new liberal ideas regarding the role of the state in ensuring that able-bodied workers could achieve what J.A. Hobson called 'full civic efficiency' (qtd in Sutton 73).

Instead, this exclusion was displaced onto the figure of the migrant, where it had always partially rested. Migrant labour constituted a significant sector of the postwar labour force in Canada, but these workers have always been situated outside the discourse of the social rights of Canadian citizenship. Currently, we confront an escalating traffic in migrant labour that is signalling a new kind of division within Canadian – and global – society.[3] As I have shown in this brief conclusion, unemployment has become a situation for the creative individual to handle; in the case of migrant labourers, it has also become a problem that can be seasonally exported. Many contemporary theorists of citizenship insist that the exclusion of the migrant worker from discourses of citizenship relies on the liberal tendency to conceptualize citizenship as a static, unitary category that is circumscribed by the state. Daiva Stasiulus and Abigail Bakan contest this liberal model with an understanding of citizenship as a 'negotiated relationship' that is 'subject to change' depending on the collective or individual action of both national and transnational actors (113). This emphasis on citizenship as *practice* also appears in the work of Mary Dietz, who contends that the radical practice of 'collective, democratic citizenship' must be animated by 'the diversity of other democratic territories historical and contemporary, male and female,' and includes as an example the 'sit-down strikes of the 1930s,' which she understands as a part of a process that was not simply a momentary engagement aimed at a final goal (socialist revolution) but that understood ongoing engagement in public debate and shared responsibility for self-government as crucial (79, 77).[4] While this book has emphasized the ways in which interwar representations of unemployment often anticipated and absorbed liberal ideologies of citizenship and the self, Dietz's argument is salubrious for its reminder that the practices of citizenship from this period might also serve as examples of collective practices not wholly defined by the state. Examining unemployment in Canada is worthless if the point is only to erect monuments to a welfare state that was always incomplete and upon which was built a concept of citizenship that grants rights to those inside but perpetually excludes the rights of those outside. It is my hope that this book reveals the making of this project in the interest of making it differently.

Notes

Abbreviations

DLC-UM   Dorothy Livesay Collection, Archives and Special Collections, University of Manitoba

DLC-QU   Dorothy Livesay Collection, Queen's University Archives, Queen's University

FPG-UM   Frederick Philip Grove Collection, Archives and Special Collections, University of Manitoba

HG-QU   Hugh Garner Collection, Queen's University Archives, Queen's University

HHS-LAC   H.H. Stevens Papers, Library and Archives Canada

LIP-LAC   Local Initiatives Program, Library and Archives Canada

MC-MU   Macmillan of Canada Fonds, The William Ready Division of Archives and Research Collections, McMaster University

RH-CU   Random House Records, Rare Book and Manuscript Library, Columbia University

TPM-UG   Theatre Passe Muraille Archives, Archival and Special Collections, University of Guelph

TWP-UG   Toronto Workshop Productions Archives, Archival and Special Collections, University of Guelph

Introduction

1 Of course the work of Watt influences all of these scholars and offers an early example of scholarship on the cultural left in Canada. As I discuss in chapters 3 and 5, the left nationalists of the 1970s also took up the study of Canada's cultural lefts, and, in Quebec, the analysis of class was undertaken

in this period by scholars such as Shek. Contemporary scholars tend to pay much more attention to the gender and race politics of Old Left histories and are in general much more critical of liberal nationalism than their New Left counterparts.

2 Irr's *The Suburb of Dissent* and Rifkind's *Comrades* are good examples, as is Carr Vellino's article 'Machine-Age Discourse.'

3 Since the publication of Rifkind's book, others have urged similar inquiries. In 2009, Irvine organized a session at the Modernist Studies Association entitled 'Old Left, New Modernisms,' from which a special issue of *Canadian Literature* was generated (Summer 2011).

4 A very limited selection would include the studies of Campeau, Crowley, Guest, Ismael, Moscovitch and Albert, and Porter.

5 The richly interdisciplinary scholarship of the arts and the state in contemporary Canada is too vast to enumerate here, but important studies include those by or edited by Berland and Hornstein, Dorland, Litt, Milz, Pennee, and Woodcock. Tippett's study of state-culture relations before the Massey Commission adds another dimension to this body of work.

6 See McKay, 'For a New Kind of History' and 'The Liberal Order Framework,' both of which were published in 2000. An introductory volume as well as the first volume of McKay's four-volume series on the left in Canada have been published: *Rebels, Reds, Radicals* and *Reasoning Otherwise.* The response generated by 'The Liberal Order Framework' is discussed and exemplified in Constant and Ducharme's *Liberalism and Hegemony.*

7 In his review of McKay's *Reasoning Otherwise* (the first instalment in a four-volume history of the left in Canada), Palmer articulates the objection that Curtis makes, arguing that McKay's use of the Gramscian conception of hegemony 'understates Gramsci's clearly multi-sided articulation of the complexities of class rule' and 'conflates what Gramsci differentiated as a "separation of powers" associated with organizing social hegemony within civil society and enforcing discipline through various vehicles of state domination' ('Radical Reasoning').

8 In particular, I am thinking of the essays collected in Constant and Ducharme's *Liberalism and Hegemony.*

9 I do not mean to neglect the tremendously important work of scholars who have read left and labour history 'otherwise.' The work of Lara Campbell, Pierson, Powell, Sangster, Rifkind, and, in the context of the United States, Rabinowitz, has influenced me greatly.

10 Prior to the introduction of national citizenship, naturalization functioned as a means of granting individuals the right to vote in federal elections and of protecting them from deportation, for example (Kelley and Trebilcock 229).

11 As Guest explains, until the 1940s, the Canadian state adopted a 'residual' approach to social security, meaning that state support of the individual was viewed as residual to family or other private help; only after the Second World War was this approach modified by the 'institutional' concept of welfare, in which social security organizations are understood as the first line of defence for the citizen (2–3). A key aspect of the move to an institutional conception of social security is the shift from the understanding of welfare measures as charity for deserving cases to the idea that social programs are rights based on age and citizenship (Guest 5).

1. Towards A Politics of Mobility

1 Canadian unemployment data were not regularly measured until 1945, when the Labour Force Survey began collecting them (Gower 28). In the first half of the 1920s, the unemployment rate spiked in the context of a postwar recession (it peaked at just under 9 per cent in 1921, a rate that masks seasonal variations); in the last three years of the decade, it hovered between approximately 3 and 4 per cent (Struthers, *No Fault* 215).

2 The period of cultural nationalism that followed the First World War also witnessed the rise of critical interest in realist fiction in Canada. MacMechan's *Headwaters of Canadian Literature*, for example, sees the 'ethos of the Canadian people to be in the land,' and, consequently, the study values realist depictions of the Canadian environment and the way of life that follows from it (Fraser, 'The Development' 291–2). This desired identification between national culture and the land is an informing principle of interwar conceptions of realism in Canada. On this point, see the first chapter, in particular, of Hill, 'The Modern,' and Willmott. One of the many postwar manifestos written for realist fiction is Lionel Stevenson's July 1924 editorial for the *Canadian Bookman*, which argues that the 'promising' new realist novels of writers like Robert Stead and Douglas Durkin witness a '*rapprochement*' of the 'raw material' of the Canadian environment and literary expression (2). I discuss the canonization of realist fiction in the wake of the Second World War in more detail in chapter 4.

3 In making this point about an unanticipated consequence of American anti-modernism – 'that its quest for authenticity helped ease the nineteenth century into a modern culture of consumption' – Mount is drawing on T.J. Jackson Lears's thesis in *No Place of Grace*.

4 Henrietta Hovey was married to Richard Hovey.

5 H.C. Miller to Grove, 13 November 1926, Correspondence 1913–1962, box 2, file 4, FPG-UM.

6 Advising Grove about the content of his lectures for the Association of Canadian Clubs, H.C. Miller (who was sponsoring the tour in the interest of
promoting *A Search for America*) suggested that the group wanted him to cover subjects such as emigration to Canada, Grove's choice of Canada over the
U.S., his work with the settlers of Manitoba, and his conception of the 'Canadian spirit and character' as compared to citizens of the U.S., Britain, and
Europe (Miller to Grove, 12 February 1928, Correspondence 1913–1962,
box 2, file 2, FPG-UM). As my reading below of the 'Nationhood' lecture
that Grove prepared for the tour indicates, the author followed through on
Miller's suggestions.

7 Spettigue's 1971 discovery of Grove's former identity as Felix Paul Greve
is documented in *F.P.G.: The European Years*. In *In Search of Myself*, Grove
claims that *A Search* was the 'story of what I had lived through since August, 1892,' but he also cautions the reader that 'the book as it was published in 1927, is, to a certain extent, fiction' (181). Divay points out that
by 1946 Grove perhaps feared that he had revealed too much of his past in
A Search for America and attempted to cover his tracks with an official autobiography ('Felix Paul Greve' 115–16). In her 1973 study, Stobie reads *A
Search* as a 'historical novel' (59). Gammel's 1992 article opts for the term
semi-autobiographical, while Russell Brown's 1994 essay describes the text
as fictional autobiography.

8 Stich reads the 'shipwreck' of the raft as the 'death of Huck Finn and Mark
Twain's America' (159).

9 My belief that Grove read both Knut Hamsun and Josiah Flynt suggests
more evidence of the fact that Grove was writing *A Search for America* around
the second decade of the twentieth century rather than, as he claimed in his
author's note to the first edition of the novel, early in the last decade of the
nineteenth century. There is already much evidence that Grove began writing *A Search* after he arrived in Manitoba in 1912. Relying in part on the testimony of Catherine Grove, Spettigue argues that the manuscript was begun
in early 1920 (*Frederick Philip Grove* 60). Given that a period of twenty years
separates Grove's alleged arrival in Montreal in 1892 and his actual arrival
in Manitoba in 1912, Divay assumes that one should likewise add twenty
years to his claim about the writing of *A Search*, which would make the initial year of composition 1914 rather than 1894 ('Frederick Philip Grove's *A
Search for America*').

10 Divay suggests this borrowing from Hamsun and also contends that Grove's
Mackenzie Farm takes many of its details from the Amenia and Sharon
Land Company near Fargo in North Dakota, a Bonanza Farm owned by
H.F. Chaffee and, subsequently, his son H.L. Chaffee. Divay contends that

Grove was employed on this farm as a bookkeeper in 1912 ('Felix Paul Greve' 128–32).

11 The titles given here are Current's translations. The essay's Norwegian title is 'Paa Præries' and the collection's title is *Kratskog: Historier og Skitser*. Current notes that part of this essay appeared in English in the U.S.-American general-interest magazine *Living Age* in August 1921, which may be how Grove first encountered it. In *In Search of Myself*, Grove acknowledges Hamsun's influence on *Pioneers* (which eventually became *Settlers of the Marsh*), although he claims the author's romanticism differed from his own realist aesthetic (356–7).

12 *Atlantic Monthly*, a Boston magazine, employed Bliss Carman in 1895 as an editor (Mount 74) and also published his poems frequently during the 1890s. It is therefore likely that Carman, who went on to produce two more 'vagabondia' collections with Richard Hovey in 1896 and 1900, knew Flynt's popular tramp writings but nevertheless chose to disarticulate his vagabond from the social conditions that Flynt documented.

13 Divay has conducted the most extensive research on Grove's years in the United States, which remained more or less a mystery long after Spettigue's research on the author's European years. Divay concludes that Grove arrived in North America in 1909, that he arrived in Montreal and went straight to New York City and then on to Pittsburgh in 1910 and Sparta, Kentucky, in 1910–11. She believes that Grove did indeed spend a season on a Bonanza Farm in the Dakotas in 1912, but that he worked as a bookkeeper rather than a farmhand ('Felix Paul Greve' 130–1).

14 Flynt's 'A Colony of the Unemployed,' published in *Atlantic Monthly* in December 1896, is an example of the research he produced from a trip to a German labour colony for unemployed workers.

15 Pacey's 1945 study of *A Search for America* similarly notices the 'abruptness of its conclusion' and its inadequacy as the 'culmination of his quest for a significant place in the American scene' (*Frederick* 31). Pacey attributes the brevity of the conclusion to Grove's condensation of his manuscript at the request of his publisher (*Frederick* 32).

16 The 1897 Alien Labour Act made it unlawful for any 'person, company, partnership or corporation, in any manner to pre-pay the transportation of, or in any other way to assist or solicit the importation or immigration of any alien or foreigner into Canada under contract or agreement ... to perform labour or service of any kind in Canada' (Dominion of Canada. Parliament, 'An Act' 73).

17 In this sense, writers of itinerant life might be linked to writers such as Mazo de la Roche, Martha Ostenso, and Raymond Knister insofar as they

all interrogate the agrarian ideal. Willmott calls writers such as de la Roche, Ostenso, and Knister 'agrarian ironists,' and notes that their dissenting vision challenged the orthodoxy of the agrarian ideal in modern Canadian writing. Willmott also places some of Grove's prairie novels in this category (148, 222), which suggests that the argument I am making here could be complicated by reading Grove's later prairie novels.

18 Addressing himself to the 'Masses' in the introductory poem to *Songs of Siberia and Rhymes of the Road* (9), Fraser was not disingenuous: according to the publisher's note in the second edition of *Songs of Siberia*, the book had 'a circulation in the Eastern provinces second only to the Holy Bible.'

19 Commonly attributed to Horace Greeley, the editor of the *New York Tribune* in the mid-nineteenth century, the imperative 'Go West, Young Man' was also the title of a 1936 Hollywood film starring Mae West.

20 Here I am indebted to Doyle's discussion of Maguire's novel (75–9), which first introduced me to its parallels with Grove's *A Search for America*.

21 The opposition of the United States and Canada in anti-modernist discourses persists well into the twentieth century, as both Litt's and Irvine's discussions of the Massey Commission make clear. Both Litt and Irvine identify the anti-modernist tendencies of the commissioners, but Irvine adds that the 1952 report 'sought to calibrate the literary culture of Canada's modernist avant-garde with its critique of modernity and mass culture' (*Editing* 220).

22 Miller to Grove, 13 March 1927, Correspondence 1913–1962, box 2, file 4, FPG-UM.

23 Miller to Grove, 30 October 1926, Correspondence 1913–1962, box 2, file 4, FPG-UM. In a 12 February 1928 letter from Miller to Grove, the publisher confirmed that *A Search for America* was selling well: the total sale was fourteen hundred copies, and he believed that the ACC tour would drive total sales to six thousand by June 1928.

24 The 'dumping' of remaindered American books on the Canadian market was just one of many problems that Canadian publishers faced during the Depression (Parker, 'Trade and Regional' 171). Miller took pride in the fact that Graphic did not seek co-publication deals with American firms (as was the regular practice at the time in Canada), but was livid that Louis Carrier's 1928 American edition was being sold in Montreal during Grove's tour for the ACC (Grove, *The Letters* 222, 261).

2. The Politics of Unemployment in Leftist Periodical Cultures, 1930–1939

1 It is estimated that the unemployment rate rose from between 2 and 4 per cent in 1929 to between 19 and 27 per cent in 1933 (Horn, *The Great* 10; Gower 28).

2 In his 1929–32 study of unemployment in Ontario, Cassidy notes that two
main sources provided the most reliable, national picture of unemployment: the Dominion Bureau of Statistics index numbers of employment
(based on voluntary returns from the 'larger employers' in eight of the
major sectors of Canadian industry) and the Dominion Department of Labour's monthly report on the percentage of unemployment among trade
unionists (a total population of about two hundred thousand workers) (19–
20). See also the first note in chapter 1. For a thorough discussion of the
exclusion of women from the category of the unemployed in 1930s Canada,
see Pierson.

3 The 1867 British North America Act had given the provinces jurisdiction
over health and welfare concerns. With the increasing industrialization and
urbanization of the late nineteenth and early twentieth centuries, however,
there was an increasing gap between provinces' responsibilities to workers
and their ability to finance health and social welfare measures (Guest 5–8).
Bennett's government capitulated with a 'New Deal' in 1935, which included an Employment and Social Insurance Act – a measure that Struthers
argues was actually designed to *reduce* the amount of money Ottawa could
be expected to spend on the unemployed (*Two Depressions* 78); however, opposition leader Mackenzie King claimed that a constitutional amendment
would be required if the federal government chose to administer an unemployment insurance program. The Privy Council agreed, and the 'New
Deal' was shelved (Guest 86–91).

4 European-born and Asian workers were disproportionately concentrated in
such sectors: the 1931 census data reveal that while 21 per cent of all European-born male workers in Canada and 21 per cent of 'Asiatic' (Chinese,
Japanese, and Indian) workers reported employment as unskilled labourers,
only 12 per cent of Canadian-born males did (Hurd 173–6). Between June
of 1930 and June of 1931, immigrant male workers lost on average 19 per
cent more time than Canadian-born men; in his 1931 study of these numbers, Hurd attributes the difference to the fact that men who were recent
immigrants were more likely to be engaged in sectors that were 'far more
sensitive to seasonal and cyclical fluctuations' (182–7).

5 For analysis of the particular effects of Depression-era unemployment on
women, see Powell. See Creese for an explanation of the situation of unemployed Chinese in Vancouver, who were neither eligible for city relief in the
early years of the Depression – almost all of them were single men and relief
went to married men with families – nor allowed to enter British Columbia's
relief camps because these camps accepted only white men (324).

6 In 1919, in the aftermath of the Russian Revolution and the Winnipeg
General Strike, the Immigration Act was revised to include the notorious

Section 41, which gave the government the power to deport individuals who sought to overthrow the government, law, or authority of Canada or who were affiliated with any organization 'entertaining or teaching the disbelief in organized government' (Kelley and Trebilcock 184). Only Canadians by birth or naturalization were exempted, although contemporary amendments to the Naturalization Act rendered this exemption for the latter group null (Kelley and Trebilcock 184–5). Hurd's analysis of the 1931 census data reveals that, between 1921 and 1931, 'foreign-born' men (excluding British-born) were 84 per cent more likely to be convicted of an indictable offence than their Canadian-born counterparts (154). While Hurd surmises that 'the economic debacle of the early thirties' was a likely factor in the sharp increases in crime in the first two years of the 1930s, Avery's interpretation of these figures attributes the increase among immigrant men, in particular, to arrests for vagrancy – the crime of unemployment (115).

7 Eighty-eight thousand immigrants entered Canada in 1931, fewer than twenty-seven thousand were permitted entrance the following year, and by 1936, the number was eleven thousand (Kelley and Trebilcock 220–21). An order-in-council in 1930 limited immigration to Canada to British subjects entering from a select group of countries and to American citizens entering from the United States, provided they had means of support while they looked for work (Shore 233).

8 Non-residents were those who could not, for whatever reason, prove continuous residence in a given place. The duration of time necessary to prove residence varied by province: in Ontario, the time period was three months in the early 1930s, but in other provinces it was as long as twelve months (Struthers, *No Fault* 51).

9 With regard to pre-Depression immigration levels, Gordon is referring in part to the Railway Agreement (1925–30), which the Bennett government inherited from the previous Liberal government. In 1925, the federal government signed an immigration agreement with the Canadian Northern Railway and the Canadian Pacific Railway; the 'Railway Agreement' gave these companies temporary control over the recruitment of '*bona fide* agriculturalists' and allowed them to recruit from officially 'non-preferred' countries, such as Lithuania, Poland, Russia, Hungary, and Germany (Kelley and Trebilcock 198). Also in place from 1922 to 1935 was the Empire Settlement Act, which is discussed in the previous chapter.

10 Although Gowan's name does not appear on the first edition of *You Can't Do That*, Mardiros indicates that Gowan attributed this omission 'to an oversight on the part of the publishers, Thomas Nelson & Sons Ltd., Toronto' (289).

11 Ringenbach describes the failures of the back-to-the-land movement that accompanied the Depression in the 1890s in the United States. According to Ringenbach, the 'rural ethic' that motivated the movement embraced the idea that full employment was possible because of the availability of arable land on the western frontier (109–10). American political economist Henry George, who had a profound influence on Canada's late nineteenth-century social-gospel movement, similarly advocated a 'frontier solution' to the problems of urban life (Cook 109).

12 Analogous carceral strategies have typified treatments of the poor and unemployed since at least the nineteenth century, when Britain's New Poor Law of 1837 encouraged the workhouse as a means of curtailing the movement of the 'undeserving' poor (Himmelfarb 183–7). Rimstead connects such nineteenth-century strategies of government to postwar investments in public housing (97).

13 Parker's *The Beginnings of the Book Trade in Canada* offers a significantly earlier date – the early 1890s – for the emergence of literary professionalism in Canada, but he emphasizes possibility over frequency (232–4).

14 For analyses of late nineteenth- and early twentieth-century periodicals from immigrant and labour groups in Canada, see Doyle; Hjartarson, 'Print Culture'; Watt, 'Literature of Protest'; and chapter 17 of Krawchuk's *Our History*. For a bibliography of the English-language literatures of social protest in Canada from the 1870s to the 1970s, see Weinrich.

15 Toby Gordon Ryan claims that *Masses* had national circulation in the major Canadian cities and even in some smaller ones (*Stage Left* 27).

16 As Irvine points out in *Editing Modernity*, this definition also has the advantage of pushing at the boundaries of the 'little magazine' movement, which has been almost exclusively associated in the work of Louis Dudek, Michael Gnarowski, and Ken Norris with the 1940s and '50s, and has thus tended to exclude the leftist, small press experiments of the interwar period (12–20).

17 Although Irvine's *Editing Modernity* considers the relation of socialism to literary modernism in Canada, it argues that radical, Third Period socialism, in particular, militated against modernist poetics. Both Brandt and McDonald cite Barbara Godard's arguments about the relation between socialism and modernism in Canada (see her 1986 review of *Exil, révolte et dissidence*). As the authors listed here acknowledge, the critical trend toward examining socialist modernisms in Canada takes cues from the work of scholars such as Foley, but also Denning and Nelson, among others.

18 The Comintern prescribed the narrow parameters of socialist realism after the 1932 Conference of the Organizational Committee of the All-Russian Union of Soviet Writers (Doyle 91). The first declaration of socialist-realist

principles, which appeared in the journal *International Literature* in 1933, characterized the method as the 'faithful description of life in all its aspects, with the victorious principle of the forces of socialist revolution' (qtd in Doyle 91). As Williams has pointed out, although this brand of realism was meant to contest the bourgeois assumptions of nineteenth-century European realism, it dissolves its own 'radical challenge' by insisting that reality (the base) can be separately known from its reflection in art (the superstructure) and that art is to be judged only by its adherence to the criteria of scientific truth (*Marxism* 6).

19 Social-democratic intellectuals formed the LSR in Toronto and Montreal in the fall and winter of 1931–2, and it eventually had branches across the country before its demise in 1942. Watt asserts that by the mid-twenties *Forum* writers were distancing themselves from the staid economic nationalism of the CAA (and their organ, the *Canadian Bookman*) and employing a critical nationalism – a 'progressive,' 'evolutionary optimism' that was not allied to a specific political or social philosophy ('Climate' 17). Horn suggests in 'The Forum during the 1930s' (*Canadian Forum*, April/May 1970) that Graham Spry purchased the *Forum* in 1935 for one dollar and, as national secretary of the LSR, encouraged the national executive of the organization to purchase the financially struggling journal (38).

20 The Fabian Society was a moderate socialist organization founded in England in 1884 to promote cautious and gradual political change. This form of socialism influenced some of Canada's Confederation-era writers, such as Archibald Lampman. The Chicago School of sociology was developed at the University of Chicago in the first decades of the twentieth century; its focus was the use of theories of human ecology to explain processes of change in human communities (e.g., urbanization and migration) (Shore xiv–xv).

21 Initially, Marsh's 1943 report met with great resistance in the King government. At the Ottawa Conference on Reconstruction in 1945 it was scarcely mentioned, but the growing electoral success of the CCF soon forced the government's hand (Guest 112–26). In 1944, the Liberals introduced two important new social security programs – the National Housing Act and the Family Allowances Act. In the 1945 federal election, the King Liberals campaigned on the slogan 'a new social order for Canada,' but the strong performance of the CCF returned them with a reduced majority (Guest 126–9).

22 Creighton authored two books of poetry, *Earth Call* (1936) and *Cross-Country* (1939), both of which were published by Macmillan of Canada. Both collections favour lyric poems devoted to nature and love, but both conclude with sections containing poems that engage with the economic and social crises of the era. 'Conference,' for example, uses two quatrains with alternating

tetrameter-dimeter lines to suggest that Depression conditions have inter-
rupted the natural, human urge to procreate because what should be 'fresh'
(new life) will become more 'dull, unwanted flesh – / More idle hands!'
(*Earth Call* 61).

23 Jameson argues that the shifting exchange relations that attend the second
industrial revolution have their cultural expression in modernist aesthetics.
It should be noted, however, that Jameson questions the notion that the
gold standard was not in itself an 'artificial and contradictory system' (261).

24 See, for example, the 'Notes and Comments' section of the February 1936
issue, which rails against the CPC's foreign traditions. Gordon Skilling
resists this line of argument in the February 1937 issue but notes that he is
opposing a significant body of opinion.

25 The CPC had shared closer ties with socialist parties in Canada (the Socialist Party of Canada and the Social Democratic Party of Canada) in the late
teens and early 1920s, but their split with the progressive left in the mid-
1920s has endured to the present (Heron 75). Not surprisingly, the federal
government did not view the CPC favourably in the 1930s. In 1931, an anti-
sedition law, Section 98 of the Criminal Code, was used to imprison eight
CPC members, including the notorious leader Tim Buck. Because Section
98 was not repealed until Mackenzie King came into office in the mid-1930s,
the CPC was technically illegal for much of the decade.

26 Filewod's research on the Workers' Theatre Movement is helpful here: he
points out that the relation between the Toronto PAC and the CPC is unclear, although he notes that the founding editor of *Masses*, Ed Cecil-Smith,
and a frequent contributor, Oscar Ryan, were both involved in the CPC
leadership ('The Comintern and the Canon' 21–2).

27 From February 1932 to May 1933, *Masses* ran a series of articles that unfa-
vourably assessed the *Forum*'s contribution to radical politics. Dorothy Livesay's poem 'Pink Ballad' (December 1932) lambastes the 'pink,' bourgeois
politics of both the CCF and the *Canadian Forum*. The gendered connota-
tions of this discourse are obvious.

28 Doyle surmises that 'Maurice Granite' is one of Ryan's pseudonyms because
he also wrote as 'Martin Stone' (97).

29 It appears that, in addition to various provincial hunger marches, there
were two NUWA-organized hunger marches to Ottawa, one in the winter of
1932 (documented in the pages of *The Unemployed Worker*, the organ of the
Vancouver branch of the NUWA) and one in the winter of 1933.

30 In February 1932, W.A. Gordon suggested in the House of Commons that
both debt and the unemployment problem were being alleviated through
the 'Colonization at Home Movement,' whereby the railways and the De-

partment of Immigration were settling new and recent immigrants on farms (Dominion of Canada, *Dominion of Canada* vol. 1: 440).

31 The *B.C. Workers' News* (1935), a CPC-affiliated paper from western Canada, offers particularly striking examples of this inter-ethnic solidarity. Its pages are full of articles calling on readers to defend the cause of Vancouver's 'Asiatic workers,' who were denied cash relief payments. On 1 February 1935, for example, the paper declared that the Chinese Protective Association had affiliated with the Provincial Workers' Council in order to contribute to the struggle for unemployment insurance 'for all workers of Canada regardless of colour or nationality' (2).

32 As Irvine notes, when Livesay revised 'A Girl Sees It!' for inclusion in her 1972 *Collected Poems*, she changed the title to the less gender-specific and politically muted 'In Green Solariums' (*Editing* 40). Gone is the exclamatory mood that is so common to her Depression-era poetry, and in its place is the quiet space of green reflection that is more common to the imagist lyrics Livesay wrote in the 1920s.

33 Livesay's 'An Immigrant' is printed on the fourth page of a four-page issue and appears across from the 'With Our Women' column, which features a letter from 'Mrs. Tim Buck' (wife of the leader of the CPC) congratulating working women's organizations for 'putting up a good fight to secure better conditions for themselves and their families' (4), as well as a letter seeking advice about a 'good, cheap cold cream,' and recipes for raisin pudding and barley coffee.

34 Irvine contends that Livesay likely composed 'An Immigrant' between 1933 and 1934, when she was living in Montreal and working for the CPC, but she may have revised it before its publication in 1936 (*Editing* 47–8, 277).

35 Both of these notations are omitted from the versions of 'An Immigrant' that appear in Livesay's *Collected Poems* and *Right Hand Left Hand*, although the name 'Nick Zynchuk' appears in parentheses below the title of the poem in each.

36 Untitled typescripts of both 'The Dispossessed' and 'In Praise of Evening' are extant (box 80, files 4 and 5, DLC-UM). Two typescripts of the former poem are filed in 'The Down and Out Series,' which contains poems later published as part of 'Depression Suite' and which is dated 1934–5. One of the typescripts is numbered 'II,' which seems to correspond to the number 'III' on the untitled typescript of 'In Praise of Evening.' In any case, I take their simultaneous publication in *New Frontier* (particularly because Livesay was an editor of the magazine) as significant.

37 The price of *New Frontier* was reduced in October 1936 to fifteen cents per issue; this price remained unchanged until the publication ceased one year later.

38 This framing of 'girls' as a threat to the paid employment of men was common in the discourse of the 1930s and permeated left and right alike (Pierson 81). Campbell shows that in fact the fear was unfounded because women were 'often clustered in sex-typed occupations, which were not hit as hard as male jobs, or in jobs that were unlikely to attract male workers,' such as service, clerical, and textile work (*Respectable Citizens* 45).

39 Livesay was not present at the 1935 Dominion Day Riot in Regina, but the section 'The West 1936' in *Right Hand Left Hand* describes how she learned about the trek and the riot while visiting Regina (183). The typescript of this poem is dated July 1936 (box 8, file 2, DLC-QU).

40 The CPC was driven underground again in 1939 by an order-in-council that declared it subversive in a wartime context (Young, *The Anatomy* 269), and thus the *Daily Clarion* ceased publication. In 1943, the CPC emerged as the Labour-Progressive Party, and it retained this name until 1959.

3. Novel Protest in the 1930s

1 Irvine reads J. Lee Thompson's 1975 survey of Depression-era Canadian poetry, which offers evidence of vibrant poetic production in this period, as a welcome 'corrective' to the 'literary-historical myth that persists in reference to the economic hardships faced by publishers in the 1930s' (*Editing* 54); however, the publication of poetry in Canada has long been financed by authors, as the publication of Dorothy Livesay's early collections or the 1936 anthology *New Provinces* make clear (Gnarowski xvii). Gerson also points to the ubiquity of author-financed poetry collections in early twentieth-century Canada in her study *Canadian Women in Print* (71).

2 International bestsellers such as *Gone With the Wind* may have negatively affected the sales of competing trade titles, but it should be noted that Macmillan of Canada also benefited from this novel because they possessed the Canadian rights to it (Young, 'The Macmillan' 128).

3 Novels authored by first- or second-generation immigrants portraying Depression-era experiences in immigrant communities, such as Vera Lysenko's *Yellow Boots* (1954) and John Marlyn's *Under the Ribs of Death* (1957), did not begin to appear until the 1950s – the period when English-language literature from immigrant communities in Canada began to emerge in a significant way.

4 Vipond characterizes the nineteenth- and early twentieth-century social-gospel novel in Canada in this way: 'The novels were sentimental and didactic: their characters were stereotyped. They were novels of society in the romantic tradition, making little attempt to depict the lives or minds of the working class or the harshness and horror of industrial squalor. They were

not novels of realism, but of romance and faith' (40). While I think Vipond overstates the *entirely* romantic quality of these narratives (see Gerson's discussion of *Roland Graeme: Knight* as 'realistic social fiction' in her 'Introduction' to the 1996 edition of that novel), Vipond's identification of romance elements is useful.

5 I cannot locate any information about the artist, Stuart Wallace. Of course, it is entirely possible that this is not the artist's real name, but I have no evidence that the artist is actually Leonard Hutchinson. I am grateful to Lora Senechal Carney for alerting me to the presence of Hutchinson, who produced woodcuts such as *Depression* (ca 1939), *Logging* (1939), and *Loading Grain* (ca 1939) in this period.

6 Pacey also notes that Gregory (1889–1944) was born in England, came to Canada at the age of seventeen, and lived in Toronto and Hamilton. He authored three novels: *Forgotten Men, Valerie Hathaway* (1933), and *Solomon Levi* (1935) ('Fiction 1920–1940' 197). There is a photograph of Gregory in the May 1935 issue of *The Canadian Bookman.*

7 McKenzie's 1939 survey of proletarian writing in Canada dismisses *Forgotten Men* as 'weak in characterization and sentimental in treatment' (59). Following McKenzie, Doyle finds the Christian allegory heavy-handed (114–15).

8 Both Irr (164) and Rifkind (*Comrades* 25–6) read *Forgotten Men* in terms of its relation to the social-gospel roots of the CCF.

9 Unfortunately, none of these brochures appears to have survived in public collections.

10 Lisson to Stevens, 30 November 1934, Correspondence 1935–6, box 64, file 81, HHS-LAC.

11 Lisson to Stevens, 6 February 1935, Correspondence 1935–6, box 64, file 81, HHS-LAC.

12 Lisson to Stevens, 5 December 1934 and Stevens to Lisson, 26 November 1934, Correspondence 1935–6, box 64, file 81, HHS-LAC.

13 Stevens's Secretary to Warren K. Cook, 7 June 1935, and Lisson to Stevens, 4 June 1935, Correspondence 1935–6, box 64, file 81, HHS-LAC.

14 It also appears that Stevens arranged through his fellow Conservative MPs to bring some Conservative Party business to Davis-Lisson. Lisson to Stevens, 27 May 1935, and Stevens to Charles Bell, 11 June 1935, Correspondence 1935–6, box 64, file 81, HHS-LAC.

15 After returning from an extended holiday in the United States in April of 1935, Lisson wrote a rather cryptic note to Stevens about his own plans to contest the riding of Hamilton East as an independent in the next federal election. Lisson to Stevens, 6 April 1935, Correspondence 1935–6, box 64, file 81, HHS-LAC. Subsequent correspondence, however, reveals that Lisson's health prevented him from pursuing this ambition.

16 'To the Honourable H.H. Stevens,' Reconstruction Party Correspondence, box 125, file 6A, HHS-LAC.
17 Lisson to Stevens, 18 June 1935, Correspondence 1935–6, box 64, file 81, HHS-LAC.
18 'Reconstruction Birth and Platform,' box 125, file 6A, HHS-LAC.
19 In her attempts to get *Waste Heritage* back into print, Baird cited demand from university instructors such as Dorothy Livesay, who 'considers it the strongest novel of its period (the dirty thirties) to be produced in Canada.' Baird to Nora Clark, 16 April 1973, First Accrual, Authors' Series, Part I, box 71, file 4, MC-MU. Livesay refers readers to Baird's 'fine novel' in the 'Vancouver 1939' section of *Right Hand Left Hand* (270).
20 See Mathews, 'Canada's Hidden Working Class Literature' and '*Waste Heritage*: The Effect of Class on Literary Structure.' Hyman and Hopkins, writing in the 1980s, read the novel with a more balanced view of its aesthetics and politics. A recent article by Wyile takes up Mathews's reading, arguing that its self-consciousness about literary form reflects Baird's own anxiety about narrating inertia. What this produces, Wyile contends, is a politicized (if not radical) novel that gives 'shape to what is otherwise shapeless' (75). Willmott, who tends to agree with Doyle's reading of the novel, is suggestive when he reads the failure of radical politics – and aesthetics – in *Waste Heritage* as an allegorical symptom of the failure of young Canada to determine its own future and to realize the 'social bonds and integration' that are the basis of an autonomous society (33–4).
21 In particular, the Sit-Down strikers were resisting the premier of British Columbia's decision in the spring of 1938 to cancel relief for the single, unemployed males who flocked to the cities in the summer months, when the province's forestry camps – provincially and federally subsidized camps that had replaced the federal relief camps in 1936 – were closed (Struthers, *No Fault* 192).
22 Baird to Hugh Eayrs, 23 August 1939, First Accrual, Authors' Series, Part I, box 71, file 4, MC-MU.
23 Unless otherwise noted, all references to *Waste Heritage* are to the 2007 University of Ottawa Press critical edition.
24 Baird to Macmillan, 10 July 1939, First Accrual, Authors' Series, Part I, box 71, file 4, MC-MU.
25 Baird wrote three articles about the novel in the mid-1970s. These were occasioned by Macmillan's reprinting of *Waste Heritage* in 1973.
26 As Doyle notes, the federal government declared the CPC illegal in 1940, and the Cold War years had a definite chilling effect on the CPC's ability to establish itself as a conventional political party in Canada (161–92).
27 The CPC's presence in relief camps was widely acknowledged in the 1930s.

The CPC was able to improve its fortunes in the 1930s as a leader of orga-
nized labour because its affiliated unions were willing, unlike craft unions,
to tackle the problem of unemployment (Palmer, *Working-Class* 208).
Mathews argues convincingly that Hep, one of the strike leaders in *Waste
Heritage*, is modelled on Steve Brodie, one of the organizers of the Relief
Project Workers' Union ('*Waste Heritage*' 74).

28 Rifkind and Hill are the only critics who have considered how race shapes
the politics of Baird's novel. See Hill, 'Critical Introduction' xxxix–xl and
Rifkind, *Comrades* 191.

29 For prophecies against Philistia (and therefore in favour of the Israelites'
right to Ashkelon), see Jeremiah 47, Amos 1, and Zephania 2. See the Book
of Samuel (especially 1:5, 7:14, and 17) for the restoration of Gath to the
Israelites.

30 For an example of a review that compares *Waste Heritage* to *Of Mice and Men*,
see Margaret Wallace's article in the 16 December 1939 issue of the (U.S.-
American periodical) *Saturday Review of Literature*. Some reviewers and later
critics also derided the novel's alleged imitation of Steinbeck's *The Grapes
of Wrath*; yet Horn's October 1974 article on *Waste Heritage* in the *Canadian
Forum* points out that Baird's novel had already gone to Macmillan when
Steinbeck's novel appeared in 1939 (38). The assumption that Baird imi-
tated Steinbeck persisted for some time, as Pacey's article on modern fiction
in the *Literary History of Canada* demonstrates. Pacey calls the novel 'social
propaganda' and claims it suffers from 'imitativeness' because it borrows
heavily from both *Of Mice and Men* and *The Grapes of Wrath* (198).

31 As Wyile observes in his 2007 article on *Waste Heritage*, the novel's 'metafictional preoccupation with the interplay between politics and literary form'
has not 'really been addressed in prior criticism' (66). Although my reading of this metafictionality differs from Wyile's in many ways, it is certainly
true that if previous generations of critics did not tend to comment on the
novel's self-consciousness, more recent readings do.

32 Bennett Cerf, telegram, 8 August 1939, Archival B41, file 1, RH-CU.

33 Baird to Cerf, 9 December 1939, Archival B93, file 2, RH-CU.

34 Marion Saunders to Bob Haas, 26 May 1939, Archival B1, file 1, RH-CU.

35 Gerson's analysis of Baird's gender in relation to the adjudication of the
1939 Governor General's award for fiction indicates the masculinist literary
environment in which Baird wrote. Using archival evidence, Gerson posits
that *Waste Heritage* was 'denied' the award because of a male-dominated 'literary power network, whose operations were governed at least as much by
personal acquaintance as by aesthetic judgment' ('The Canon' 52).

36 Hugh Eayrs to Haas, 1 June 1939, Archival B2, file 1, RH-CU. Drawing on

John Gray's 1978 autobiography, Young suggests that Eayrs's ill health in the late 1930s (he died in 1941) led him to make 'capricious' and 'rash' publishing decisions ('The Macmillan' 129).

37 Carl Eayrs to Hugh Eayrs, 1939, First Accrual, Authors' Series, Part I, box 71, file 4, MC-MU.

38 Saunders to Hugh Eayrs, 2 June 1939, First Accrual, Authors' Series, Part I, box 71, file 4, MC-MU.

39 State censorship of supposedly seditious literature was not uncommon during the two world wars or during the interwar period in Canada. During the Depression, the state frequently attempted to monitor and restrict access to communist art. As Cecil-Smith notes in his 1976 foreword to the agitprop play *Eight Men Speak*, for example, the play was first performed by the Workers' Experimental Theatre in Toronto in 1933 before the provincial government of Ontario banned further performances and threatened the licences of theatres that dared to show the play (Wright and Endres 22–4).

40 Saunders to Hugh Eayrs, 9 June 1939, First Accrual, Authors' Series, Part I, box 71, file 4, MC-MU.

41 Carl Eayrs to Hugh Eayrs, 1939, First Accrual, Authors' Series, Part I, box 71, file 4, MC-MU.

42 Haas to Hugh Eayrs, 30 June 1939, Archival B5, file 1, RH-CU.

43 Saunders to Cerf, 5 July 1939, Archival B11, file 1, RH-CU.

44 Although controversial, *The Grapes of Wrath* was a bestseller in the United States: initially published in April 1939, it was in its seventh printing by August 1939 (Lingo 358). For a discussion of the banning of *The Grapes of Wrath* in Kern County, California, see Lingo's full article. Baird's correspondence to Bennett Cerf indicates that in 1939 she was reading and enjoying modern authors like Steinbeck, Dos Passos, and Clifford Odets.

45 Random House had done the exact opposite with a more marketable Canadian author, Morley Callaghan. *They Shall Inherit the Earth* and *Now That April's Here* had both been printed by Random House in New York and sold to Macmillan of Canada. Random House estimated the sales of *Waste Heritage* correctly: by January 1940, the novel had not sold more than six hundred copies in the United States, and Random House never ordered more than the initial one thousand and forty copies that it received in 1939 (Cerf to Baird, 18 January 1940, Archival B96, file 2, RH-CU; Hugh Eayrs to Cerf, 7 October 1939, First Accrual, Authors' Series, Part I, box 71, file 4, MC-MU).

46 Baird to Cerf, 11 July 1939, Archival B15, file 1, RH-CU.

47 Baird to Cerf, 11 July 1939, Archival B15, file 1, RH-CU.

48 Baird to Macmillan, 10 July 1939, First Accrual, Authors' Series, Part I, box 71, file 4, MC-MU.

49 Baird to Cerf, 5 October 1939, Archival B53, file 2, RH-CU.
50 Cerf to Baird, 9 October 1939, Archival B56, file 2, RH-CU.
51 Cerf to Baird, 16 November 1939, Archival B73, file 2, RH-CU.
52 Hugh Eayrs to Cerf, 14 September 1939, Archival B47, file 2, RH-CU. Eayrs commented on the parallel in his letter to Cerf, but I have not been able to locate any extant dust jackets.
53 Hugh Eayrs to Baird, 6 November 1939, First Accrual, Authors' Series, Part I, box 71, file 4, MC-MU. The regulations, which acted as supplements to the existing War Measures Act, barred the publication of material likely to cause disaffection with the war effort, to influence relations among countries involved in the war, or to prejudice military recruitment (Dominion of Canada, Standing Interdepartmental Committee 44).
54 All the changes to the Canadian text were made such that no additional lines and very few additional letters were added to the text. The pagination of the two is therefore the same. For a discussion and analysis of the exact changes that were made to the Canadian *Waste Heritage*, see Mason, 'State Censorship.'
55 Hugh Eayrs to Cerf, 21 November 1939, First Accrual, Authors' Series, Part I, box 71, file 4, MC-MU.
56 Baird to Cerf, 13 November 1939, Archival B71, file 2, RH-CU. Baird was somewhat mistaken, as she later admitted to Cerf. *Waste Heritage* was not being targeted specifically: the Defence of Canada Regulations applied broadly to all published materials.
57 For example, Baird supported Cerf's campaign to have the novel's title changed from *Plow These Men Under* (one of Baird's suggestions) to *Waste Heritage*. However, as mentioned briefly above, she changed her mind in August of 1939 and wrote an urgent letter and telegram to Cerf, imploring him to consider a new suggestion, *Wrath to Come*. Cerf's reply to the telegram was a firm 'no': 'The final title for the book, then, is *Waste Heritage*' (Cerf, telegram, 8 August, 1939, Archival B41, file 1, RH-CU).

4. The Postwar Compact and the National Bildungsroman

1 Rose's 1958 study of the Regent Park project provides a useful account of the 'slum clearance' and the factors that motivated it. He notes, for example, that despite federal concentration on home ownership in the postwar period – what he calls a 'national fetish' (18) – the need for 'low-rental' housing constituted the 'essence of the housing problem' (13). Federal, provincial, and municipal governments wrangled over the funding of the Regent Park project, and, in 1948, the Central Mortgage and Housing Cor-

poration agreed to provide about half the estimated cost of acquiring and clearing the building site (79).

2 According to Garner's autobiography, *Storm Below* sold fourteen hundred copies in hardcover and more than twenty thousand copies as a White Circle paperback (*One Damn* 102).

3 Garner to Robin Ross-Taylor, 5 February 1948, box 1, file 1, HG-QU.

4 Ellen Elliott to Garner, 15 January 1947 and 27 February 1947, box 1, file 1, HG-QU.

5 The parent company of Collins, based in Scotland, entered the paperback market in 1934 with a series of reprints (priced at sevenpence per volume) that included Somerset Maugham's novel *The Painted Veil* and several detective novels by, among others, Agatha Christie (McCleery 10).

6 Eayrs to Baird, 28 December 1951, First Accrual, Authors' Series, Part I, box 71, file 4, MC-MU. The Canadian publishing industry experienced an anti-communist witch hunt of its own in the wake of the 1945 defection of Russian cipher clerk Igor Gouzenko, resulting, for example, in the attempted censorship of Vera Lysenko's history of Ukranian settlement in Canada, *Men in Sheepskin Coats* (1947) and Dorothy Livesay's uneasiness regarding her communist past (Campbell, 'Lorne Pierce').

7 Ross-Taylor to Garner, 12 April 1948, box 1, file 1, HG-QU.

8 Garner to Ross-Taylor, undated, box 1, file 1, HG-QU.

9 Garner to Ross-Taylor, undated, box 1, file 1, HG-QU.

10 In 1949, Bob Weaver rejected 'The Go-Boys' for his Canadian Short Stories series on CBC Radio, calling it derivative and lacking in 'insight into an actual experience' (Weaver to Garner, 16 August 1949, box 1, file 2, HG-QU). Weaver later became a great supporter of Garner's short fiction.

11 I am thinking here of Williams's identification of dominant, residual, and emergent formations, and his discussion of the incorporation of oppositional practices by dominant ones (*Marxism* 121–6).

12 Garner also used the pseudonym 'Jarvis Warwick' for his sensational novel *Waste No Tears: The Novel about the Abortion Racket*, which appeared in Export Publishing's News Stand Library in 1950.

13 'My Memories of the Great Depression,' box 22, file 24, HG-QU.

14 'Purchase Request for Scripts,' box 3, file 25, HG-QU.

15 'Spain, 38 Years Later,' box 23, file 11, HG-QU. This typescript is dated 'Nov 11 1975' and bears a handwritten note signed by Garner: 'Article for "Weekend" magazine, commissioned by Julie Bayliss, and then turned down by her, 1975.' There is more evidence for a New Left revival of the Popular Front and the Spanish Civil War than I am able to cite here: a wonderful example that does not concern Garner (as far as I know) is the conference

held at York University in March 1976, The Social and Cultural Aftermath of the Spanish Civil War. At this conference, Dorothy Livesay presented a paper, 'Canadian Poetry and the Spanish Civil War,' which was reprinted in 'the Thirties' issue of *CV/II* in May 1976.

16 Garner to Farr, 19 February 1968 and 1 May 1968, box 3, file 25, HG-QU.

17 'Ryerson Press Release,' box 2, file 24, HG-QU.

18 As Friskney's work on McClelland and Stewart's New Canadian Library series indicates, those critics who were central to defining a Canadian literary canon in the postwar period demonstrated a marked preference for realist fiction (157–9). Lecker's 'The Canonization of Canadian Literature' also makes the connection between postwar cultural nationalism and literary realism.

19 'Cabbagetown.' Fall Catalogue, Ryerson Press, 1968, box 3, file 26, HG-QU.

20 The 1950 edition omits this scene from Chapter Thirteen of 'Transition.' See page 118 in the 1950 edition.

21 'Garner's Classic of Depression Back in Print,' *Collingwood Enterprise-Bulletin* 12 September 1968 and Bob Noble, 'Garner Reprint,' *Winnipeg Free Press* 19 October 1968, box 25, file 7, HG-QU.

22 Ross Hayball, 'Their Nobility's Even Greater Resurrected,' *Globe and Mail* 12 October 1968, box 25, file 7, HG-QU.

23 This critical reception of the 1968 *Cabbagetown* arguably influenced the reception of subsequent Garner titles. In a 1971 review of Garner's novel *A Nice Place to Visit*, for example, Waddington argues that 'Garner has often been praised for his good heart when it is really his good ear and sharp eye that deserve our admiration … his concern with truth places his work in the realm of social realism' (72–3).

24 McGraw-Hill Company of Canada purchased the venerable Canadian publishing house Ryerson Press in 1970 and thus contributed to the general crisis in Canadian publishing in that decade (Parker, 'Trade and Regional' 173). As Garner reports in his autobiography, the sale caused a 'terrible flap among the ranks of the Canadian Nationalist Brigade' and prompted the 1970 Ontario Royal Commission on Book Publishing (*One Damn* 246; Parker, 'Trade and Regional' 173). Despite his leftist politics in the interwar period, Garner had little sympathy for the nationalist and anti-imperialist discourse of the New Left and remained with McGraw-Hill Ryerson after the sale. Stuewe observes that such actions did little to endear Garner to the nationalist critics of the 1970s (*The Storms* 187–8).

25 A young Bob Rae, for example, writing for the University of Toronto student newspaper *The Varsity*, condemns Garner's tremendous tendency to

'sentimentalize,' noting 'the occasional purple passage' that was 'more reminiscent of Victorian melodrama than the "realistic school" of which the young Garner was obviously trying to become a member' (Bob Rae, 'Cabbagetown,' *The Varsity* 29 November 1968, box 25, file 7, HG-QU). Other critics in the period also found Garner's didactic narrative intrusions distasteful: Barry Callaghan, 'A Convincing Portrait of Spiritual Poverty,' *Toronto Telegram* 5 October 1968; Mari Pineo, 'Canadian Classic – Perhaps,' *Vancouver Sun* 27 September 1968; and Jamie Portman, 'Social Document of the Thirties,' *Calgary Herald Magazine* 22 November 1968, 7, box 25, file 7, HG-QU.

26 At the hobo jungle in Manitoba at the beginning of 'Transition' in the 1950 edition, Ken notes the presence of 'foreigners' who 'spoke together in their own language before picking up their packs and moving off through the trees' (83). This sense of difference becomes the means by which Ken distinguishes himself from those who turn to leftist political activity. By contrast, in the 1968 edition Ken cannot tell that one of the transients he is speaking to at the Manitoba camp is a 'foreigner,' and, in response to a racist comment, the unnamed transient observes: 'That's the trouble in this goddamn country, nobody sticks together. The Englishman hates the Frenchman, an' the two of them hate the Jew, and the Jew hates everybody, and everybody hates the hunkies. The only guy that benefits is the capitalist' (175).

27 Interestingly, Garner's short story 'Step-'n-a-Half,' which appears in his 1971 collection *Violation of the Virgins,* counters this public/private, male/female dichotomy. The story is based on Garner's own 1968 road trip to Mexico with his wife Alice, and the story's protagonist Ed is a thinly disguised middle-aged, middle-class Garner. While driving, Ed encounters two hitchhikers – a pregnant, young 'Spanish American' girl and her 'bearded hippie' companion (40–1). The eponymous female character alludes to an infamous Depression-era 'railway bull' who is mentioned in *Cabbagetown.* The hippie mistreats the girl, and though Ed wants to help her and offers the couple a ride, he ends up being merely a witness as she murders her companion in his backseat. This complicates the heroic rescue plot and suggests the young woman's ability to contest the containment of such a plot, which might otherwise have positioned her as utterly subject to the male power of the public sphere embodied by the road.

28 For commentary on Purdy's reactivation of Bliss Carman's late nineteenth-century vagabondia poetics, see Bentley (110–11) and Solecki (55).

29 If one takes the examples of Marlyn and Vera Lysenko as representative, it is clear that for the sons and daughters of first-generation immigrants, the

creative labour of writing about the Depression was often delayed by the exigencies of earning money in the 1930s. During the 1930s, Lysenko, a recent graduate of the University of Manitoba, worked as a nurse and high school teacher in Alberta and then, after 1936, as a journalist, salesperson, teacher, factory hand, night school instructor, domestic servant, and research clerk in various cities in Ontario ('Vera Lysenko'). Unemployed during the Depression, John Marlyn sailed for England and found work as a reader for a film studio. It was not until he returned to Canada and found employment as a writer for various government departments in Ottawa that he began work on *Under the Ribs of Death* (New 715–16).

30 In Coleman's more recent take on *Under the Ribs of Death* (in the final chapter of his book *White Civility*), he reads the novel more positively as an example of a resistant 'wry civility' that challenges masculinist, Anglo-Canadian norms (212–16).

5. New Left Culture and the New Unemployment

1 Women's labour-force participation increased from just over 14 per cent of the labour market in 1955 to just under 30 per cent by 1980. The rate of unemployment for women remained higher than the rate for males throughout most of the 1970s (Keck 359, 4).

2 Moscovitch and Drover claim that Canada's welfare state did not arrive until the 1960s, when Lester Pearson's minority government introduced programs such as the Canada Assistance Plan (1966). While social expenditures accounted for only 4 per cent of the GNP in 1946, they represented 15 per cent by the mid-1970s. Moscovitch and Drover contend that rather than offering evidence of the influence of socialism on the Canadian state, such social expenditures 'legitimize capitalism as a social system, growing in size relatively and absolutely' (30–6).

3 With a budget of $180 million in its first granting year, the LIP was the larger of the two programs (Canada, *The Local Initiatives Program* 1–2).

4 The Canadian government's decision to move away from the interventionist labour market policy that had reigned since the Second World War did not achieve lower unemployment rates, which continued to rise dramatically in the late 1970s, reaching a postwar high of just over 8 per cent in 1978 (McBride 152–3; Muszynski 273).

5 A 1973 review of the LIP indicates that while youths (meaning workers between fourteen and twenty-five years of age) represented only 25 per cent of Canada's labour force, they constituted approximately 48 per cent of the nation's unemployed (Canada, *Local Initiatives Program, 1972–73* 2).

6 NFB photographer Joan Latchford's photo essay 'Tripping on the Trans-Can' documents the phenomenon of youth hitchhiking in the early 1970s, and it appears alongside Crystal Luxmore's more recent essay in the online July/August 2008 issue of *The Walrus*. Luxmore concedes that the road-tripping youth culture 'idealized "the bum"' and that its 'professed anti-materialism was less substance than style,' but is candid about her envy: 'How awesome is it that hundreds of thousands of teenagers just upped and traveled across the country, staying in youth-run hostels (like the former Bastille on the Plains of Abraham) for fifty cents a night? Now that is some sweet love.'

7 'Indian Band Gets LIP Grant,' *St John's Daily News* 4 December 1972, volume 80, file 11 (Press Coverage of Special Employment-Creating Program Announced on September 4, 1972: December 4, 1972 to January 3, 1973), LIP-LAC.

8 Of the many wonderful ironies that form the history of the LIP, the most startling is the fact that Pierre Vallières, a prominent member of the Front de Libération du Québec who had just been released from prison in the wake of the October Crisis, was found working on an LIP-funded project. In the wake of the discovery, which landed in the waiting lap of the Progressive Conservative Party, Robert Stanfield (the leader of the opposition) accused the prime minister of hiring his 'FLQ friends' on LIP projects (qtd in Keck 167).

9 In the last lecture in the 1978 Collège de France series, Foucault describes the processes of such incorporation in his discussion of how movements of 'counter-conduct' inform the development of the state (333–57).

10 The 'Fundraising' file in the Theatre Passe Muraille archives that deals with the period 1970–84 contains applications to the Province of Ontario Council for the Arts for the 1969–70 and 1970–1 seasons. Both indicate that Rochdale College (which received LIP grants for a medical clinic and for Coach House Press) formed the basis of the theatre's financial support ($10,000 per year). Both applications make it clear that funding from the Canada Council had not yet been received and was not anticipated (TPM-UG). In Herbert Whittaker's review of *Buffalo Jump* in the *Globe and Mail* (22 May 1972), Thompson is quoted as saying that he wanted to avoid dependence on subsidies but that Passe Muraille received a small amount – $16,000 – from the Ontario Arts Council and the Canada Council combined for the 1971–2 season (20). It is certainly true that the effects of the LIP and the OFY have been somewhat mythologized in the history of the alternative theatre movement. See, for example, Bolt's recollections in her 1982 interview with Zimmerman ('Carol Bolt' 268) and Zimmerman's subsequent assump-

tion that the collective play-making methodology of *Buffalo Jump* was enabled by job-creation grants (*Playwriting Women* 31). In the early 1970s, Passe Muraille did produce plays with large casts, but Thompson financed these with 'occasional runaway hits'; the 'regular work' thus provided, the 'good wages on the hit shows,' and Thompson's 'habitual husbandry' all enabled actors to remain with the company (Johnston 122).

11 Friedlander agrees with Filewod, but Johnston and Rubin disagree and leave Luscombe's theatre out of their histories of the alternative theatres (Johnston 17–23; 'The Toronto Movement').

12 Although *Next Year Country* differs from *Buffalo Jump*, the Globe Theatre was also influenced by the documentary theatre of the 1970s. Filewod points out that Ken and Sue Kramer, who founded the Regina theatre in 1968, were familiar with the documentary theatre of British director Peter Cheeseman, whose work also influenced Paul Thompson (*Collective Encounters* 18–19).

13 'Buffalo Jump – House Program,' TPM-UG.

14 A wonderful example of this exploration of gendered labour occurs in act 2, when the strikers mockingly discuss Mrs Dougherty, a resident of Regina, who wants to 'make a quilt' representing 'the relief camp marchers going to Ottawa' (2.19–20). Also at the beginning of act 2, Mrs Mountjoy of Golden, British Columbia, knits a sweater and sings a song that clearly links her 'private' labour to 'public' politics (2.56). See Sangster (98–102) for a thorough discussion of the gendered division of political and cultural labour on the left in the first part of the twentieth century.

15 Bolt stages a decisive moment here that recalls the 1934 production of the fourth act of the agitprop play *Eight Men Speak* at a meeting organized by the Toronto Progressive Arts Club – a meeting called to protest both the continued imprisonment of Tim Buck and other prominent communists and to resist the fact that provincial authorities had shut down performances of the play after its first night. According to Endres, the 'Red Squad' – a special unit of the Toronto Police Force – was present at the meeting and arrested A.E. Smith, the leader of the communist front organization, the Canadian Labour Defense League, for sedition (Introduction xxviii).

16 Drawing on the insights of both Scobie and Davey (in 'Recontextualization in the Long Poem'), Jones's theorization of the 'documentary collage' in *That Art of Difference* examines the intersections of postmodernism and documentary forms. Miller (in 'Documentary/Modernism') and Denning have both argued that Depression-era documentaries might be understood as alternative, experimental modernisms, and these arguments are put to good use in Rifkind's *Comrades and Critics*.

17 For example, see John Yardley Jones's 1972 cartoon from the *Toronto Sun*,

which is reproduced in McKinnie's article 'Bees, Horseshoes.' Dennis Brath-waite's 'A Cry of Agony from a Depression Freak,' which appeared in the *Toronto Star* on 11 November 1971, bemoans the fact that he got through the 1930s without a 'nickel in unemployment insurance or welfare' and now must 'pay substantial taxes to support healthy young kids on welfare' or 'to support other people's children in a lot of unproductive and in some cases downright foolish make-work programs' (9).

18 The Lady Poet alludes to or quotes from William Hervey Allen's popular historical novel of Napoleonic Europe, *Anthony Adverse* (1933); Richard Lovelace's 1649 poem about the English Civil War, 'To Lucasta, Going Off to the Wars'; Charles Dickens's and Rafael Sabatini's novels of the French Revolution, *A Tale of Two Cities* (1859) and *Scaramouche* (1921); and Alfred, Lord Tennyson's ballad, 'The Charge of the Light Brigade' (1854). This last clearly comments on the 'buffalo jump' theme of the play, which critiques the way in which strikers are sacrificed by Bennett's unwillingness to address the issue of unemployment.

19 As Keck points out, in the review of the LIP that occurred during the summer of 1972, federal policy makers expressed fears that the LIP was actually *inflating* unemployment numbers because its projects drew people into the labour market who otherwise would not have been seeking work. As a result, the 1972–3 program was limited to those who were currently receiving unemployment insurance or social assistance (173). Cohen's government-commissioned report on the 1971 OFY program argues that its impact on total student unemployment had been small (i.e., OFY inhibited the increase of unemployment rather than diminishing the problem) (57). Given this, and given that those who did get OFY grants managed to save very little money to pay for tuition (65), Cohen suggests that more structural changes are necessary, such as the elimination of the cost of education to the student (67). The OFY, he concludes, was not 'truly an employment program' because it benefited so few – many of whom came from middle-class backgrounds – and did 'nothing to alter the conditions which create student unemployment' (83).

20 Briefly joined in the early 1970s, labour-market and arts policy were perhaps at odds from the beginning: if the former emphasizes the treatment of the population through abstracted, general types – via policy instruments such as unemployment insurance – the latter, particularly in the late twentieth and early twenty-first centuries, privileges individual expression and unique exception.

21 Bolt misinterprets Luscombe's method to some extent, although she is correct about his use of objectives. Luscombe admits in a 1984 interview

that his search for 'unit objectives' does not begin with actors but with play-wrights and directors: 'I'm not interested in watching an actor look for an idea. You have to begin with an idea and look for its theatrical shape' (qtd in Filewod, *Collective Encounters* 54).

22 'In Case Your Mother Never Told You, This Was the Depression,' *Winnipeg Tribune* (*TV Times*) 31 January 1974, 'Ten Lost Years – Reviews and Articles,' TWP-UG.

23 'Ten Lost Years (First National Tour),' TWP-UG.

24 'Bad-Language Plays Offend Audiences,' *Lethbridge Herald* 28 October, 1974, 'Ten Lost Years – Reviews and Articles,' TWP-UG.

25 'Ten Lost Years (First National Tour),' TWP-UG.

26 For example, in the speech that accompanied the presentation of Winch with an honorary doctor of laws from the University of British Columbia in 1973, he was celebrated for his pivotal role in ending the Vancouver Sit-Down Strike ('The Title').

27 Henderson's reading of Foucault's concept of governmentality is useful here: 'Power is organized and exercised in liberal societies through a strat-egy that harnesses individual modes of self-government to wider campaigns to govern others. This strategy aims to minimize the expenditure of force and to streamline the exercise of state power by coordinating "totalizing" with "individualizing" forms of power' (19).

28 Canadian Painting in the Thirties, curated by Charles C. Hill, was exhibited at the National Gallery before touring to Toronto and Vancouver, and, in reduced form, to Calgary, Edmonton, Saskatoon, and Montreal. It inspired Derek May's NFB documentary film *Pictures from the 1930s* (1977).

29 Mathews's *Canadian Literature: Surrender or Revolution* and Cappon's *In Our Own House*, also published in the late 1970s, articulate similar theses.

30 Richard confirms that he had difficulty finding a publisher for *Journal d'un hobo*; many houses in Paris turned it down before his friend Gaston Miron suggested that he try Parti pris ('Jean-Jules' 50). Parti pris accepted it but Richard claims it was edited to curb its sexual candour ('Jean-Jules' 50–1).

31 The actual eastward trek of the jobless by train that appears in chapter 11 of *Journal d'un hobo* is represented as part of the 'Marche de la Faim,' which sent a delegation to Ottawa from various parts of the country. In the novel, the march occurs in the late 1930s, but the actual NUWA-organized Hunger March to Ottawa occurred in either 1932 or 1933. See my chapter 2, note 30. Biographical information about Richard is scanty and often inaccurate, but a 1972 interview with him clarifies his role in the Hunger March: along with three other workers from camps for the unemployed in Quebec, four delegates from Toronto, and four from Vancouver, Richard met with R.B.

Bennett to demand, according to Richard, better wages in the camps, and, according to *The Unemployed Worker* (5 March 1932), non-contributory unemployment insurance ('Jean-Jules' 42–3). An article entitled 'Jean-Jules Richard' in the spring 1952 issue of *New Frontiers* also provides some details about Richard's role in the Hunger March.

32 Tremblay offers a thorough analysis of how the androgynous ideal in *Journal d'un hobo* alludes to Plato's Aristophane, whose discourse on the subject represents the original human as a hermaphroditic whole (65).

33 For interesting comparisons between Baird's *Waste Heritage* and Potrebenko's short fiction, see Rimstead (245, 264–5).

34 Rebick and the former members of the Vancouver Women's Caucus that she interviewed for her book *Ten Thousand Roses* use the term 'caravan' for this event (35–46); in its April and May issues from 1970, *The Pedestal* refers to it as a 'cavalcade.'

35 It is these sectors of the labour market – clerical, sales, and service – where most of the jobs for women were created in the 1950s, '60s, and '70s (Keck 3–4).

Conclusion

1 Two recent book-length studies include Kamboureli and Miki's *Trans.Can. Lit* and Dobson's *Transnational Canadas.*

2 Conrad Black's apologia for the president's New Deal in the *Globe and Mail* (24 October 2008) (based on Black's 2003 biography) offers one good example of this positive reading of these figures.

3 For analyses of Canada's historical reliance on migrant labour and the intensification of this reliance in recent years, see Knowles (161–70), Satzewich, and Sharma.

4 Both liberal and communitarian (or civic republican) concepts of citizenship are tied to the nation-state: the former views citizenship as a legal status based on rights and duties and the latter emphasizes the public good and participation in political community over individual interests (Delanty 51; Mouffe, 'Democratic Citizenship' 225–7). By contrast, radical democratic citizenship is less tied to the nation but is not necessarily antithetical to it because it is rooted in the idea of subnational social movements as forming participatory democracy (Delanty 37–8, 51–3).

Works Cited

Note that citations for material (short stories, poems, editorials, manifestos, and literary reviews) from non-scholarly periodicals appear in the text.

Adorno, T.W. *The Culture Industry*. Ed. J.M. Bernstein. New York: Routledge, 1991. Print.

Allen, Richard. *The Social Passion: Religion and Social Reform in Canada, 1914–28*. Toronto: U of Toronto P, 1971. Print.

Anderson, Benedict. 'Staging Antimodernism in the Age of High Capitalist Nationalism.' Jessup 97–103.

Arnold, Kathleen R. *Homelessness, Citizenship, and Identity: The Uncanniness of Late Modernity*. Albany: State U of New York P, 2004. Print.

Arrighi, Giovanni. *The Long Twentieth Century: Money, Power, and the Origins of Our Times*. London: Verso, 1994. Print.

Avery, Donald. *'Dangerous Foreigners': European Immigrant Workers and Labour Radicalism in Canada, 1896–1932*. Toronto: McClelland and Stewart, 1979. Print.

Baird, Irene. 'Sidown, Brothers, Sidown.' *Laurentian University Review* 9 (1976): 81–6. Print.

– *Waste Heritage*. Toronto: Macmillan, 1939. Print.

– *Waste Heritage*. New York: Random House, 1939. Print.

– *Waste Heritage*. 1939. Ed. Colin Hill. Ottawa: U of Ottawa P, 2007. Print.

Baldwin, Harold. *A Farm for Two Pounds: Being the Odyssey of an Emigrant*. London: John Murray, 1935. Print.

Benjamin, Walter. 'The Work of Art in the Age of Mechanical Reproduction.' *Illuminations: Essays and Reflections*. Ed. Hannah Arendt. Trans. Harry Zhon. New York: Schocken Books, 2007. 217–51. Print.

Bennett, Donna. 'Conflicted Vision: A Consideration of Canon and Genre in English-Canadian Literature.' Lecker, *Canadian Canons* 131–49.

Bennett, Tony. 'Marxism and Popular Fiction.' *Popular Fictions: Essays in Literature and History.* Ed. Peter Humm, Paul Stigant, and Peter Widdowson. London: Methuen, 1986. 237–65. Print.

Bentley, D.M.R. *The Gay]Grey Moose: Essays on the Ecologies and Mythologies of Canadian Poetry, 1690–1990.* Ottawa: U of Ottawa P, 1992. Print.

Berland, Jody, and Shelley Hornstein, eds. *Capital Culture.* Montreal: McGill-Queen's UP, 2000. Print.

Bliss, Michael. Preface. *Report on Social Security for Canada.* By Leonard Marsh. Toronto: U of Toronto P, 1975. ix–x. Print.

Boire, Gary. 'Callaghan, Edward Morley.' New 169–71.

Bolt, Carol. 'An Interview with Carol Bolt.' By Rota Lister. *World Literature Written in English* 17.1 (1978): 144–53. Print.

– *Buffalo Jump.* Toronto: Playwrights' Co-op, 1972. Print.

– 'Carol Bolt.' By Robert Wallace and Cynthia Zimmerman. *The Work: Conversations with English-Canadian Playwrights.* Toronto: Coach House P, 1982. 264–76. Print.

Bourdieu, Pierre. *The Field of Cultural Production: Essays on Art and Literature.* Ed. Randal Johnson. Cambridge: Polity P, 1993. Print.

Bourinot, Arthur S. *Under the Sun.* Toronto: Macmillan, 1939. Print.

Brandt, Di. 'A New Genealogy of Canadian Literary Modernism.' *Wider Boundaries of Daring: The Modernist Impulse in Canadian Women's Poetry.* Ed. Di Brandt and Barbara Godard. Waterloo: Wilfrid Laurier UP, 2009. 1–25. Print.

Broadfoot, Barry. *Ten Lost Years, 1929–1939: Memories of Canadians Who Survived the Depression.* Toronto: Doubleday, 1973. Print.

Brodie, Janine. 'Citizenship and Solidarity: Reflections on the Canadian Way.' *Citizenship Studies* 6.4 (2002): 377–94. Print.

Brooks, Sheila A., and Alice K. Hale, eds. *The Depression in Canadian Literature.* Toronto: Macmillan, 1976. Print.

Brown, Lorne A. 'Unemployment Relief Camps in Saskatchewan, 1933–1936.' MacDowell and Radforth 523–46.

Brown, Russell. 'The Road Home: Meditation on a Theme.' *Context North America: Canadian/U.S. Literary Relations.* Ed. Camille R. La Boussière. Ottawa: U of Ottawa P, 1994. 23–48. Print.

Buci-Glucksmann, Christine. 'State, Transition, and Passive Revolution.' *Gramsci and Marxist Theory.* Ed. Chantal Mouffe. London: Routledge and Kegan Paul, 1979. 207–36. Print.

Callaghan, Morley. *They Shall Inherit the Earth.* 1935. Toronto: McClelland and Stewart, 1992. Print.

Campbell, Lara. *Respectable Citizens: Gender, Family, and Unemployment in Ontario's Great Depression.* Toronto: U of Toronto P, 2009. Print.

Campbell, Robert Malcolm. *Grand Illusions: The Politics of the Keynesian Experience in Canada, 1945–1975*. Peterborough: Broadview P, 1987. Print.

Campbell, Sandra. 'Lorne Pierce of the Ryerson Press and Vera Lysenko's *Men in Sheepskin Coats* (1947): Resisting the "Red Scare."' *Historical Perspectives on Canadian Publishing*. McMaster University, n.d. Web. 15 January 2010.

Campeau, Georges. *From UI to EI: Waging War on the Welfare State*. Vancouver: U of British Columbia P, 2004. Print.

Canada. *Canada's Economic Action Plan*. Government of Canada, n.d. Web. 10 June 2010.

– *The Local Initiatives Program*. Ottawa: Manpower and Immigration, 1973. Print.

– *Local Initiatives Program, 1972–73: A Profile*. Ottawa: Manpower and Immigration, 1973. Print.

– *Projects by People: The Local Initiatives Program*. Ottawa: Information Canada, 1972. Print.

Canadian Council on Social Development. *Youth '71: An Inquiry into the Transient Youth and Opportunities for Youth Programs in the Summer of 1971*. Ottawa: Canadian Council on Social Development, 1971. Print.

Canadian Labour Congress. 'Recession Watch Bulletin' 3 (Fall 2009): 1–20. Print.

Cappon, Paul, ed. *In Our Own House: Social Perspectives on Canadian Literature*. Toronto: McClelland and Stewart, 1978. Print.

Cardinal, Linda. 'Citizenship Politics in Canada and the Legacy of Pierre Elliott Trudeau.' *From Subjects to Citizens*. Ed. Pierre Boyer, Cardinal, and David Headon. Ottawa: U of Ottawa P, 2004. 163–78. Print.

Carman, Bliss. *Low Tide on Grand Pré*. New York: Charles L. Webster, 1893. Print.

Carman, Bliss, and Richard Hovey. *Songs From Vagabondia*. 1894. New York: Greenwood, 1969. Print.

Carr Vellino, Brenda. 'Machine-Age Discourse, Mechanical Ballet, and Popular Song as Alternative Document in Dorothy Livesay's "Day and Night."' *Studies in Canadian Literature* 32.2 (2007): 43–58. Print.

The Case of Charlie Gordon. Dir. Stuart Legg, NFB, 1939. *NFB*. Web. 10 April 2009.

Cassidy, H.M. *Unemployment and Relief in Ontario, 1929–1932: A Survey and Report*. Toronto: J.M. Dent, 1932. Print.

Cecil-Smith, E. Foreword. Wright and Endres. 22–4.

Chen, Zhongming. 'The Politics of Fiction: Social Realism in English-Canadian Novels, 1920–55.' Diss. U of Calgary, 1989. Print.

Clarke, Austin. *Nine Men Who Laughed*. Markham: Penguin, 1986. Print.

Cohen, Andrew. *Report of the Evaluation Task Force to the Secretary of State: Opportunities for Youth '71*. Department of the Secretary of State. Ottawa: n.p., 1972. Print.

Cole, W.H. 'The Railroad in Canadian Literature.' *Canadian Literature* 77 (Summer 1978): 124–30. Print.

Coleman, Daniel. 'Immigration, Nation, and the Canadian Allegory of Manly Maturation.' *Essays on Canadian Writing* 61 (1997): 84–104. Print.

– *Masculine Migrations: Reading the Postcolonial Male in New Canadian Narratives.* Toronto: U of Toronto P, 1998. Print.

– *White Civility: The Literary Project of English Canada.* Toronto: U of Toronto P, 2007. Print.

Constant, Jean-François, and Michel Ducharme, eds. *Liberalism and Hegemony: Debating the Canadian Liberal Revolution.* Toronto: U of Toronto P, 2009. Print.

– 'A Project of Rule Called Canada.' Introduction. Constant and Ducharme 3–31.

Cook, Ramsay. *The Regenerators: Social Criticism in Late Victorian English Canada.* Toronto: U of Toronto P, 1985. Print.

Cooley, Dennis. *The Vernacular Muse.* Winnipeg: Turnstone, 1987. Print.

Creese, Gillian. 'Exclusion or Solidarity? Vancouver Workers Confront the "Oriental Problem."' MacDowell and Radforth 311–32. Print.

Creighton, Alan. *Earth Call.* Toronto: Macmillan, 1936. Print.

Cresswell, Tim. *The Tramp in America.* London: Reaktion, 2001. Print.

Crowley, Brian Lee. *Fearful Symmetry: The Fall and Rise of Canada's Founding Values.* Toronto: Key Porter, 2009, Print.

Current, Richard Nelson. Introduction. Hamsun, *Knut Hamsun* 1–13.

Curtis, Bruce. '"After Canada": Liberalisms, Social Theory, and Historical Analysis.' Constant and Ducharme 176–200.

Curtis, Susan. 'The Son of Man and God the Father.' *Meanings for Manhood: Constructions of Masculinity in Victorian America.* Ed. Mark C. Carnes and Clyde Griffen. Chicago: U of Chicago P, 1990. 67–78. Print.

Daniells, Roy. 'Crawford, Carman, and D.C. Scott.' Klinck Vol. 1 422–37. Print.

Davey, Frank. 'Economics and the Writer.' Gerson and Michon 103–12.

– 'Recontextualization in the Long Poem.' *Reading Canadian Reading.* By Davey. Winnipeg: Turnstone P, 1988. 123–36. Print.

Daymond, Douglas M., and Leslie G. Monkman, eds. *Towards a Canadian Literature: Essays, Editorials and Manifestos.* Vol. 2. Ottawa: Tecumseh P, 1985. Print.

Delanty, Gerard. *Citizenship in a Global Age.* Buckingham: Open UP, 2000. Print.

Denning, Michael. *The Cultural Front: The Laboring of American Culture in the Twentieth Century.* London/New York: Verso, 1996. Print.

Derksen, Jeff. 'Poetry and the Long Neoliberal Movement.' *West Coast Line: A Journal of Contemporary Writing and Criticism* 40.3 (Winter 2007): 4–11. Print.

Dietz, Mary. 'Context Is All: Feminism and Theories of Citizenship.' Mouffe 63–85.

Divay, Gaby. 'Felix Paul Greve / Frederick Philip Grove's Passage to America: The Discovery of the Author's Arrival in North America and Its Implications.' *New Worlds: Discovering and Constructing the Unknown in Anglophone Literature.* Ed. Martin Kuester, Gabriele Christ, and Rudolf Beck. München: Verlag Ernst Vögel, 2000. 111–32. Print.

– 'Frederick Philip Grove's *A Search for America*: 1927 and Beyond.' *A Search for America: Electronic Edition Based on the Book's First 1927 Edition.* By Frederick Philip Grove. Ed. Divay, Jan Horner, and Barry Pomeroy. U of Manitoba Archives and Special Collections, 2005. Web. 5 June 2009.

Djwa, Sandra. 'The *Canadian Forum*: Literary Catalyst.' *Studies in Canadian Literature* 1.1 (1976): 7–25. Print.

– *The Politics of the Imagination: A Life of F.R. Scott.* Toronto: Douglas and McIntyre, 1987. Print.

Dobson, Kit. *Transnational Canadas: Anglo-Canadian Literature and Globalization.* Waterloo: Wilfrid Laurier UP, 2009. Print.

Dominion of Canada. *Dominion of Canada Official Report of Debates of the House of Commons.* Sixth Session – 17th Parliament. Vol. 4, 1935. Ottawa: J.A. Patenaude, 1935. Print.

– *Dominion of Canada Official Report of Debates of the House of Commons.* Third Session – 17th Parliament. Vol. 1, 1932. Ottawa: F.A. Acland, 1932. Print.

– Parliament. 'An Act to Restrict the Importation and Employment of Aliens.' *Statutes of Canada.* Second Session – 8th Parliament, March–June 1897. Ottawa: Samuel Dawson Law Printer, 1897. 73–5. Print.

– Standing Interdepartmental Committee on Emergency Legislation. *Defence of Canada Regulations.* Ottawa: J.A. Patenaude, 1939. Print.

Dorland, Michael, ed. *The Cultural Industries in Canada: Problems, Policies, and Prospects.* Toronto: J. Lorimer, 1996. Print.

Dowler, Kevin. 'The Cultural Industries Policy Apparatus.' Dorland 328–46.

Doyle, James. *Progressive Heritage: The Evolution of a Politically Radical Literary Tradition in Canada.* Waterloo, ON: Wilfrid Laurier UP, 2002. Print.

Druick, Zoë. *Projecting Canada: Government Policy and Documentary Film at the National Film Board.* Montreal: McGill-Queen's UP, 2007. Print.

Duffy, Dennis. 'Losing the Line: The Field of Our Modernism.' *Essays on Canadian Writing* 39 (1989): 164–90. Print.

'Economy: Unemployment Rate.' *How Canada Performs.* The Conference Board of Canada, July 2009. Web. 11 June 2010.

Eichler, Margrit, and Marie Lavigne. 'Women's Movement.' *The Canadian Encyclopedia.* Historica-Dominion Institute, 2010. Web. 18 May 2010.

Endres, Robin. Introduction. Wright and Endres xi–xxxvi.

Ewald, François. 'Insurance and Risk.' *The Foucault Effect: Studies in Governmen-*

tality. Ed. Graham Burchell, Colin Gordon, and Peter Miller. London: Harvester Wheatsheaf, 1991. 197–210. Print.

Falk, Richard. 'The Decline of Citizenship in an Era of Globalization.' *Citizenship Studies* 4.1 (2000): 5–17. Print.

Farmer, Bernard J. *Go West, Young Man*. London: Thomas Nelson and Sons, 1936. Print.

Feldman, Leonard. *Citizens without Shelter: Homelessness, Democracy, and Political Exclusion*. Ithaca: Cornell UP, 2004. Print.

Fetherling, Doug. *Hugh Garner*. Toronto: Forum, 1972. Print.

Filewod, Alan. *Collective Encounters: Documentary Theatre in English Canada*. Toronto: U of Toronto P, 1987. Print.

– 'The Comintern and the Canon: Workers' Theatre, *Eight Men Speak* and the Genealogy of Mise-en-Scène.' *Australasian Drama Studies* 29 (October 1996): 17–32. Print.

– 'Performance and Memory in the Party: Dismembering the Workers' Theatre Movement.' *Essays on Canadian Writing* 80 (Fall 2003): 59–77. Print.

Fingard, Judith. 'The Winter's Tale: The Seasonal Contours of Pre-Industrial Poverty in British North America, 1815–1860.' MacDowell and Radforth 81–105. Print.

Flynn, Kevin. 'Destination Nation: Writing the Railway in Canada.' Diss. McGill, 2002. Print.

Flynt, Josiah. *Tramping with Tramps: Studies and Sketches of Vagabond Life*. New York: Century, 1899. Print.

Foley, Barbara. *Radical Representations: Politics and Form in U.S. Proletarian Fiction, 1929–1951*. Durham: Duke UP, 1993. Print.

Foucault, Michel. *Security, Territory, Population: Lectures at the Collège de France, 1977–78*. Ed. Michael Senellart. Trans. Graham Burchell. New York: Palgrave Macmillan, 2007. Print.

Frank, David, and Donald Macgillivray. Introduction. Fraser, *Echoes* 9–25.

Fraser, Dawn. *Echoes from Labour's War: Industrial Cape Breton in the 1920s*. Toronto: New Hogtown P, 1976. Print.

– *Songs from Siberia and Rhymes of the Road*. Glace Bay: The Eastern Publishing Co., n.d. Print.

Fraser, Nancy. 'Rethinking the Public Sphere: A Contribution to the Critique of Actually Existing Democracy.' *Habermas and the Public Sphere*. Ed. Craig Calhoun. Cambridge: MIT Press, 1992. 109–42. Print.

Fraser, Nancy W. 'The Development of Canadian Realism During the 1920s.' *Dalhousie Review* 57 (Summer 1977): 287–99. Print.

Friedlander, Mira. 'Survivor: George Luscombe at Toronto Workshop Productions.' *Canadian Theatre Review* 38 (1983): 44–52. Print.

Fripp, E.F.G. *The Outcasts of Canada: Why Settlements Fail.* Edinburgh: William Blackwood and Sons, 1932. Print.

Friskney, Janet. *New Canadian Library: The Ross-McClelland Years, 1952–1978.* Toronto: U of Toronto P, 2007. Print.

Frye, Northrop. 'Conclusion.' Klinck Vol. 2 333–61. Print.

Gammel, Irene. 'Two Odysseys of "Americanization": Dreiser's *An American Tragedy* and Grove's *A Search for America.' Studies in Canadian Literature* 17.2 (1992): 129–47. Print.

Garner, Hugh. *Cabbagetown.* Toronto: Collins, 1950. Print.

– *Cabbagetown.* Toronto: Ryerson, 1968. Print.

– 'A Conversation with Hugh Garner.' By John Moss. *Journal of Canadian Fiction* 1.2 (1972): 50–5. Print.

– Foreword. Munro vii–ix.

– *Hugh Garner's Best Stories.* Toronto: Ryerson, 1963. Print.

– 'An Interview with Hugh Garner.' By Allan Anderson. *Tamarack Review* 52 (December 1969): 19–33. Print.

– *One Damn Thing after Another.* Toronto: McGraw-Hill Ryerson, 1973. Print.

– 'Step-'n-a-Half.' *Violation of the Virgins and Other Stories.* By Garner. Toronto: McGraw-Hill Ryerson, 1971. Print.

Gaskell, Philip. *A New Introduction to Bibliography.* 1972. New Castle: Oak Knoll P, 1995. Print.

Gerson, Carole. *Canadian Women in Print, 1750–1918.* Waterloo: Wilfrid Laurier UP, 2010. Print.

– 'The Canon between the Wars: Field-Notes of a Feminist Archaeologist.' Lecker, *Canadian Canons* 46–56.

– Introduction. *Roland Graeme: Knight.* By Agnes Maule Machar. Ottawa: Tecumseh, 1996. vii–xxiv. Print.

Gerson, Carole, and Jacques Michon, eds. *History of the Book in Canada.* Vol. 3. Toronto: U of Toronto P, 2007. Print.

– 'Editors' Introduction.' Gerson and Michon 3–9.

Gnarowski, Michael. Introduction. *New Provinces: Poems of Several Authors.* Ed. Gnarowski. 1936. Toronto: U of Toronto P, 1976. vii–xxiii. Print.

Godard, Barbara. 'Notes from the Cultural Field: Canadian Literature from Identity to Hybridity.' *Essays on Canadian Writing* 72 (2000): 209–47. Print.

– Rev. of *Éxil, révolte et dissidence: Étude comparée des poésies québécoise et canadienne (1925–1955),* by Richard Giguère. *University of Toronto Quarterly* 56.1 (1986): 197–201. Print.

Goldstein, Philip. *Post-Marxist Theory: An Introduction.* Albany: State U of New York P, 2005. Print.

Gower, Dave. 'A Note on Canadian Unemployment Since 1921.' *Perspectives on Labour and Income* 4.3 (1992): 28–30. Print.

Grainger, Martin Allerdale. *Woodsmen of the West.* 1908. Toronto: McClelland and Stewart, 1996. Print.

Gramsci, Antonio. *Selections from the Prison Notebooks.* Ed. and Trans. Quintin Hoare and Geoffrey Nowell Smith. New York: International Publishers, 2008. Print.

Gray, James. *The Winter Years: The Depression on the Prairies.* Toronto: Macmillan, 1966. Print.

Grayson, L.M., and Michael Bliss, eds. *The Wretched of Canada: Letters to R.B. Bennett, 1930–1935.* Toronto: U of Toronto P, 1971. Print.

Gregory, Claudius. *Forgotten Men.* Hamilton: Davis-Lisson, 1933. Print.

– *The Printed Word.* Hamilton: Davis-Lisson, 1938. Print.

Grove, Frederick Philip. *In Search of Myself.* Toronto: Macmillan, 1946. Print.

– *The Letters of Frederick Philip Grove.* Ed. Desmond Pacey. Toronto: U of Toronto P, 1976. Print.

– 'Nationhood.' *It Needs to Be Said … By Grove.* 1929. Ottawa: Tecumseh, 1982. 135–63. Print.

– *Our Daily Bread.* Toronto: Macmillan, 1928. Print.

– 'Postscript to *A Search for America.*' *Queen's Quarterly* 49.3 (1942): 197–213. Print.

– *A Search for America.* Ottawa: Graphic, 1927. Print.

Guest, Dennis. *The Emergence of Social Security in Canada.* Vancouver: U of British Columbia P, 1985. Print.

Hage, Rawi. *Cockroach.* Toronto: House of Anansi, 2008. Print.

Hale, Alice K., and Sheila A. Brooks, eds. *The Depression in Canadian Literature.* Toronto: Macmillan, 1976. Print.

Hamsun, Knut. *Knut Hamsun Remembers America: Essays and Stories, 1885–1949.* Trans. and Ed. Richard Nelson Current. Columbia: U of Missouri P, 2003. Print.

– *On the Cultural Life of Modern America.* Trans. and Ed. Barbara Gordon Morgridge. Cambridge: Harvard UP, 1969. Print.

– 'On the Prairie.' Hamsun, *Knut Hamsun* 72–9.

Harrison, Dick. 'Fiction of the 1930s.' *The Dirty Thirties in Prairie Canada.* 11th Western Studies Conference. Ed. R.D. Francis and H. Ganzevoort. Vancouver: Tantalus, 1980. 77–87. Print.

Henderson, Jennifer. *Settler Feminism and Race Making in Canada.* Toronto: U of Toronto P, 2003. Print.

Henderson, Jennifer, and Pauline Wakeham. 'Colonial Reckoning, National Reconciliation? Aboriginal Peoples and the Culture of Redress in Canada.' *ESC* 35.1 (March 2009): 1–26. Print.

Heron, Craig. *The Canadian Labour Movement: A Short History.* Toronto: James Lorimer, 1989. Print.

Hill, Charles. *Canadian Painting in the Thirties*. Ottawa: The National Gallery of Canada, 1975. Print.

Hill, Colin. 'Critical Introduction.' *Waste Heritage*. By Irene Baird. Ottawa: U of Ottawa P, 2007. ix–lvii

– 'The Modern-Realist Movement in English-Canadian Fiction, 1919–1950.' Diss. McGill U, 2003. Print.

Himmelfarb, Gertrude. *The Idea of Poverty: England in the Early Industrial Age*. New York: Knopf, 1984. Print.

'History of Federal Ridings Since 1867: General Elections, 18th Parliament.' *Elections Canada*. Parliament of Canada, n.d. Web. 21 December 2009.

Hjartarson, Paul. 'On the Textual Transmission of F.P. Grove's *A Search for America*.' *Papers of the Bibliographic Society of Canada* 25 (1986): 59–81. Print.

– 'Print Culture, Ethnicity, and Identity.' *History of the Book in Canada*. Ed. Yvan Lamonde, Patricia Lockhart Fleming, and Fiona A. Black. Vol. 2. Toronto: U of Toronto P, 2005. 43–54. Print.

– 'Staking a Claim: Settler Culture and the Canonization of "Frederick Philip Grove" as a "Canadian" Writer.' *Pioneering North America*. Ed. Klaus Martens. Würzburg: Königshausen and Neumann, 2000. 19–30. Print.

Hoar (Howard), Victor, ed. *The Great Depression: Essays and Memoirs from Canada and the United States*. Vancouver: Copp Clark, 1969. Print.

– *The Mackenzie-Papineau Battalion: Canadian Participation in the Spanish Civil War*. Toronto: Copp Clark, 1969. Print.

Hoerder, Dirk. *Labor Migration in the Atlantic Economies: The European and North American Working Classes during the Period of Industrialization*. Westport: Greenwood, 1985. Print.

Hopkins, Anthony. 'Thematic Structure and Vision in *Waste Heritage*.' *Studies in Canadian Literature* 11.1 (1986): 77–85. Print.

Horn, Michiel. *The Dirty Thirties: Canadians in the Great Depression*. Toronto: Copp Clark, 1972. Print.

– *The Great Depression of the 1930s in Canada*. Ottawa: The Canadian Historical Association, 1984. Print.

– 'The Great Depression: Past and Present.' *Journal of Canadian Studies* 11 (1976): 41–50. Print.

– *The League for Social Reconstruction: Intellectual Origins of the Democratic Left in Canada, 1930–1942*. Toronto: U of Toronto P, 1980. Print.

Horowitz, Gad. 'Conservatism, Liberalism, and Socialism in Canada: An Interpretation.' *Canadian Journal of Economics and Political Science* 32.2 (1966): 143–71. Print.

Hughes, Kenneth J. Introduction. Phillips 11–41.

Hurd, W. Burton. *Racial Origins and Nativity of the Canadian People*. 1931. Census Monograph No. 4. Ottawa: J.A. Patenaude, 1937. Print.

Hutcheson, Sydney. *Depression Stories*. Vancouver: New Star Books, 1976. Print.

Hyman, Roger Leslie. 'Wasted Heritage in *Waste Heritage*: The Critical Disregard of an Important Novel.' *Journal of Canadian Studies* 17.4 (1982–3): 74–87. Print.

Irr, Caren. *The Suburb of Dissent: Cultural Politics in the United States and Canada during the 1930s*. Durham: Duke UP, 1998. Print.

Irvine, Dean. 'Among *Masses*: Dorothy Livesay and English Canadian Leftist Magazine Culture of the Early 1930s.' *Essays on Canadian Writing* 68 (1999): 183–212. Print.

– ed. *The Canadian Modernists Meet*. Ottawa: U of Ottawa P, 2005. Print.

– *Editing Modernity: Women and Little-Magazine Cultures in Canada, 1916–1956*. Toronto: U of Toronto P, 2008. Print.

Irvine, William. *You Can't Do That: A Play in Three Acts*. Toronto: Thomas Nelson, 1936. Print.

Ismael, Jaqueline, ed. *The Canadian Welfare State: Evolution and Transition*. Edmonton: U of Alberta P, 1987. Print.

– Introduction. Ismael xi–xxii.

'Jack Winter.' *Canada's Playwrights: A Biographical Guide*. Ed. Don Rubin and Alison Cranmer-Byng. Toronto: CTR Publications, 1980. 185–8. Print.

Jameson, Fredric. 'Culture and Finance Capital.' *Critical Inquiry* 24.1 (1997): 246–65. Print.

Jessup, Lynda, ed. *Antimodernism and Artistic Experience: Policing the Boundaries of Modernity*. Toronto: U of Toronto P, 2001. Print.

– 'Antimodernism and Artistic Experience.' Introduction. Jessup 3–9.

Johnston, Denis. *Up the Mainstream: The Rise of Toronto's Alternative Theatres*. Toronto: U of Toronto P, 1991. Print.

Jones, Manina. *That Art of Difference: 'Documentary-Collage' and English-Canadian Writing*. Toronto: U of Toronto P, 1993. Print.

Jones, W.M. 'Relief Land Settlement.' *Canada's Unemployment Problem*. Ed. L. Richter. Toronto: Macmillan of Canada, 1939. 261–95. Print.

Kamboureli, Smaro. *Scandalous Bodies: Diasporic Literature in English Canada*. Don Mills: Oxford UP, 2000. Print.

Kamboureli, Smaro, and Roy Miki, eds. *Trans.Can.Lit: Resituating the Study of Canadian Literature*. Waterloo: Wilfrid Laurier UP, 2007. Print.

Kaplan, Caren. *Questions of Travel*. Durham: Duke UP, 1996. Print.

Keck, Jennifer. 'Making Work: Federal Job Creation Policy in the 1970s.' Diss. U of Toronto, 1995. Print.

Kelley, Ninette, and Michael Trebilcock. *The Making of the Mosaic: A History of Canadian Immigration Policy*. 2nd ed. Toronto: U of Toronto P, 2010. Print.

Kertzer, Jonathan. *Worrying the Nation: Imagining a National Literature in English Canada*. Toronto: U of Toronto P, 1998. Print.

Klinck, Carl F., gen. ed. *Literary History of Canada*. 2nd ed. 4 vols. Toronto: U of Toronto P, 1976. Print.

Knowles, Valerie. *Strangers at Our Gates: Canadian Immigration and Immigration Policy, 1540–2006*. Rev. ed. Toronto: Dundurn P, 2007. Print.

Krawchuk, Peter. *Our History: The Ukrainian Labour-Farmer Movement in Canada, 1907–1991*. Trans. Mary Skrypnyk. Toronto: Lugus, 1991. Print.

Lawson, Alan. 'Postcolonial Theory and the "Settler" Subject.' *Essays on Canadian Writing* 56 (1995): 20–36. Print.

League for Social Reconstruction. *Canada and Socialism*. Toronto: Stafford, 1935. Print.

– *Democracy Needs Socialism*. Toronto: Thomas Nelson, 1938. Print.

– *Social Planning for Canada*. Toronto: Thomas Nelson, 1935. Print.

Lears, T.J. Jackson. *No Place of Grace: Antimodernism and the Transformation of American Culture, 1880–1920*. New York: Pantheon, 1981. Print.

Lecker, Robert, ed. *Canadian Canons: Essays in Literary Value*. Toronto: U of Toronto P, 1991. 131–49. Print.

– 'The Canonization of Canadian Literature: An Inquiry into Value.' *Critical Inquiry* 16.3 (1990): 656–71. Print.

Lewis, David, and F.R. Scott. *Make This Your Canada: A Review of CCF History and Policy*. Toronto: Central Canada, 1943. Print.

Lingo, Marci. 'Forbidden Fruit: The Banning of *The Grapes of Wrath* in the Kern County Library.' *Libraries and Culture* 38.4 (2003): 351–79. Print.

Litt, Paul. *The Muses, the Masses, and the Massey Commission*. Toronto: U of Toronto P, 1992. Print.

Liversedge, Ronald. *Recollections of the On to Ottawa Trek*. Ed. Victor Hoar. Toronto: McClelland and Stewart, 1973. Print.

Livesay, Dorothy. *Collected Poems: The Two Seasons*. Toronto: McGraw-Hill Ryerson, 1972. Print.

– 'The Documentary Poem: A Canadian Genre.' *Contexts of Canadian Criticism*. Ed. Eli Mandel. Chicago: U of Chicago P, 1971. 267–81. Print.

– *Right Hand Left Hand*. Erin: Press Porcepic, 1977. Print.

Lofty. *Adventures and Misadventures, or, an Undergraduate's Experiences in Canada*. London: John Bale, 1922. Print.

Lukács, Georg. 'Reportage or Portrayal?' *Essays on Realism*. By Lukács. Ed. Rodney Livingstone. Trans. David Fernbach. 1971. London: Lawrence and Wishart, 1980. 47–75. Print.

– *Studies in European Realism*. Trans. Edith Bone. London: Hillway, 1950. Print.

MacDowell, Laurel Sefton, and Ian Radforth, eds. *Canadian Working-Class History*. Toronto: Canadian Scholars' P, 1992. Print.

MacMechan, Archibald. *Headwaters of Canadian Literature*. 1924. Toronto: McClelland and Stewart, 1974. Print.

Malkki, Liisa. 'National Geographic: The Rooting of Peoples and the Territori-
    alization of National Identity among Scholars and Refugees.' *Cultural Anthro-
    pology* 7.1 (1992): 24–44.
A Man and His Job. Dir. Alistair M. Taylor, NFB, 1943. *NFB*. Web. 16 April
    2009.
Mandel, Eli. Introduction. *Under the Ribs of Death*. By John Marlyn. 1957. Toron-
    to: McClelland and Stewart, 1964. 7–14. Print.
Manley, John. '"Communists Love Canada!": The Communist Party of Canada,
    the "People," and the Popular Front, 1933–1939.' *Journal of Canadian Studies*
    36.4 (2002): 59–84. Print.
– '"Starve, Be Damned!" Communists and Canada's Urban Unemployed, 1929–
    39.' *The Canadian Historical Review* 79.3 (1998): 466–91. Print.
Mardiros, Anthony. *William Irvine: The Life of a Prairie Radical*. Toronto: James
    Lorimer, 1979. Print.
Marsh, Leonard C. *Canadians In and Out of Work: A Survey of Economic Classes and
    Their Relation to the Labour Market*. Toronto: Oxford UP, 1940. Print.
– *Employment Research: An Introduction to the McGill Programme of Research in the
    Social Sciences*. Toronto: Oxford UP, 1935. Print.
– *Report on Social Security for Canada*. Toronto: U of Toronto P, 1943. Print.
Marshall, T.H. *Social Policy*. London: Hutchinson, 1965. Print.
Marx, Karl. *Capital*. Vol. 1. 1867. Trans. Ben Fowkes. New York: Vintage, 1977.
    Print.
– *The German Ideology*. Part 1. 1946. Ed. C.J. Arthur. London: Lawrence and Wis-
    hart, 1970. Print.
– 'On the Jewish Question.' *Early Writings*. By Marx. Trans. T.B. Bottomore.
    London: C.A. Watts, 1963. 1–40. Print.
Mason, Jody. '"Sidown, Brother, Sidown!": The Problem of Commitment and
    the Publishing History of Irene Baird's *Waste Heritage*.' *Papers of the Bibliograph-
    ical Society of Canada* 45.2 (2007): 143–61. Print.
– 'State Censorship and the Reconsideration of Irene Baird's *Waste Heritage*.'
    Canadian Literature 191 (Winter 2006): 192–5. Print.
Massey, Doreen. *Space, Place and Gender*. Cambridge: Polity, 1994. Print.
Mathews, Robin. 'Canada's Hidden Working Class Literature.' *Canadian Dimen-
    sion* (November-December 1997): 37. Print.
– *Canadian Literature: Surrender or Revolution*. Ed. Gail Dexter. Toronto: Steel
    Rail, 1978. Print.
– '*Waste Heritage*: The Effect of Class on Literary Structure.' *Studies in Canadian
    Literature* 6.1 (1981): 65–81. Print.
McBride, Stephen. 'Trends and Priorities in Job Creation Programs.' Ismael
    151–70.

McCallum, Todd. 'The Great Depression's First History? The Vancouver Archives of Major J.S. Matthews and the Writing of Hobo History.' *The Canadian
Historical Review* 87.1 (2006): 79–107. Print.

McCleery, Alistair. 'The Paperback Evolution: Tauchnitz, Albatross, and Penguin.' *Judging a Book by Its Cover: Fans, Publishers, Designers, and the Marketing
of Fiction.* Ed. Nicole Matthews and Nickianne Moody. Hampshire: Ashgate,
2007. 3–17. Print.

McDonald, Larry. 'Socialism and the English Canadian Literary Tradition.' *Essays on Canadian Writing* 68 (1999): 213–41. Print.

McGann, Jerome. 'The Socialization of Texts.' *The Book History Reader.* Ed.
David Finkelstein and Alistair McCleery. London: Routledge, 2002. 39–46.
Print.

McGauley, Tom. Introduction. Hutcheson vii–x.

McKay, Ian. 'For a New Kind of History: A Reconnaissance of 100 Years of Canadian Socialism.' *Labour / Le Travail* 46 (2000): 69–125. Print.

– 'The Liberal Order Framework: A Prospectus for a Reconnaissance of Canadian History.' Constant and Ducharme 617–45.

– *Reasoning Otherwise: Leftists and the People's Enlightenment in Canada, 1890–1920.*
Toronto: Between the Lines, 2008. Print.

– *Rebels, Reds, Radicals: Rethinking Canada's Left History.* Toronto: Between the
Lines, 2005. Print.

McKenzie, Ruth I. 'Proletarian Literature in Canada.' *Dalhousie Review* 19
(1939): 49–64. Print.

McKinnie, Michael. 'Bees, Horseshoes, and Puppets for the Elderly: The Local
Initiatives Program and the Political Economy of Canadian Theatre.' *Contemporary Theatre Review* 15.4 (2005): 427–39. Print.

McKnight, David. 'Small Press Publishing.' Gerson and Michon 308–18.

McPherson, Hugo. 'Fiction 1940–1960.' Klinck 205–33.

Miller, Muriel. *Bliss Carman: Quest and Revolt.* St John's: Jesperson, 1985. Print.

Miller, Tyrus. 'Documentary/Modernism: Convergence and Complementarity
in the 1930s.' *Modernism/Modernity* 9.2 (2002): 225–41. Print.

Milz, Sabine. 'Cultural Policy-Making at a Time of Neoliberal Globalization.'
ESC 33.1–2 (March/June 2007): 85–107. Print.

Moffat, Ken. *A Poetics of Social Work: Personal Agency and Social Transformation in
Canada, 1920–1939.* Toronto: U of Toronto P, 2001. Print.

Moscovitch, Alan, and Jim Albert, eds. *The 'Benevolent' State: The Growth of Welfare
in Canada.* Toronto: Garamond P, 1987. Print.

Moscovitch, Alan, and Glenn Drover. 'Social Expenditures and the Welfare
State: The Canadian Experience in Historical Perspective.' Moscovitch and
Albert 13–43.

Mouffe, Chantal, ed. *Dimensions of Radical Democracy: Pluralism, Citizenship, Community*. London: Verso: 1992. Print.

– 'Democratic Citizenship and the Political Community.' Mouffe 225–39.

Mount, Nick. *When Canadian Literature Moved to New York*. Toronto: U of Toronto P, 2005. Print.

Moyes, Lianne. 'Homelessness, Cosmopolitanism and Citizenship: Robert Majzels' *City of Forgetting*.' *Études Canadiennes / Canadian Studies* 64 (2008): 123–38. Print.

Munro, Alice. *Dance of the Happy Shades*. Toronto: McGraw-Hill Ryerson, 1968. Print.

Murray, Heather. 'The Canadian Writers Meet: The Canadian Literature Club of Toronto, Donald G. French, and the Middlebrow Modernist Reader.' *Papers of the Bibliographical Society of Canada* 46.2 (2008): 149–83. Print.

– 'The CANLIT Project and the Question of a National Reader.' Department of English Production of Literature Doctoral Speakers Series, Carleton University, Ottawa. 27 November 2009. Lecture.

Muszynski, Leon. 'The Politics of Labour Market Policy.' *The Politics of Economic Policy*. Ed. G. Bruce Doern. Toronto: U of Toronto P, 1985. 251–301. Print.

Neatby, H. Blair. *The Politics of Chaos: Canada in the Thirties*. 1972. Toronto: Copp Clark Pittman, 1986. Print.

Nelson, Cary. *Revolutionary Memory: Recovering the Poetry of the American Left*. New York: Routledge, 2001. Print.

New Hogtown Press. Preface. Wright and Endres vii–x.

New, W.H., ed. *Encyclopedia of Literatures in Canada*. Toronto: U of Toronto P, 2001. Print.

– 'John Marlyn.' New 715–16.

Norris, Ken. *The Little Magazine in Canada 1925–80*. Toronto: ECW, 1984. Print.

'Novel of Depression Years Reissued.' Review of *Waste Heritage*, by Irene Baird. *Quill and Quire* (June 1974): 6. Print.

'Opportunities for Youth [archival description of textual record].' Library and Archives Canada. Canada, 19 March 2008. Web. 17 December 2009.

Orwell, George. 'Boys' Weeklies.' *Dickens, Dali and Others*. By Orwell. New York: Harcourt Brace, 1946. 76–114. Print.

Pacey, Desmond. 'Fiction, 1920–1940.' Klinck Vol. 2 168–233.

– *Frederick Philip Grove*. Toronto: Ryerson, 1945. Print.

Pal, Leslie. 'Tools for the Job: Canada's Evolution from Public Works to Mandated Employment.' Ismael 33–62. Print.

Palmer, Bryan. 'Radical Reasoning.' Review of *Reasoning Otherwise*, by Ian McKay. *Underhill Review* (Fall 2009). Web. 1 April 2010.

– *Working-Class Experience.* Rev. ed. Toronto: McClelland and Stewart, 1992. Print.

Parker, George. 'The Agency System and Branch-Plant Publishing.' Gerson and Michon 163–8.

– *The Beginnings of the Book Trade in Canada.* Toronto: U of Toronto P, 1985. Print.

– 'Trade and Regional Publishing in Central Canada.' Gerson and Michon 168–78.

Pennee, Donna Palmateer. 'Looking Elsewhere for Answers to the Postcolonial Question: From Literary Studies to State Policy in Canada.' *Is Canada Postcolonial? Unsettling Canadian Literature.* Ed. Laura Moss. Waterloo: Wilfrid Laurier UP, 2003. 78–94. Print.

Penner, Norman. *The Canadian Left.* Scarborough: Prentice-Hall, 1977. Print.

– *From Protest to Power: Social Democracy in Canada, 1900–Present.* Toronto: James Lorimer, 1992. Print.

Phillips, Donna, ed. *Voices of Discord: Canadian Short Stories from the 1930s.* Toronto: New Hogtown, 1979. Print.

Pierson, Ruth Roach. 'Gender and the Unemployment Insurance Debates in Canada, 1934–1940.' *Labour / Le Travail* 25 (Spring 1990): 77–103.

Porter, Ann. *Gendered States: Women, Unemployment Insurance and the Political Economy of the Welfare State in Canada.* Toronto: U of Toronto P, 2003. Print.

Potrebenko, Helen. *Taxi!* Vancouver: New Star Books, 1975. Print.

Powell, Mary Patricia. 'A Response to the Depression: The Local Council of Women in Vancouver.' *The Depression in Canada: Responses to Economic Crisis.* Ed. Michiel Horn. Toronto: Copp Clark Pitman, 1988. 12–29. Print.

Purdy, Al. *The Cariboo Horses.* 1965. Toronto: McClelland and Stewart, 1972. Print.

Pyke, Magnus. *Go West, Young Man, Go West.* Ottawa: Graphic Publishers, 1930. Print.

Querengesser, Neil, and Jean Horton. Introduction. *Dry Water.* By Robert Stead. Ed. Querengesser and Horton. Ottawa: U of Ottawa P, 2008. xi–xli. Print.

Rabinowitz, Paula. *Labor and Desire: Women's Revolutionary Fiction in Depression America.* Chapel Hill: U of North Carolina, 1991. Print.

Radforth, Ian. *Bushworkers and Bosses: Logging in Northern Ontario, 1900–1980.* Toronto: U of Toronto P, 1987. Print.

Rebick, Judy. *Ten Thousand Roses: The Making of a Feminist Revolution.* Toronto: Penguin Canada, 2005. Print.

Reimer, Robert J. 'Hugh Garner and Toronto's Cabbagetown.' MA thesis. U of Waterloo, 1971. Print.

'Report of the Royal Commission on National Development in the Arts, Letters, and Sciences, 1951 (Literature).' Daymond and Monkman 387–94.

Richard, Jean-Jules. 'Jean-Jules Richard au présent.' Interview by Reginald Martel. *Liberté* 14.3 (1972): 40–52. Print.

– *Journal d'un hobo: l'air est bon à manger.* Montreal: Parti pris, 1965. Print.

Rifkind, Candida. *Comrades and Critics: Women, Literature, and the Left in 1930s Canada.* Toronto: U of Toronto P, 2009. Print.

– 'Too Close to Home: Middlebrow Anti-Modernism and the Poetry of Edna Jacques.' *Journal of Canadian Studies* 39.1 (2005): 90–114. Print.

– 'The Hungry Thirties: Writing Food and Gender During the Depression.' *Essays on Canadian Writing* 78 (Winter 2003): 163–91. Print.

Rimstead, Roxanne. *Remnants of Nation: On Poverty Narratives by Women.* Toronto: U of Toronto P, 2001. Print.

Ringenbach, Paul. *Tramps and Reformers, 1873–1916: The Discovery of Unemployment in New York.* Westport: Greenwood, 1973. Print.

Rose, Albert. *Regent Park: A Study in Slum Clearance.* Toronto: U of Toronto P, 1958. Print.

Ross, Malcolm. Introduction. *Such Is My Beloved.* By Morley Callaghan. Toronto: McClelland and Stewart, 1957. v–xiii. Print.

– ed. *Poets of the Confederation.* Toronto: McClelland and Stewart, 1960. Print.

Roy Gabrielle. *Bonheur d'occasion.* Montreal: Boréal, 1993. Print.

Rubin, Don, ed. *Canadian Theatre History: Selected Readings.* Toronto: Copp Clark, 1996. Print.

– 'The Toronto Movement.' Rubin 394–403.

Rubin, Joan Shelley. *The Making of Middlebrow Culture.* Chapel Hill: U of North Carolina P, 1992. Print.

Ryan, Toby Gordon. 'Canadian Theatre in the 30s: A New Kind of Arts Organization.' Rubin, *Canadian Theatre* 106–13.

– *Stage Left: Canadian Theatre in the Thirties.* Toronto: CTR Publications, 1981. Print.

Sangster, Joan. *Dreams of Equality: Women on the Canadian Left, 1920–1950.* Toronto: McClelland and Stewart, 1989. Print.

Satzewich, Vic. *Racism and the Importation of Foreign Labour: Farm Labour Migration to Canada since 1945.* New York: Routledge, 1991. Print.

Schofield, Anakana. 'Reader, Hail That Cab!' *Globe and Mail,* 24 July 2009. Web. 18 May 2010.

Scobie, Stephen. 'Amelia, Or: Who Do You Think You Are? Documentary and Identity in Canadian Literature.' *Canadian Literature* 100 (Spring 1984): 264–85. Print.

Scott, F.R. *The Dance Is One.* Toronto: McClelland and Stewart, 1973. Print.

Sharma, Nandita. *Home Economics: Nationalism and the Making of 'Migrant Workers' in Canada.* Toronto: U of Toronto P, 2006. Print.

Shek, Ben-Zion. *Social Realism in the French-Canadian Novel.* Montreal: Harvest House, 1976. Print.

Shore, Marlene. *The Science of Social Redemption: McGill, the Chicago School, and the Origins of Social Research in Canada.* Toronto: U of Toronto P, 1987. Print.

Simpson, Mark. *Trafficking Subjects: The Politics of Mobility in Nineteenth-Century America.* Minneapolis: U of Minnesota P, 2005. Print.

Slaughter, Joseph R. 'Enabling Fictions and Novel Subjects: The Bildungsroman and International Human Rights Law.' *PMLA* 21.5 (2006): 1405–23. Print.

Smiley, Donald V. *The Rowell/Sirois Report.* 3 vols. Toronto: McClelland and Stewart, 1963. Print.

Smith, Cedric, and Jack Winter. 'Ten Lost Years.' 1974. *The CTR Anthology: Fifteen Plays from the Canadian Theatre Review.* Ed. Alan Filewod. Toronto: U of Toronto P, 1993. 133–89. Print.

Smith, Jean Edward. *FDR.* New York: Random House, 2007. Print.

Smith, Neil. *The Endgame of Globalization.* New York: Routledge, 2005. Print.

Solecki, Sam. *The Last Canadian Poet: An Essay on Al Purdy.* Toronto: U of Toronto P, 1999. Print.

Solie, Karen. 'Jean-Jules Richard.' New 965–6.

Souchotte, Sandra. Introduction. *Buffalo Jump, Gabe, Red Emma.* By Carol Bolt. Toronto: Playwrights Co-Op, 1976. 7–13. Print.

Spettigue, D.O. *FPG: The European Years.* Ottawa: Oberon, 1973. Print.

– *Frederick Philip Grove.* Toronto: Copp Clark, 1969. Print.

Stasiulus, Daiva, and Abigail Bakan. 'Negotiating Citizenship: The Case of Foreign Domestic Workers in Canada.' *Feminist Review* 57 (Autumn 1997): 112–39. Print.

Steinbeck, John. *The Grapes of Wrath.* 1939. New York: Penguin, 1992. Print.

Stevenson, Lionel. 'Manifesto for a National Literature.' Daymond and Monkman 203–8. Print.

Stich, K.P. 'Extravagant Expressions of Travel and Growth: Grove's Quest for America.' *Studies in Canadian Literature* 6.2 (1981): 155–69. Print.

St John, Edward. *The Graphic Publishers Limited, 1925–1932.* Ottawa: The Historical Society of Ottawa, 1992. Print.

Stobie, Margaret. *Frederick Philip Grove.* New York: Twayne, 1973. Print.

Stott, William. *Documentary Expression and Thirties America.* New York: Oxford UP, 1973. Print.

Struthers, James. 'Canadian Unemployment Policy in the 1930s.' *Readings in Ca-*

nadian History: Post-Confederation. 4th ed. Ed. R. Douglas Francis and Donald
    B. Smith. Toronto: Harcourt Brace Canada, 1994. 375–89. Print.
– *No Fault of Their Own: Unemployment and the Canadian Welfare State, 1914–1941.*
    Toronto: U of Toronto P, 1983. Print.
– 'Shadows from the Thirties: The Federal Government and Unemployment
    Assistance, 1941–1956.' Ismael 3–32.
– 'Two Depressions: Bennett, Trudeau, and the Unemployed.' *Journal of Cana-*
    dian Studies 14.1 (1979): 70–80. Print.
Stuewe, Paul. *Hugh Garner and His Works.* Toronto: ECW, 1984. Print.
– *The Storms Below: The Turbulent Life and Times of Hugh Garner.* Toronto: James
    Lorimer, 1988. Print.
Sutton, David. 'Liberalism, State Collectivism and Social Relations of Citizen-
    ship.' *Crises in the British State 1880–1930.* Ed. Mary Langan and Bill Schwarz.
    London: Hutchinson, 1985. 63–79. Print.
Szalay, Michael. *New Deal Modernism: American Literature and the Invention of the*
    Welfare State. Durham: Duke UP, 2000. Print.
Thompson, Lee Briscoe [J. Lee Thompson]. '"Emphatically Middling": A Criti-
    cal Examination of Canadian Poetry in the Great Depression.' Diss. Queen's
    U, 1975. Print.
Tippett, Maria. *Making Culture: English-Canadian Institutions and the Arts before the*
    Massey Commission. Toronto: U of Toronto P, 1990. Print.
'The Title and Degree of Doctor of Laws Conferred at Congregation, May 31
    1973: Harold Edward Winch.' University Archives. University of British Co-
    lumbia, n.d. Web. 9 May 2010.
Tremblay, Victor-Laurent. 'L'Androgyne dans *Journal d'un hobo* de Jean-Jules
    Richard.' *Studies in Canadian Literature* 21.2 (1996): 62–88. Print.
Turner, Brian S. 'Contemporary Problems in the Theory of Citizenship.' *Citizen-*
    ship and Social Theory. Ed. Turner. London: Sage, 1993. 1–18. Print.
'Vera Lysenko Fonds.' *Library and Archives Canada.* Canada, 19 March 2008.
    Web. 15 January 2010.
Vipond, Mary. 'Blessed Are the Peacemakers: The Labour Question in Canadi-
    an Social Gospel Fiction.' *Journal of Canadian Studies* 10 (1975): 32–43. Print.
Waddington, Miriam. 'Garner's Good Ear.' *Canadian Literature* 50 (Autumn
    1971): 72–5. Print.
Walters, William. *Unemployment and Government: Genealogies of the Social.* Cam-
    bridge: Cambridge UP, 2000. Print.
Warken, Arlette. 'Fredrick Philip Grove and Knut Hamsun: Northern European
    Perceptions of the New World.' *American and Canadian Literature and Culture:*
    Across a Latitudinal Line. Ed. Klaus Martens and Paul Morris. Saarbrücken:
    Amarant, 2008. 28–39. Print.

Waterston, Elizabeth. 'Travel Books on Canada, 1920–1960.' Klinck Vol. 2
    108–18.

Watt, F.W. 'Climate of Unrest: Periodicals in the Twenties and Thirties.' *Canadian Literature* 12 (Spring 1962): 15–27. Print.

– 'Literature of Protest.' Klinck Vol. 1 473–89.

Weinrich, Peter. *Social Protest from the Left in Canada, 1870–1970.* Toronto: U of
    Toronto P, 1982.

Whitehorn, Alan. *Canadian Socialism: Essays on the CCF-NDP.* Don Mills: Oxford
    UP, 1992. Print.

Wiebe, Rudy. Afterword. *Fruits of the Earth.* By Frederick Philip Grove. Toronto:
    McClelland and Stewart, 1989. 351–9. Print.

Wilbur, J.R.H. 'H.H. Stevens and the Reconstruction Party.' *Canadian Historical
    Review* 45.1 (1964): 1–28. Print.

– *H.H. Stevens, 1878–1973.* Toronto: U of Toronto P, 1977. Print.

Williams, Raymond. *The Country and the City.* London: Chatto and Windus, 1973.
    Print.

– *Marxism and Literature.* Oxford: Oxford UP, 1977. Print.

Willmott, Glenn. *Unreal Country: Modernity in the Canadian Novel in English.* Montreal: McGill-Queen's UP, 2002. Print.

Wolff, Janet. 'On the Road Again: Metaphors of Travel in Cultural Criticism.'
    Resident Alien: Feminist Cultural Criticism. Cambridge: Polity P, 1995. 115–34.
    Print.

Woodcock, George. *Strange Bedfellows: The State and the Arts in Canada.* Vancouver: Douglas and McIntyre, 1985. Print.

Wright, Richard, and Robin Endres, eds. *Eight Men Speak and Other Plays from the
    Canadian Workers' Theatre.* Toronto: New Hogtown P, 1976. Print.

Wyile, Herb. '"Draw a Squirrel Cage": The Politics and Aesthetics of Unemployment in Irene Baird's *Waste Heritage.*' *Studies in Canadian Literature* 32.1
    (2007): 62–81. Print.

Young, David. 'The Macmillan Company of Canada in the 1930s.' *Journal of Canadian Studies* 30.3 (Fall 1995): 117–33. Print.

Young, Walter D. *The Anatomy of a Party: The National CCF, 1932–1961.* Toronto:
    U of Toronto P, 1969. Print.

Zimmerman, Cynthia. *Playwriting Women: Female Voices in English Canada.* Toronto: Simon and Pierre, 1994. Print.

Index